Preaching to the Nations

Acknowledgements

I would like to thank some of the many people who have helped me in my dialogue with the New Testament. In particular, I would like to thank friends and colleagues at Ripon College Cuddesdon who helped me to get started on the project, and students at the College and at SEITE who contributed through their comments, questions and criticisms. Professor Christopher Evans, my first New Testament teacher at King's College London and now in retirement in Cuddesdon, was an enormous support, encouragement and guide throughout my time at the College, as was Dr Ruth Edwards when she joined the staff team. Professor Chris Rowland and other friends in the New Testament seminar in Oxford were a tremendous help, and it was a privilege to be with them.

My own family have been more than patient over the long period this book has been in the making, especially alongside all the other pressing demands at college and more recently at SEITE. Thank you, Linny, Peter, James and Katie. Thank you also to Lucy Gasson, alas no longer with SPCK, for her encouragement at an early stage, as well as to the present team in the Publications Department. Jennifer Wild has an incredible eye for detail, and I am greatly indebted to her for her hard work and interest at the editing stage.

Alan Le Grys
Rochester
September 1998

Preaching to the Nations

The Origins of Mission in the Early Church

ALAN LE GRYS

First published in Great Britain in 1998

Society for Promoting Christian Knowledge
Holy Trinity Church
Marylebone Road
London NW1 4DU

British Library Cataloguing-in-Publication Data

A catalogue record for this book is available from the British Library

ISBN 0-281-05148-8

Typeset by Wilmaset Ltd, Birkenhead, Wirral
Printed in Great Britain by
Redwood Books, Trowbridge, Wiltshire

Contents

CONTENTS

Abbreviations

JNTS	Journal of New Testament Studies
LXX	Septuagint
N-A26	*Novum Testamentum Graece*, ed. Nestle-Aland (26th edn, Deutsche Bibelgesellschaft 1979)
NRSV	New Revised Standard Version
TDNT	Theological Dictionary of the New Testament abridged in one volume
CE	Common Era (= AD)
BCE	Before Common Era (= BC)
ET	English Translation

Preface

This book started life as a series of conversations about the biblical background for Christian mission. It seemed to me that a good many churchgoers simply take it for granted that 'proclaiming the Good News' is a basic 'gospel imperative' – something Jesus told his disciples to do, and therefore something the Church has always done. By contrast, there is a similar 'taken-for-grantedness' in many New Testament circles that the development of a universal mission outside Judaism was a highly controversial innovation in the first post-Easter period. These two ways of viewing the origins of mission are simply poles apart, the one hardly making any contact with the other.

In some respects, this is just another example of the disturbing gap between New Testament scholarship and regular church congregations. If anything, perhaps, the gap is becoming wider as less interest is shown in scholarship by congregations made up of people who are suspicious, fearful or simply bored by the demands of academic research. The outcome, however, is that such congregations may become ill-informed, and have to rely on naive soundbites or dogmatic assertions based on a pre-critical use of the Bible.

This book is an attempt to bridge the gap between faith and scholarship in one limited area related to Christian mission. Biblical texts lifted out of context can be shaped by any competent preacher to fit another agenda. The process is probably inevitable, and it is one way in which the formative faith of scripture is recycled to speak again to the changing circumstances facing the contemporary Church. Nevertheless, it is perhaps worth pausing occasionally to consider the historical context which may have generated these scriptures in the first place, if only to reflect on the legitimacy of the way in which these texts are now used.

I hope the book may be of some help to those who want to think more widely about the background to the New Testament, as well as the role of mission and evangelism in the church today.

Introduction:
The Mission Imperative

There has been a considerable surge of interest in mission over recent years – not least among the churches in Great Britain. The initiative taken by Anglican bishops at the 1988 Lambeth Conference to launch a Decade of Evangelism was widely endorsed by other Christian communities, and the growing tide of publications on evangelism is eloquent testimony to the mood of the moment.[1] As far as these churches are concerned, mission is high on the agenda.

Mission, however, can mean different things to different people. The English word comes from the Latin root *missio*, meaning 'a sending'. The question is, however, who is sending whom to do what? At a theoretical level, the answer is relatively straightforward: Christian mission is modelled on the *missio dei* – the sending out by God of Jesus and the Holy Spirit to engage in loving service within the world. But in practice this begs a number of questions. How does God reach out? In what way is his activity connected with the particular person called Jesus? What is the role of the Holy Spirit? What constitutes 'loving service'? And, last but by no means least (in terms of New Testament studies), who are the people to whom God reaches out? Any number of different answers are possible, and they all add colour to the precise meaning given to the concept of mission.

One well-established model in the Church of England has been to see a strong connection between 'sending out' in mission and a 'reaching out' in pastoral care: Christian ministers (lay and ordained) are sent by the church to exercise a ministry of care and compassion to those in genuine need. At the heart of this approach is a conviction that God is involved in every aspect of human existence, even the most secular and mundane. Mission is seen as an extension of the incarnation, a sacramental presence within the world through which the church says 'God cares'.[2] This pastoral model tends to focus on relationships with individuals, but it can be applied to the wider community as well. In this case, the minister is perceived to be commissioned by the church to proclaim a prophetic critique of the social structures which cause neglect in the first place.

But perhaps the dominant model in most recent thinking is the equally traditional idea of mission as evangelism – the confident proclamation of the gospel in the hope of attracting new members into a Christian way of life. At the heart of this understanding is a passionate belief that Christians are sent by God to proclaim the gospel to non-believers. Mission, therefore, is any activity which presents to those outside the community of believers the convictions, values and practices of the group, with the intention of persuading them to accept these values as their own. The precise content of the 'Good News' may vary from church to church, but will almost certainly be rooted in an understanding of the ministry, life and death of Jesus Christ, and related to an infectious belief that God has acted once and for all in Christ in order to establish a new relationship with anyone prepared to accept his gracious love.[3] The desired response is that non-believers take up the invitation to receive salvation and participate as full members of the receiving congregation.

But although this particular model is at the forefront of much contemporary Christian thinking, it has not always been so. There have been long periods when most Christians were hardly interested in evangelism at all.[4] Indeed, it probably remains true that mission is not a major issue for most congregations most of the time. Millions of Eastern Orthodox Christians, many northern European Catholics and quite a number of 'middle of the road' Protestants have little or no interest in the subject, and probably even less experience. Despite the endorsement of the Lambeth bishops, even Anglicans are split over the issue: in practice, enthusiasts who press for outreach programmes are likely to be met with lukewarm embarrassment from the rest of the congregation who feel distinctly uneasy about 'this sort of thing'.

Rightly or wrongly, mission tends to be identified with a particular strand of enthusiastic evangelical Christianity,[5] and generates silent misgiving among those who are not so sure about the implications in a changing multicultural, multi-ethnic, environment.

In fact, evangelism has had a decidedly patchy history in Europe. After the great sagas of the early centuries, it was held by many that there was no need for further outreach because 'Christendom' had already been firmly established. Apart from occasional prayers for divine compassion on non-believers such as 'Jews, Turks, Infidels and Hereticks',[6] evangelism was a marginal matter, of interest only to those who dared to venture abroad to heathen lands. It only resurfaced as an issue around the Counter-Reformation, when the dramatic advances of the breakaway Protestant communities inspired Roman Catholics to find new ways of reasserting influence and reversing a serious decline in membership.[7] *Plus ça change, plus c'est la même chose.*

A similar pattern of renewed concern for mission can be detected in other boundary situations where the influence of Christianity is perceived to be in decline. Indeed, it is possible to plot the history of evangelism against the changing patterns of social, political and economic currents within a given society which drive the church to make some kind of response. This is well exemplified in the history of the nineteenth-century missionary movement where faith so often followed the flag. Nevertheless, this would not be an isolated example.[8] Although there have been noble exceptions of dedicated Christian service in every century, the overall impression is that mission is as subject to fashion as most other ecclesiastical matters, and that the rise of interest in evangelism is not always unrelated to pragmatic concerns about power and influence.

If there is a contemporary resurgence of interest in mission, therefore, it presses the question, why now? Part of the answer must surely lie in the remarkable revival of evangelical Christianity in recent decades: in this context, an increase in missionary activity might be expected. But this merely pushes back the underlying question: why is there a remarkable revival of evangelical Christianity at this particular point in history? No doubt the reasons are complex, and a careful response would need to take account of all the variables, not least the well-established trend towards conservative religious and social views worldwide.[9] But behind the renaissance in evangelism there is more than a hint that western churches are responding as much to a perceived decline in influence as to theological altruism.[10] To put it bluntly, mission is becoming a matter of survival.

Yet there is no doubt that evangelism has a respectable theological pedigree. Whatever mixed motives lie behind the present revival, many believers see evangelism as a matter of obedience to a simple gospel imperative:

> [Jesus said] 'All authority in heaven and on earth has been given to me. Go therefore and make disciples of all nations, baptizing them in the name of the Father and of the Son and of the Holy Spirit, and teaching them to obey everything that I have commanded you.' (Matthew 28.19f)[11]

It follows that mission is a non-negotiable obligation. The task of inviting non-believers to enter into a new relationship of obedience to God is simply part of the package of Christian discipleship.

It may come as a shock, therefore, to discover that probably the majority of New Testament scholars suspect that the so-called Great Commission in Matthew 28.19f says more about Matthew than it does about the historical Jesus. This is just one more example of the widening gap between biblical scholarship and the average churchgoer. The conspiracy of silence from the pulpit continues as preachers do what comes naturally and patronize the congregation on the pretext of protecting them from hostile scholarship. Pushing their own expensive theological education to one side, too many ministers foster an unthinking and naive approach to Scripture. A superficial reading of the text combined with highly selective canon leaves the average churchgoer ill-equipped to handle the Bible with any degree of maturity, caught between the Scylla of neo-fundamentalism and the Charybdis of ignoring Scripture altogether.

On the other side of the great divide, scholars are increasingly drawn into heavily defended ivory-towers and have little to say outside the charmed but introverted guild of academic experts. As more and more Christians are attracted towards dogmatic forms of theological discourse, the need for a sensible conversation between the two worlds has rarely been greater.

But if that conversation is to develop, it is clear that the stunning advances in New Testament scholarship over the past two decades must be allowed to have an impact on basic Christian thinking. It is no longer acceptable to hide behind surface readings of the text. Christians interested in maturity of faith must wrestle with precisely the same ambiguities and complexities as everyone else.

And this includes the scriptural texts which tell the story of Jesus. The recent 'third wave' of historical Jesus research insists on giving full credit to the first-century context within which he lived. It shows that Jesus was a child of his times, a product of his Jewish heritage.[12] It is against this background that his ministry and teaching must be plotted.

It is extremely unlikely, therefore, that Jesus saw himself in the same terms as later Christian orthodoxy – as the second person of the holy and undivided Trinity. It is possible that he saw himself as 'Son of God', but probably in no greater sense than other charismatic leaders or even ordinary Jews at that time saw themselves as 'sons of God'.[13] But it is even more likely that Jesus saw himself as an agent of God, called and set apart for a special purpose. Commissioned like most of the Hebrew prophets before him, Jesus believed he had been sent on a mission to call Israel to renewal before the final day of judgement.[14]

To renew Israel. Absolute certainty is not possible, but it will be argued that almost certainly Jesus restricted his ministry to the people of Israel. He may have enjoyed an occasional encounter with Gentiles on a one-to-one basis, but in the first century this was well within range of normal Jewish behaviour. There is little or no evidence that Jesus set out on a systematic mission to preach to the Gentiles, or that he expected his disciples to do so later. Most Jews at that time simply got on with the business of living with non-Jewish neighbours as best they could. Frequently, they ignored each other, apart from occasional social contact or a flicker of religious interest based on curiosity. Only at times of national tension did the temperature rise across the ethnic boundary. Otherwise most people got on with the more pressing business of scraping together a daily living.

Matthew suggests that Jesus saw himself as someone sent by God 'to the lost sheep of the house of Israel' (Matthew 15.24). The language of sending is particularly striking in this context, and is reminiscent of the 'agency motif' found in some forms of early Jewish thought.[15] This holds that a senior figure in a position of authority – say a king or the head of a family or business – might appoint someone else – usually a close relative – to act as a deputy or 'agent' in business affairs or matters of state. This is rather like a modern ambassador, sent on behalf of a foreign government, and treated in that capacity with all the courtesy and protocol appropriate to a head of state. But only in that capacity; they have little independent authority of their own. If they are recalled, diplomatic privileges are withdrawn; if the head of state visits, they take a back seat in the presence of the one who sent them. They have an enhanced status, therefore, but only by virtue of their position as the authorized representative of someone who is unable to be there in person.

This agency motif is worked out most fully in John's Gospel, where Jesus is sent to do the will of the Father (e.g. John 5.30; see also John 4.34; 6.39 etc.). It is only because of his status as God's designated representative that Jesus can say 'the Father and I are one' (John 10.30); otherwise it remains true that 'the Father is greater than I' (John 14.28). As God's chosen agent, Jesus is sent to carry out the Father's instructions. But he has no other authority than that of the chosen delegate.

In the same Gospel, Jesus delegates some of his authority to the disciples after his resurrection: 'As the Father has sent me, so I send you' (John 20.21). Within the limits of the agency motif, this commissioning gave them no independent status, only the authority to act as chosen representatives appointed to carry out the instructions of the senior figure. They are delegates, not representatives free to make up their own minds. They are sent out on a mission to carry on where Jesus left off.

What they thought this meant in practice probably developed over an extended period of time. John's Gospel, for example, gives out mixed messages: on the one hand, 'God so loved the world that he gave his only Son, so that everyone who believes in him may not perish but may have eternal life' (John 3.16 – said to be the most quoted verse in the Bible); on the other hand, the world appears to be so hostile that the disciples need to be protected from it (John

17.11ff). Because of this hostility, John specifically restricts the all-embracing love command of the Synoptic Gospels (Mark 12.33 and parallels) and limits it to the Christian community: 'I give you a new commandment, that you love one another. By this everyone will know that you are my disciples, if you have love for one another' (John 14.34f).[16]

This ambivalence towards 'the world' continues to echo in Christian experience. In perhaps the most extreme form, it becomes the 'call to the ghetto' of the Book of Revelation,[17] an uncompromising demand for Christian exclusivism. But this is very different from the more open approach of leaders such as Paul, who in 1 Corinthians 7—10 sees marriage with unbelievers and invitations to dinner parties with pagan neighbours as paradigms of 'missionary opportunity'. Others in the early Christian churches were perhaps less sanguine about dialogue with non-believers, and some scholars suspect Revelation may even have been written as a conscious attempt to roll back Pauline liberalism.[18]

As today, Christian attitudes towards non-believers continued to oscillate between these twin poles of openness and introversion. But in this respect, early Christianity was similar to Judaism: it continued to maintain open, perhaps even friendly, contact with outsiders most of the time unless hostility or social pressure caused the community to turn in on itself. All that changed were the constituents. For most first-century Jews, the outsiders were the Gentiles, whereas by the time the gospels had been written the outsiders, for the Christian community, included non-believing Jews. This is taken to an extreme form in John's Gospel, where non-believing Jews are lumped together as 'the Jews' (as if Jesus and the twelve were not) who are now given the chilling title of 'children of the devil' (John 8.44).

In short, the primary point of reference for Jesus and his disciples was Israel. Jesus may have had a wider vision than some of his contemporaries about God's ultimate graciousness – for example, there is evidence that he thought God would admit sinners into the Kingdom before they had even repented.[19] But these are Jewish sinners, not Gentile ones. Jesus is simply inviting the fringe or excluded members of Israel to share in the eschatological feast; he is not adjusting the ethnic boundaries. In fact, there is little evidence that Jesus thought he was creating anything new: few of the people who came to meet him were invited to join a new community, and most apparently went straight home afterwards. Still less did he call Gentiles to 'convert' to a new religious movement (for example, the Canaanite woman in Matthew 15.21–8). The obvious exception proves the rule: in Mark 5.1–20, the cured demoniac certainly goes off to proclaim 'how much Jesus had done for him', but there is no indication in the text that either he or those who heard him became members of the new Jesus Movement.[20]

The evidence is compelling. Jesus did not extend his mission beyond the boundaries of Israel, nor did he expect to form a new community.[21] On the contrary, he saw himself as a prophetic agent of renewal within the existing Covenant of Scripture. In the same way, he commissioned his disciples to act as his delegates after his death. As Jews, they had a similar outlook: they were not concerned about the Gentiles most of the time, but they were not especially hostile either. It is possible that they caught the attention of a few Gentiles who were already sympathetic to Judaism. But such outsiders came as God-fearers or proselytes, Gentile adherents to Judaism, not as Christians per se. The primary Jewish focus of the Jesus movement remained intact.

The rumour of change only begins to surface in Acts – and it emerges as a novel concept, forged out of conflict and dissent. Acts was written at a comparatively late date, and is often regarded as a highly idealized account of early church history.[22] This makes it difficult to assess: although Luke almost certainly had access to a certain amount of reliable information, he shaped and moulded his account of the first Christian communities in order to present his own distinctive perspective. It is tempting to dismiss his account as hopelessly compromised, but it remains the only significant source of information about those earliest days of the church.

Reading between the lines, therefore, it appears that the first Christians initially remained in close contact with the local synagogue. In the first century, however, many of these synagogues attracted Gentile sympathizers, so these people also heard the Christian preachers by default. It due course, some Christians began to realize that Gentile adherents tended to respond more positively than the rest of the congregation to the proclamation of

Jesus as Messiah. Gradually, over an extended period of time, a few of them were drawn into the Jewish-Christian circle. They, in turn, had the effect of altering the ethnic balance within the community, although the first Christian communities remained predominantly Jewish. Their increasing influence caused ripples of unease among the Jewish membership, especially when it came to eating their sacred meal together (the Eucharist: see Galatians 2.12).

In Jerusalem, further friction led eventually to the violent scenes which lie behind the Stephen incident, and Jewish Christians sympathetic to the Gentiles were expelled from the synagogue. This expulsion meant that a number of 'liberal' believers were dispersed over a wide area of the eastern Mediterranean, and through their continued preaching, the circle of people who came into contact with followers of 'the Way' (Acts 9.2) was steadily extended. Through their action, Christianity was in the process of emerging from an exclusively Jewish context within Palestine into the pagan environment of the Graeco-Roman world.

It was within this context that Paul first came into contact with followers of the Way at Damascus (Acts 9.10–22). From the outset, Paul thus belonged to a branch of Jewish Christianity which had already built up closer links with Gentile sympathizers. Although he probably continued the established practice of preaching only to Jews – at least for a while – his experience of the Hellenistic world persuaded him to take an increasingly open view of those Gentiles who were prepared to listen. He became a strong advocate for these people; so strong, in fact, that even his colleagues in the Hellenistic Jewish-Christian community began to feel uncomfortable (Galatians 2). Matters came to a head at Antioch, and thereafter Paul is found preaching freely among the Gentiles. It would seem that Paul – or at least the group of like-minded people around him – succeeded for the first time in breaking the predominantly Jewish mould of Christianity and establishing a fully independent movement.

But it is curious he was able to succeed. Not in the dramatic way suggested in some of the more exaggerated accounts of early Christianity, of course, but none the less in a way which was sufficiently successful to give the fledgling community a foothold among the religions of the ancient world. It is perhaps worth considering why he was able to succeed even to that small degree:

what were the social and cultural factors which enabled Christians like Paul to present a persuasive case and attract a handful of adherents?

Attitudes towards new religious groups in the Graeco-Roman world were generally tolerant – within limits. Religion was seen as part of the fabric which held society together, and was therefore viewed primarily in terms of social obligation. But since most local cults were polytheistic, individuals were generally free to worship as many gods as they wished, just so long as they continued to pay their respects to the local cult as well. There is evidence that some people were just becoming aware of other options around this time, and beginning to explore the possibility of exercising a more personal choice in matters of religion. The birth of Christianity coincides with the growth of the mystery cults supported by voluntary associations of the like-minded – groups of adherents to Isis, Dionysus and numerous other gods. Christianity arrived on the scene just in time to witness the development of a religious 'market place' in the Graeco-Roman world.

The major exception to the 'live and let live' religious policy of the ancient world was Judaism. The issue that set it apart was not that Jews had a distinctive loyalty to the God of Israel: most communities were devoted to their own particular deities. The problem was rather Jewish exclusivity: 'Hear, O Israel: the Lord is our God, the Lord alone' (Deuteronomy 6.4). Alone among the religions of the Roman Empire, Judaism contested the very existence of other gods, and defined polytheism as idolatry. Consequently, Judaism could become the target of ridicule and abuse, especially at times of local tension or social unrest. Even so, the general atmosphere of religious diversity ensured that most Jews were tolerated most of the time, even if they were regarded as eccentric. Some Gentiles were more sympathetic, however, and conceded a grudging admiration for what was an ancient and venerable religion. Opinion was split, therefore, between a minority who were attracted to the ethical and theological rigour of the Hebrew Scriptures, and the majority who saw no further than the popular perspective of amusement tinged with suspicion. But those already broadly sympathetic to Judaism were ripe for the harvest when a charismatic Jewish-Christian preacher like Paul came to the local synagogue to preach a form of

Judaism which accepted them as Gentiles and without the rather painful process of circumcision.

Nevertheless, the cost of conversion for such people remained enormously high. In many situations, transfer of allegiance to another religion was viewed by the family or the local community as a form of treason – a betrayal of the ancestral gods. The trauma of crossing cultural boundaries is familiar enough even in twentieth-century societies where children who 'marry out' of one ethnic group may find themselves ostracized by their family and friends. Similar circumstances in the ancient world produced similar consequences: converts might not be physically attacked or abused – most of the time – but they were likely to find themselves despised at home and in the local community.

Christianity had to offer a very attractive package, therefore, to counteract both the natural inertia which makes most people resistant to change, and the fear of social rejection. Of course only a tiny minority of Gentiles were prepared to take the risk, and it is not always clear why they did so. However, such evidence as there is suggests that the balance was often tipped by the sense of release commonly experienced by people who became Christians. In other words, Christianity offered 'salvation', rescue from a rigidly hierarchial world which they felt was controlled by blind fate.

Christianity also tended to attract people who for one reason or another felt particularly vulnerable in their present social context, and were therefore open to the possibility of change. The first Christian communities attracted a higher proportion than usual of the marginalized and outcast – not only those positively rejected by society or forced into menial service, but others higher up the social scale who still felt ill at ease with the mixed messages they received from their friends and neighbours. The church as a community of believers offered all of these people a home for the homeless.[23]

It is a measure of the importance of Paul that eventually – after a lot of hostility and heartache – his novel view of the Gentile mission prevailed. Thereafter, after the ideological battle had been won, all other forms of Christianity were post-Pauline by definition. And since history is generally written by the winners, it is this broadly Pauline perspective which is embedded in the later strands of the New Testament literature, including the gospels. Although these may be based on earlier oral tradition, nevertheless the narratives have been reshaped by the experience of the later church. We have no direct access to the historical Jesus, only to Jesus as seen by Matthew, Mark, Luke and John and others in the post-Pauline church.

This is why the gospels take mission to the Gentiles for granted: they were written after the heat of the controversy had begun to diminish. From the point of view of the evangelists, the risen Lord had spoken through the experience of the community telling them to 'Go [. . .] and make disciples of all nations'. By the time our gospels were written, the battle for a universal Christian mission had already been won.

And that remains the canonical view of the church to this day: mission to all people is a gospel imperative. Yet it is important to recognize that this was in New Testament terms a major innovation. As the contemporary church continues to struggle with the pressure of how to live faithfully before God in an increasingly indifferent world, it is worth recalling the similar pressures and conflicts which shaped the proclamation of the gospel in the formative days of early Christianity. It may help contemporary believers to live more comfortably with the continuing conflicting motives which haunt Christian mission. The church is called to live again with many of the same issues as those who first came to recognize the power of God in Christ.

The theology of mixed motives is intriguing, however. Although the disputes within the early church were fought by fallible human beings fired by competing ideals and group interests in a power struggle against opponents, it was precisely in this mess of conflicting interests that God's universal mission to all humanity was finally established. And that, perhaps, is the hope of salvation for the church today: if God could do it once, perhaps he can do it again.

PART ONE

The Concept of Mission in First-Century Judaism

❋ 1 ❋
Mission and the
Hebrew Scriptures[1]

Jesus was a first-century Jew, a child of his time and culture. As a real human being, he was shaped by the world-view of the community in which he lived, just like everyone else. Further, as a person who established a reputation for being a powerful teacher, he had to use the same language and theological values as his contemporaries in order to communicate his beliefs. In short, if Jesus is to be understood as a believable historical personality, he has to be placed within a specific cultural framework coloured by the Jewish assumptions and attitudes which made his teaching plausible.

However, the kind of Judaism Jesus experienced was far from monolithic. Before the Jewish War (66–72 CE), Judaism was going through a period of transition as it adapted to changing social circumstances, and a rich diversity of different theological attitudes and practices were tolerated.[2] Although many a Christian preacher is often heard insisting otherwise, it is simply not true that all Jews in the first century believed one thing and that Jesus believed something completely different. First-century Judaism was perfectly capable of living with a considerable degree of dissent. And, as happens, most of the controversy stories reported in the gospels fall comfortably within range of the theological disagreement tolerated in Judaism at that time.[3]

Various dissenting Jewish groups are known from this period, including the Pharisees, Sadducees and Essenes.[4] Each of these movements drew on a common Jewish heritage, but in distinctive ways. The Pharisees tended to be theological innovators, the people most determined to maintain Judaism as a living faith capable of

3

adapting to an unstable world order. But Pharisaism was itself a diverse movement made up of teachers who often disagreed with each other, quite apart from anyone else. Their preferred theological method was argument and controversy. During the ministry of Jesus they were still a relatively small minority, though they were already influential. Other religious leaders argued with them over many issues, but ordinary folk probably found them rather pious extremists. To say Jesus disagreed with Pharisees, therefore, is to say he was an ordinary first-century Jew. Most people disagreed with Pharisees, including the Pharisees who disagreed with Pharisees.[5] It would be rather surprising if Jesus had not been involved in controversy with them from time to time.

The Sadducees tended to be the political and theological conservatives, people who regarded theological innovation as a potential threat to their self-understanding and the stability of the status quo. They were probably associated with the priestly élite based in and around the temple in Jerusalem, though this is not entirely clear. As a broadly aristocratic group, they were the people most likely to be in regular contact with the Roman governor. So again, it is hardly surprising that the chief priests and Sadducees only make an impact on the gospel narratives after Jesus reaches the temple (e.g. Mark 11.18–19, 27–33), but thereafter they dominate the proceedings as Jesus is dispatched backwards and forwards between the Jewish and Roman authorities (e.g. Mark 14.53—15.15).

The Essenes were in some respects the most radical of the dissenters, and had perhaps fallen out with both Pharisees and Sadducees over the interpretation of the Law, especially the sacrificial regulations relating to the temple cult. They appear to be connected with the community at Qumran responsible for the Dead Sea Scrolls.[6] This community consisted of people who had retreated from mainstream Judaism in order to create a 'pure' community wholly dedicated to a rigorous understanding of the Torah. Their answer to theological disagreement was to withdraw into a semi-monastic ghetto of the religiously like-minded, cut off as much as possible from the rest of humanity, whom they tended to regard as irredeemable sinners heading for destruction. Not surprisingly, therefore, they appear to have had little impact on the group of people found around Jesus.

Alongside these established groups, other movements came and went. The Jewish historian Josephus mentions a 'fourth philosophy', by which he seems to mean a group of political rebels often called the Zealots.[7] But he also mentions a lone prophetic figure named Bannus who looks strangely familiar alongside the figure of John the Baptist.[8] John appears to be the leader of a Jewish renewal movement based around the River Jordan, and was already a significant religious leader in his own right by the time Jesus appeared on the scene.[9]

Whatever else these groups and movements show, they suggest that Judaism in the first half of the first century was full of energy and diversity, as well as dissent. It was within this setting that the 'Jesus Movement' (for want of a better term to describe the group of people who associated with Jesus before the crucifixion) first appeared. Like other groups, this new movement drew on the dynamic heritage of Jewish culture and experience. They shared a common outlook and lived with broadly the same assumptions and social values. Despite the arguments and disagreements with other Jewish groups, all these movements had far more in common with each other than with those outside Judaism.

Central to this common heritage was the Hebrew Bible which helped to shape Judaism in all its variant forms. During Jesus' lifetime, the canon of the Hebrew Scriptures had not yet reached a fixed form. Nor is it clear how widely known the individual books were, except that it is unlikely that every synagogue had a copy of all the texts later considered to be scriptural. All the books of the later Bible had already been through a complex process of textual revision as succeeding generations adapted the material to reflect changing conditions. The Hebrew Scriptures represent several centuries of theological insight and religious dissent, covering perhaps a period of anything up to a thousand years.[10] The texts reflect the conflicting cross-currents of debate within early Israelite and later Jewish communities.

The full range of theological diversity in the Hebrew Bible is often marginalized by Christian theologians eager to explain the origins of mission.[11] It seems to be assumed by many commentators that there was a fixed pattern of interpreting Scripture which made it obvious to everyone in Judaism that it was only a matter of time before the Gentiles would come to worship the Jewish God. But although there are certainly some texts which could be read this way – though usually only by Christian theologians who have already made the connection on other grounds – it turns out there is hardly any evidence that they were, in fact, read this way by any of Jesus' contemporaries.[12]

Already within the Hebrew Scriptures there are the roots of the diversity found in later Judaism. This is hardly surprising, since it was precisely these Scriptures which helped to provide a framework for belief and dissent within first-century Judaism. In Jesus' lifetime, there was no fixed attitude towards the Gentiles based on scriptural expectation. On the contrary, at the risk of generalizing, it is possible to detect competing strands which contributed to an ongoing debate and left plenty of room for a range of views. For the sake of simplicity, two of the most prominent of these strands in Scripture may be singled out for attention and labelled the 'universalist' and the 'exclusivist' traditions respectively.

Universalism

'Universalism' in the Hebrew Scriptures may be defined as the belief that there is only one God, the maker of all things. This is the Jewish God, who may have chosen to enter into a close relationship with Israel through the Covenant, but nevertheless remains the universal God of all creation. Further, the 'favoured nation' status given to Israel brought with it a primary responsibility to be 'a light to the nations' (Isaiah 42.6) – to show the non-believing Gentiles the reality of Israel's God and his saving power.

The obvious place to start a review of the universalist tradition is with the creation narratives of Genesis 1—2, although these are almost certainly not the earliest evidence of the universalist tendency.[13] That honour probably goes to material now found in the Psalms, and perhaps Deutero-Isaiah (Isaiah 40—55 or 40—66, depending on which scholarly analysis is accepted[14]). But even these are relatively late texts.[15] It is likely that the universalist tendency only began to surface well into the exilic period, perhaps even as an attempt to make sense of a changing world order.[16]

Of the two creation accounts in Genesis, the more primitive is almost certainly Genesis 2.4ff. This reflects the outlook of an early peasant stage in the development of Israel, and focuses on agricultural features such as the planting of a garden, the need for water to irrigate the crops, and the creation of humanity to enjoy the fruit of the garden in primeval bliss – until, that is, the curse of sin intervenes and forces Adam to become a labourer cast out of his own land (Genesis 3.17ff).

By contrast, the first (and later) story in Genesis 1 reflects the priestly concerns of the post-exilic age, and takes a keen interest in the cosmic power of God to create stability. It catalogues the regular rhythm of nature, and sees this as the context out of which the appropriate liturgical festivals emerge.[17] The balance and natural rhythm of creation is to be maintained through the observance of proper regular worship.

Thus, both the Genesis creation stories reflect the ideological interests of their respective authors. The theology of a universal creator God is, in reality, a vehicle for more immediate concerns about contemporary social reality. All that the two accounts have in common is a belief that the God of Israel is the sovereign creator; otherwise, the accounts reflect very different experiences and concerns.

Even so, the effect of the combined narrative is to make both Jews and Gentiles descendants of the same stock, born of Adam. They share a common heritage, a point which was never lost in later Jewish tradition.[18] Nevertheless, the focus remains sharply on Israel, not on the Gentile nations. The promised land is the centre of the universe.[19]

The idea of common descent is repeated in both the Noah and Abraham cycles. Divisions between warring clans emerge as early as the story of Cain and Abel, and God decides to re-establish a new humanity in his universal covenant with Noah (Genesis 9.1–17), through whom all later generations descend, both Jew and Gentile. Thus it is only in the Abraham saga that the distinction between Israel and the nations is finally established. Following a dispute between Hagar and Sarah, the children of Sarah inherit the promise that they will enter Israel, whereas the children of Hagar are excluded. From this point on, the theme of election dominates the narrative: everyone may be created by God, but only some are chosen.

This new distinction is reflected in the technical terms which are used to describe Israel in contrast to the other nations. The word usually translated as 'Gentile' (gōy in Hebrew, ethnos in the Septuagint) simply means 'people', and could be applied to any community, including Israel. However, the word takes on a more limited meaning in Scripture, as it is employed to make a clear sociological distinction between 'them' (the Gentiles) and 'us' (the Israelites).[20]

But if at an earlier stage the people of Israel was just one among many, so too was the God of Israel. One of the key words in Hebrew for God is plural (Elōhīm) – it literally means 'gods'. It even doubles up occasionally for other supernatural beings – angels, for example, in Psalm 8.5.

The monotheism of later Judaism should not be read back into these earlier traditions, therefore. In the social environment of the period, heaven was believed to be a mirror image of down-to-earth experience. As humanity had different tribes and social groupings, so did heaven. Each community had its own representative in heaven, who could be expected to support the local cause in time of conflict: the gods would battle it out on behalf of their earthly counterparts. The important thing was that 'our' god should be stronger than 'yours', so 'we' could win. Such a world-view almost certainly lies behind the contest in 1 Kings 17f between Ba'al and Yahweh. The story revolves around a deliberate parallel projection of political events and religious interpretation. The theology is entirely nationalistic, and the outcome is cultural.

Monotheism only began to evolve when the God of Israel was perceived not just as one god among many, but as the supreme deity – the strongest and most powerful Lord in charge of the heavenly hosts (army). In the competitive atmosphere of neighbouring cults, the God of Israel had now become the divine champion, president of the heavenly council. This view can be found in Psalm 95.3–7, which is perhaps a cultic celebration of the supremacy of Israel's god. Although this is a significant development, nevertheless the theology remains thoroughly nationalistic – 'we' win and 'you' lose. Only later is the concept of monotheism further refined, so that the gods of other nations are no longer merely inferior, but actually deceptive. They are now false gods and vain idols (e.g. Psalm 114.3–8).

Religious belief and ethnic identity in the Hebrew Scriptures are thus closely linked. As one of the ten commandments puts it, 'I am the Lord your God, [...] you shall have no other gods before me. You shall not make for yourself an idol [... nor] bow down to them or worship them: for I, the Lord your God, am a jealous God [...]' (Deuteronomy 5.8f). This does not deny the existence of other gods – on the contrary, it presupposes them. What it condemns is not polytheism, but treason – betrayal of the communal identity.[21]

The 'universalist' element in Hebrew thought, therefore, emerges out of a background of ethnic and religious struggle. Even monotheism, one of the key elements of later Judaeo-Christian thought, was born out of socio-political experience. The sovereign God of Israel is the creator God because he is the supreme champion, the most powerful above all other gods. Throughout the process, Israel remains centre stage.

This is true even in the two collections in the Bible which express the universalist theme most strongly – the Psalms and Deutero-Isaiah. A good example is Psalm 47.1f:

Clap your hands all you peoples;
  shout to God with loud songs of joy.
For the Lord, the Most High, is awesome,
  a great king over all the earth.

Similar themes are found in Psalms 93, 97, 98 and 99, as well as others. Based, perhaps, on earlier Canaanite material, these hymns reflect the common culture of the Semitic world. They are eloquent testimony to the common cultural heritage Israel shared with the 'nations' (Gentiles), whether this is recognized or not.[22] Religious poems perhaps from a pagan past share a witness to the one creator God.

Nevertheless, as they now stand, these Psalms continue to speak from the perspective of Israel.[23] Universalism is rooted in the concept of election. All peoples must shout for joy because, as the Psalmist goes on to say,

He subdued peoples under us,
  and nations under our feet.

> He chose our heritage for us,
>> the pride of Jacob whom he loves.
> (Psalm 47.3f)

The point of celebrating the universal power of God is to highlight the privileged position of Israel over the nations as 'the pride of Jacob whom he loves'. The political agenda is never far away, even in worship.

This remains true in the widely discussed universalist material of Deutero-Isaiah. In one of the classic 'Suffering Servant' passages, God appoints his (unnamed) servant to 'bring forth justice to the nations':

> He will not grow faint or be crushed
>> until he has established justice in the earth;
>> and the coastlands wait for his teaching.
> Thus says the Lord,
>> who created the heavens and stretched them out,
>> who spread out the earth and what comes from it,
>> who gives breath to the people upon it
>> and spirit to those who walk in it:
> I am Lord, I have called you in righteousness.
> (Isaiah 42.4–6a)

The creation theme is clear: the Lord created the heavens, spread out the earth, and gives breath to all the people. Yet the message proclaimed is a call to righteousness and justice, key terms which are defined in terms of the exclusive Covenant with the chosen people of Israel. Even in universalist passages such as this, the theme of election is never far away.

The Servant Song in Isaiah 42 lays out the claims of Israel's God. The 'glory of the Lord' shouts aloud against his foes (Isaiah 42.12f), and those who trust in other (false) gods will be 'turned back and utterly put to shame' (Isaiah 42.17). The people of Israel are robbed and plundered (Isaiah 42.22), given up by God because of their sin (Isaiah 42.24). But now, God's anger is spent, and his chosen people are to be restored. This is not a disinterested celebration of a common cause. The nations are gathered together (Isaiah 43.9) solely for the purpose of hearing God proclaim that Israel is:

> my servant whom I have chosen.
> [. . .]
> Before me no god was formed,
> nor shall there be after me.
> I, I am the Lord,
> and besides me there is no saviour.
> (Isaiah 43.10f)

Universalism in Deutero-Isaiah thus continues to have a sharp nationalistic streak. Creation is recalled not to recognize the equality of nations before God, but to assert power over those who had previously defeated Israel. Theology emerges out of the fire of experience; monotheism is a function of the hope for political revival.

Similar points might be made about other universalist texts in Deutero-Isaiah, such as Isaiah 49 and Isaiah 56. The Isaianic servant is given to be a 'light to the nations that my salvation may reach the ends of the earth' (Isaiah 49.6), but the result is that

> 'Kings shall see and stand up,
> princes [. . .] shall prostrate themselves,
> because of the Lord, who is faithful,
> the Holy One of Israel, who has chosen you.'
> (Isaiah 49.7)

In Isaiah 56.6ff, the worship of foreigners will be acceptable to the Lord only if they join themselves to the community of Israel. Only then will 'my house' be 'called a house of prayer for all peoples' (Isaiah 56.7). Altogether, there are but a tiny handful of texts in the Hebrew Bible which suggest that Gentiles might be able to approach God independently of Israel.[24] Overwhelmingly, the dominant motif is of a God who compels foreigners to recognize the folly of rejecting his people. Universalism turns out to mean recognition of the primacy of Israel, and submission to the people of God.

It is worth registering one or two other obvious points about these passages. Firstly, they are addressed to Israel, not to the Gentiles. These are not 'missionary' texts, therefore, but messages of hope to a dispirited nation. They are theological responses to military humiliation.

11

Secondly, they emphasize that the initiative for witnessing to the Gentiles lies with God, not Israel. It is God's action which will compel the nations to believe. If the Isaianic servant is to be identified with the whole community of Israel, as some suggest,[25] then this community is appointed to witness not through missionary enterprise, but through righteous (and passive) suffering. The redeeming power of God is shown not by preaching but by silent example.[26]

Thirdly, the universalist promise in Deutero-Isaiah is focused on Zion, the city of God. In Isaiah 49.14, Zion is forsaken and desolate, but will be restored. In the oracle, God says:

I will soon lift up my hand to the nations,
    and raise my signal to the peoples;
    and they shall bring your sons in their bosom,
    and your daughters shall be carried on their shoulders.
Kings shall be your foster fathers,
    and their queens your nursing mothers.
With their faces to the ground they shall bow down to you,
    and lick the dust of your feet.
(Isaiah 49.22f)

Thus, not only will foreign nations submit to God, but Jerusalem will become the symbol of Israel's redemption 'before the eyes of all the nations' (Isaiah 52.10). By Isaiah 60.1–16, this has become a promise that the nations will pour into Jerusalem, bringing expensive and exotic gifts as an offering to God. This suggests a reversal of the contemporary political imbalance: Israel, which had been laid waste by the nations, was now in a position to receive back the tribute of the nations. The temple had been destroyed, but the nations would flood in to acknowledge Zion alone as the place of legitimate worship. This is a crucial point: in Deutero-Isaiah, so often cited as the paradigm text for later Christian mission, the movement is essentially inwards towards Jerusalem, not outwards in mission. It is centripetal, not centrifugal.[27]

Finally, the promise of tribute from the Gentiles belongs to the indefinite (but imminent) future. It is not a present reality. In due course, this future dimension in Isaiah would develop in Judaism into a full-scale eschatological expectation.[28] Mission became (for some) a function of eschatology.

Beyond these obvious texts relating to the Gentiles, some scholars suggest that others may be making implicit claims. Legrand, for example, notes a number of texts calling on Israel to recognize the legitimate rights of the stranger and the alien. Laws in the Pentateuch (e.g. Deuteronomy 10.18ff) instruct Israel to remember their own experience as a vulnerable minority in Egypt, so that they may treat foreigners with the same care and compassion they would wish for themselves.[29]

But it is questionable how much light these texts throw directly or indirectly on Jewish perceptions of the Gentiles. These laws deal exclusively with intra-communal relationships, concerning the 'stranger in your midst' – that is, they are about good community relations, not about the status of Gentiles as such. They suggest little interest in outsiders except inasmuch as they impinge on the life of the Jewish community. It is theologically motivated, to be sure, but presents more a humanitarian concern for the resident alien than an expression of missionary outreach.

Senior and Stuhlmueller suggest other indirect examples in Scripture of an implied acceptance of Gentiles. In particular, they discuss the process of acculturation through which Israel took over aspects of pagan religious thought and practice, and suggest this reflects a readiness to learn from the Gentiles. Examples include the appropriation and development in the Torah of laws common to most Semitic peoples in the ancient world, or the use of themes from Canaanite myths in some of the Psalms (e.g. Psalm 104). Even the prophet Hosea based his critique of Israel on concepts borrowed from Canaanite fertility cults. Israel was apparently ready to share the common wisdom and heritage of the nations.[30]

But again, it may be questioned whether the evidence cited will support the claims made. The texts do not seem to show any genuine openness to the Gentiles, and all the material borrowed from neighbouring cultures is firmly reworked from the perspective of Israel. Thus, although there are strands of thought which are not hostile to the Gentiles, all of these traditions operate on their own terms. They are enlisted to speak of God's relationship with Israel, not to claim responsibility for mission.

Israel was thus ready to acknowledge the dependence of Gentiles on the one creator God, but this was always the God of Israel.

Worship by the Gentiles meant worship in Zion. One day, God would reverse the defeat of his elect by the Gentiles, who would then be forced to make amends by offering an acceptable sacrifice of praise in the shape of tribute to Israel. In the meantime, perhaps the most that could be said is that individual Gentiles might be used by God (e.g. the Persian King Cyrus is anointed by God in Isaiah 45.1), and that they should be treated humanely when they lived within the boundaries of Israel. But, that is far from being a universal concept of mission, even an eschatological one.

Exclusivism

It can be seen from this review of supposedly universalist texts that the theological framework for an exclusivist trend was already in place. Under the right conditions, the concept of election could be pushed to the point where it would undermine universalism entirely. It was a but short step from the view that Gentiles should submit to the God of Israel to the unequivocal demand for a sharp ethnic boundary to exclude the non-Jew. It required only the appropriate sociological conditions for that step to be taken, and those conditions occurred around the time of Ezra and Nehemiah. In the aftermath of defeat by Babylon and the ensuing exile, the demoralized Israelites began the task of re-grouping around a new focal point as a holy people set apart from their pagan neighbours.

Historical analysis of the events surrounding the restoration of Israel is an enormously difficult task.[31] But a key element in the theological reconstruction was the development of a pattern of thought modelled on the teaching set out in the book of Deuteronomy. This may be called the 'sin-punishment-restoration' pattern: God sets out the requirements of the Law; Israel sins, is punished, forgiven and restored. The community must learn from its past mistakes: Israel had been destroyed because the chosen people had been utterly unfaithful to God. The remedy was repentance – a renewed determination to be loyal to the Covenant, and to make sure no falling away ever happened again. From now on, Israel had to be exclusively faithful and recognize the responsibilities of election. Israel is precisely not like the other nations.

Something like this seems to lie behind the reforms of Ezra. Israel must close ranks, exclude the foreigner, if the calamity of sin is to be avoided in the future. Thus, Ezra reports:

> The officials approached me and said, 'The people of Israel, the priests, and the Levites have not separated themselves from the peoples of the lands with their abominations [. . .] they have taken some of [the Gentiles'] daughters as wives for themselves and for their sons. Thus the holy seed has mixed itself with the peoples of the lands, and in this faithlessness the officials and leaders have led the way.' (Ezra 9.1f)

Ezra prays and makes a confession for the people, and goes into mourning (Ezra 10.1–8). He assembles the community and instructs them to renew the Covenant through the expulsion of foreign wives: 'By the first day of the first month they had come to the end of all the men who had married foreign women.'

Senior and Stuhlmueller, amongst others, attempt to interpret this strand of thought from a predominantly theological perspective: Israel perceives itself called to faithful obedience in order to witness to a world hostile to God.[32] But this reads like special pleading, a last-ditch attempt to avoid the logic of the text. The emphasis on election at the time of Ezra grew out of a response to social reality; it was not born out of a nascent wish to become missionaries. Outreach was almost certainly the last thing the post-exilic community had in mind. On the contrary, in all likelihood theology and social reality interacted to promote a predictable sectarian response – a tightening up of the communal boundaries around Israel to the exclusion of the Gentiles. One immediate outcome was the rift between the Jews and the Samaritans, which almost certainly began around this time. The foreigner or outsider pollutes God's people by their very presence. There could be no 'mixing of the seed' (Ezra 9.2). A holy God demands exclusive rights within the community.

The result was that 'zeal for the Law' became almost a badge for faithful Judaism. Perhaps this even helps to explain Paul's later objection to the Torah – he knew from his own experience the barrier it put up between Jew and Gentile (see especially Romans 3—5).[33]

This exclusivist line of thought was further developed in later Jewish literature. The book of Tobit, for example, is a moral tale warning against the dangers of intermarriage with Gentiles. Such warnings took on fresh meaning in times of crisis. Some of this apocryphal and pseudepigraphal literature contains both universalist and exclusivist material, showing that at least some Jews had little difficulty in combining the two traditions. The Wisdom of Ben Sirach contains a bitter denunciation of the Gentiles (Sirach 36.1–17) alongside more universalist material (Sirach 36.21ff). The author apparently saw no problem in holding the two elements in tension – and it is done (as in Deutero-Isaiah) by appealing to the centrality of Jerusalem (Sirach 36.18ff).

Other literature, however, was more single-minded. The book of Jubilees stresses Israel's special status as the elect people of God, and calls for complete separation from the uncleanness of Gentiles. 4 Ezra is even more hostile. Within this exclusivist trajectory of biblical thought, to be a Gentile was to be a sinner almost by definition.[34]

The Protest against Excessive Exclusivism
But the growing exclusivist tendency was not allowed to pass unchallenged. A number of biblical and pseudepigraphal texts suggest that some Jews clearly felt uneasy about the move to exclude Gentiles. Within the Hebrew Scriptures, the two most obvious examples of such protest literature are the books of Ruth and Jonah.

Ruth records a folk tale about a Moabite woman married into a Jewish family.[35] When her first husband dies, Ruth elects to return with her mother-in-law Naomi to Israel, where she meets Boaz, a distant relative from the same family. The story records their marriage, and ends by citing Ruth and Boaz as ancestors of one of the greatest heroes of the Bible – King David. For this author, even great folk heroes could be of Gentile descent.[36]

Equally clear is the book of Jonah.[37] Jonah is a good upright child of the Covenant, and naturally refuses to preach repentance to the pagan people of Nineveh. He tries to run away, but is caught by God and literally washed up where he started. With the greatest reluctance, he finally goes off to preach to the city. In the process, he provides the only example of a missionary sermon in the entire Hebrew Bible. As he predicted, though still to his horror, the people of Nineveh repent.

At this point, Jonah goes off in a tantrum and sits under a castor-bean plant. In its shade, he rails against God for allowing Gentiles off the hook. God strikes down the plant, causing Jonah to become even more temperamental. God then draws the moral of the story:

'You are concerned about the bush, for which you did not labour and which you did not grow; it came into being in a night and perished in a night. And should I not be concerned about Nineveh, that great city, in which there are more than a hundred and twenty thousand persons who do not know their right hand from their left, and also many animals?' (Jonah 4.10–11)

Many a preacher has commented on the charming interest in the 'many animals' tacked on to the end of the narrative. But the real point is that Jonah has no right to be indignant when the Gentiles repent – they are as much a part of God's creation as the silly bush about which Jonah was so concerned.

Jonah may be said to be the nearest thing in ancient Jewish literature to a missionary tract, yet it is not directed at Gentiles so much as at Jewish exclusivism. It is an appeal for tolerance, not for proselytizing activity. Nor was it read as such. Even though the book was obviously treasured sufficiently to be brought into the canon of Scripture, there is no evidence that it inspired a Jewish mission. It was not meant to.

Both Ruth and Jonah are therefore examples of early Jewish protest literature. A similar background may lie behind the book of Esther, which sets out the framework for the Hebrew feast of Purim.[38] Esther is married to Persian King Ahasuerus (Xerxes I), and through her privileged position is able to prevent a massacre of Jews. Despite the intensely nationalistic tone of the book, Esther's marriage to a Gentile is seen as providential. God is able to use even such a marriage as a way of protecting Israel.

Thus, although exclusivism dominated much Jewish thought towards the end of the biblical period, it was not the only possible theological perspective. Two conflicting trends bounced off each other, acting as catalysts for further thought and reflection. Both came easily to be held together in the canon because they were both similarly rooted in the same idea of the primacy of Israel. Even the protests of Ruth and Jonah define Gentiles in terms of their relationship with the chosen people. Universalism and exclusivism are not as incompatible as is sometimes suggested.

Universalism and Election:
Opposing Poles but Similar Attitudes

Jewish attitudes towards the Gentiles in the first century were thus influenced by many factors, including the need for social pragmatism within the interpretative framework provided by the emerging Hebrew canon. Scripture contained two closely related but opposing views: the tendency to assert the universal sovereignty of God over all peoples, versus the tendency to assert the exclusive rights of the Jews as the chosen people of God. The only major difference was one of emphasis, not one of substance. Both views shared a common acceptance of the concept of election: Israel had been called to be a unique witness to the saving power of the one God.[39]

Social pressures over an extended period continued to push Judaism to develop a strong sense of ethnic identity, in sharp contrast to the surrounding pagan culture. The exclusivist trajectory tended to become increasingly dominant towards the end of the biblical period, though it may be suggested (somewhat tentatively) that this was a result of the significant social and political changes experienced by Israel at this time. The bitter struggle of the Maccabean rebellion persuaded the community to tighten ranks around the Torah. This led to disputes about the interpretation of the Law, which, coupled with the complex intrigues of the Hasmonean era, led in turn to the extensive fragmentation of Judaism into competing sects.

Sectarian patterns of behaviour tend to emphasize perceived differences between competing groups, so in time even membership of the 'real' community of Israel was to become a matter of dispute. Opinions ranged from the exclusivism of Qumran to the more pragmatic attitudes of the *'am hā 'āretz* (people of the land, ordinary people). But however fragmented Judaism became, it held together around the belief that God had chosen Israel to be faithful to the Covenant. Faithfulness to the Law thus became a natural symbol for Judaism, widely recognized by Jew and Gentile alike. In the various theological and sociological struggles of the period, the significance of the Law as a central symbol for the community ensured that the exclusivist trend would tend to predominate.

Thus, Legrand cannot be correct when he writes 'Election does not cut off Israel from the nations.'[40] Whilst it is true that Israel needed other people to define itself, election, by definition, raises Israel above the surrounding nations. Unlike them, Israel is called to be holy and faithful. Exclusivism is built into the system.

❋ 2 ❋

Judaism and Mission:
Jewish and Gentile Perceptions
of One Another

The absence in the Scriptures of a theological rationale for mission is reflected in the practice of first-century Judaism. There is evidence that some Jews sought to explain their distinctive customs to non-Jews, either in order to promote a more positive image of the synagogue or to defend Judaism from a perceived threat. A trickle of Gentiles chose to attach themselves to local Jewish communities, and there are isolated examples of individuals opting to become full proselyte members. But there is simply no evidence of any systematic missionary activity organized by Jews in order to convert the Gentiles.[1]

Judaism in the first century was as much an issue of ethnic identity as religious belief.[2] Both Jews and Gentiles tended to regard their respective ancestral religion as the norm, and managed to live most of the time within the recognized social boundaries without too much difficulty.

Ethnic identity is sustained by a number of factors. Usually established by birth, it has to be confirmed through regular feedback during the ordinary course of day-to-day experience. The modern concept of nationality is by no means an exact parallel, but will perhaps illustrate the point: I am British not simply because I was born in Britain (alas, this proves nothing under recent immigration rules), but because I grew up within a community which describes itself as British and accepts me as belonging to the same group. This has given me a sense of personal identity rooted in British nationality, though this self-awareness is not enough by itself – I could be seriously deluded. So the claim to British status has to be confirmed through routine feedback from other people, British and non-British alike (for example, I have a British passport). Self-identity is thus a complex affair; but certain elements are fundamental. These include a sense of belonging ('I know this is who I am') and regular feedback from in-group or out-group members who confirm (or deny) my membership.[3]

Most groups use symbols and ceremonies to help focus identity and provide a boundary between 'them' and 'us'.[4] The central social markers in Judaism were circumcision, Sabbath observance and the kosher food laws, all of which were widely recognized throughout the Graeco-Roman Empire as essential features which set the Jews apart. Such symbols enabled people to locate themselves socially and fashion their behaviour accordingly.

Estimates of the Jewish population in the first century are hard to find, but Meeks suggests that there may have been around five to six million Jews living in the Diaspora.[5] This compares with an overall population for the Roman Empire of between 50 and 80 million people.[6] Such estimates are little more than calculated guesses and need to be treated with caution. But, assuming the figures are roughly correct, Jews in the Diaspora made up (say) about 6 per cent of the total population.

Jewish communities were found in most major settlements.[7] The dispersion from Palestine had probably begun around the time of the Assyrian invasion, c. 722 BCE. After annexation, it had been Assyrian policy to deport a proportion of the defeated population in order to discourage potential rebellions from building up in the future. Defeated groups from other parts of the Empire were brought in to replace the deported people.[8] In the case of the northern kingdom of Israel (2 Kings 17.5f), this reshuffle meant the replacement of Israelites by fresh settlers who intermarried with the surviving indigenous population, and thus created the Samaritan community of later New Testament times.

The southern kingdom of Judah survived the Assyrians (only just – see 2 Kings 17—20 and the parallel passage in Isaiah 36—39) and remained a semi-autonomous region until the rise of the Babylonian Empire a century later. A series of political miscalculations at that time caused the invasions of 597 BCE and 586 BCE, and the

21

subsequent destruction of Jerusalem. The Babylonians, however, adopted a more humane policy of deportation: rather than removing the community en bloc, only some people – usually from the leadership classes – were forced into exile. Many of these eventually resettled in the new Jewish communities established around Babylon, and stayed there even after the Restoration. Remarkably in the light of subsequent Arab–Israeli tension, many of their descendants remain in the region to this day.

Migration from Palestine continued throughout the Persian and Macedonian period, though largely on a voluntary basis. The rapidly developing network of Hellenistic cities attracted a number of Jews through the generous incentives offered in the form of citizenship rights and other privileges. War and civil conflict, coupled with periods of severe economic difficulty in Palestine, fed the dispersion, so that around the beginning of the first century, the Greek historian Strabo could write: 'This people [the Jews] has already made its way into every city, and it is not easy to find any place in the habitable world which has not received this nation and in which it has not made its power felt.'[9] Other first-century Jewish authors such as Philo and Josephus (roughly contemporaries of Jesus and Paul) made similar points. Jewish communities were well established and recognized throughout the Graeco-Roman world. Most people knew about the Jews.

Reactions, however, tended to be mixed. In his study of the rise of anti-Semitism,[10] John Gager describes the widely diverging views on Judaism found in the literature of this period. The earliest evidence suggests a substantial degree of tolerance on both sides. Judaism was known as a 'philosophy', and equated with some of the classic teachings of ancient Greece. On the other hand, many Jews were happy to mix and associate with Gentiles, not only in the Diaspora where contact with them was practically unavoidable, but even in Palestine – provided only that the ban on the worship of foreign idols within the Holy Land was respected.

The first signs of hostility begin to surface around the time of the Maccabean revolt (c. 167 BCE), when a small group of rebels took advantage of the power vacuum created by the declining Ptolomaic and Seleucid Empires to establish a brief period of Jewish independence.

In one sense, the Maccabean revolt may be seen as a violent protest against the dominant culture of the Hellenistic empires – in the same way, perhaps, that some contemporary Islamic states react against the creeping imperialism of western culture. Paradoxically, though, the violence of the reaction highlights the extent to which Hellenization had already successfully invaded Palestine. In his massive study of the cultural interaction between Jews and Gentiles during the second temple period, Hengel demonstrates the extent to which Greek values had penetrated Jewish thought. However much some Jews protested,[11] the speed at which the Hebrew Scriptures were translated into Greek is a powerful indicator of growing Hellenistic influence. To a large extent, the cultures enriched each other.

But in the period immediately before the Maccabean revolt, the imperial government implemented a new policy of aggressive Hellenization. The symbolic markers of national identity were singled out for particular attention – circumcision, Sabbath, kosher food laws and the temple cult (1 Maccabees 1.41–50). Some members of the Jewish aristocracy even encouraged these developments, and actually petitioned the imperial authorities for permission to build a gymnasium in Jerusalem – a key feature of any truly Greek city.[12] This obviously put ordinary Jews under tremendous pressure to adopt a Greek way of life, and the predictable result was a backlash in the form of the Maccabean resistance movement.[13]

The impact of the Maccabean revolt on Jewish and Gentile relations should not be underestimated. The shock of the confrontational policies of the Seleucid king Antiochus Epiphanes came to a head in 167 BCE, when the temple in Jerusalem was defiled by the 'desolating sacrilege' of pagan sacrifice (see Daniel 12.11). A number of Jews compromised and conformed to imperial policy. But others resisted with their lives. This provoked a major guerrilla war which lasted for twenty-five years, until Judah eventually achieved a fragile independence in 142/141 BCE.

Independence had been won not only through the military struggle but also through a series of complicated political manoeuvres centred on the appointment of the high priest. These plots and counter-plots became incredibly tangled, and led to social fragmentation as different groups fell out with each other and competed for power. Several of these groups were the immediate ancestors of the later Pharisees, Sadducees and Essenes.

Many of the internal disputes focused on different understandings of the Jewish Law. Thus, at times of civil unrest, the attitude of an individual towards the Torah could literally become a matter of life and death. People were forced to take sides and face tough decisions. Much of the literature of the period reflects an atmosphere of passion and foreboding as it calls on the reader to resist the temptation to capitulate, on the grounds that God will surely intervene in the near future to bring this intolerable situation to an end.[14]

One consequence of this was that the Torah was pushed firmly on to the centre stage: from now on, ethnic identity was inextricably bound up with attitudes towards the Law. This development had the knock-on effect of sharpening up the ethnic boundaries, forcing the distinction between those who were obedient to the Law and those who were not. This reached an extreme form in the Qumran community, but had a subtle impact on most walks of life. At the very least, zeal for the Law gave Judaism a reputation for being 'anti-social' and exclusive, and these charges colour Gentile perceptions of Judaism from the Maccabean period onwards. Attitudes forged in the complex struggle for national identity and religious survival were interpreted by Gentiles as stand-offish arrogance.

Gentile Perceptions of Judaism

Perhaps the clearest example of Gentile hostility to Judaism is found in the Roman historian Cicero. He called Judaism a 'barbaric superstition' from a 'nation born to slavery'. He suggests that 'practice of their sacred rites was at variance with the glory of our Empire, the dignity of our name, and the customs of our ancestors.'[15]

In a similar vein, other Roman authors took offence at the key ethnic symbols of circumcision, Sabbath and *kasruth*, the dietary laws of the Scriptures. The weekly Sabbath rest was seen by some as an excuse for laziness, and the food laws invited ridicule. Juvenal and Martial contributed calculated insults of one kind or another, and the slander first attributed to the Greek author Mnaseas (*c.* 200 BCE) – that Jews worshipped the head of an ass in the temple in Jerusalem – is frequently repeated. Petronius offers a particularly vicious variation of this when he suggests that Jews worshipped a 'pig-god' This presumably reflects a (deliberate?) misunderstanding of the Jewish refusal to eat pork.[16]

It has often been assumed that such derisory remarks were representative of Roman attitudes generally. Gager, however, shows that such judgements need to be carefully qualified. Many of these citations reflect the intellectual prejudices of the upper literary classes, and attitudes of other people lower down the social scale could be more accommodating. Varro (c. 50 BCE), for example, praises Judaism for the prohibition of images and for a strongly monotheistic faith. He is more representative, perhaps, of a popular 'common-sense' approach which could be genuinely sympathetic towards Judaism as a religion.

Hostile attitudes were often complicated by a number of factors, including local tensions and difficulties. Thus, it is not always easy to discern whether inter-community problems were really religious, cultural, political or any combination of these. Alexandria provides a good example. A large Jewish community had been established since the fifth century BCE,[17] but as a readily identifiable group distinct from the majority, Jews frequently became the focus for local resentment. Occasionally, this erupted into violence. The situation was made worse by the Roman civil war in 31 BCE, when the indigenous Egyptian population supported the defeated Anthony, whereas the Jewish community had largely supported the victorious Augustus. The entire Jewish population was promptly rewarded by the future Emperor with the confirmation of privileges hitherto established only by local custom.

This encouraged some Jews to push their luck by petitioning Rome for the full citizenship rights which would give them exemption from the punitive taxes levied on non-citizen 'provincials'. Their intervention stirred up further anti-Jewish resentment, and this finally erupted into full-scale rioting from around 38 to 41 CE. The resultant disorder and loss of life led to official action against the Jews, and their expulsion from a number of cities. The Emperor Claudius was forced to intervene, issuing an edict telling both sides to behave: the riots were to stop, but Jewish privileges were to continue as before. On the other hand, Jews were not to aspire to greater power, but were to keep a low profile during the local games, a particular source of grievance amongst the non-Jewish population. Thus, Roman policy was characteristically directed towards maintaining the status quo, but it was by no means unsympathetic to Judaism. Clearly, Claudius was not unduly influenced by Cicero, or by any of the other prominent literary figures who abused the Jews. Broadly speaking, like most imperial authorities from the fifth century BCE onwards, he was quite willing to tolerate religious diversity. All he asked in return was that Jews kept the peace by maintaining good order and refraining from provocative action.[18]

Local politics and competing interests were therefore the major cause of tension. Some of the hostility undoubtedly sprang from simple racial prejudice, but it should be kept in context: Dominic Crossan notes the contempt the upper classes held routinely for anyone they considered to be beneath them. Cicero reckoned tradesmen and small-scale merchants were vulgar, for example, though professionals and wealthy merchants were socially acceptable. At the top of the pile were teachers and land-owners; at the bottom were labourers, mechanics, food sellers and entertainers, regardless of nationality.[19]

Some of this upper-class prejudice undoubtedly fed the literary jibes, but nevertheless it is important to register the reported grounds for complaint. In his account of the life of the Emperor Tiberius, the Roman historian Suetonius writes:

> Foreign religions, the Egyptian and Jewish religious rites, he
> suppressed, and compelled those who were engaged in that
> superstition to burn their religious vestments with all their
> apparatus. The Jewish youth he dispersed, under pretence of
> military service, into provinces of unhealthy climate; the rest of
> that race, and those who adopted similar opinions, he expelled
> from the city, on pain of perpetual slavery if they did not obey. He
> also banished the astrologers; but when they petitioned him, and
> promised that they would forsake their art, he pardoned them.[20]

Judaism is thus treated as one group among many described as foreign 'superstition'. It receives extended attention, perhaps because it was seen as a particularly powerful threat. Even so, it is a question of degree, not of kind. Fear of the consequences of religious competition seems to lie at the root of the problem, yet this highlights the extent to which a number of foreign cults, and not only Judaism, had penetrated the life of the capital.

The expulsion of Jews from Rome is also reported by Tacitus, and by Josephus, who alone links it to an incident involving a high-ranking Roman woman called Fulvia. She was apparently a Jewish proselyte who had been introduced to four Jews who turned out to be embezzlers. Fulvia was persuaded to part with substantial amounts of cash on the pretext it would be sent to the temple in Jerusalem. When the fraud was exposed, Fulvia told her husband Saturninus, who complained to his friend the Emperor, who duly responded by expelling the entire Jewish community from the city. Not surprisingly, Josephus is deeply critical of his four compatriots for causing such grief and for giving his people a bad name![21]

There was yet another expulsion during the reign of Claudius, though the dating in this case is the subject of considerable scholarly argument.[22] Traditionally set at 49 CE, it could have occurred as early as 41 CE, following riots in the city. In his report, Suetonius suggests that the problem was 'disturbances made at the instigation of Chrestus',[23] a comment which may be the first known non-Christian reference to Jesus. This expulsion of Jews probably lies behind the references in the New Testament to Prisca and Aquila (Romans 16.3 and Acts 18.2ff).

Jewish Perceptions of Gentiles

For some New Testament commentators, Jewish attitudes towards Gentiles are summed up in the uncompromising comment of Rabbi Eliezer ben Hyrcanus (c. 90 CE): 'No Gentile will have any part in the world to come.'[24] However, although it is not difficult to find some support for this hostile approach, a more careful review of the evidence suggests that his was just one view among many.

Negative views towards Gentiles

Not surprisingly, some of the most hostile material comes from the time of the Maccabean revolt and the Hasmonean (post-Maccabean) intrigues. Given the general level of anxiety at this time, it is probably hardly surprising Gentiles are singled out for attention.

This is especially clear in the writings of the Dead Sea Scrolls.

Putting to one side some of the eccentric accounts of the community at Qumran which have recently attracted a fair amount of media attention, it seems clear the founder members of the community had withdrawn into the wilderness following a bitter dispute between themselves and the followers of the 'Wicked Priest' (presumably the high priest in Jerusalem).[25] It should be immediately clear from this that the scrolls do not reflect ordinary Jewish attitudes. They were compiled by a community with an extraordinarily strong sense of corporate identity and a long history of conflict over religious matters. This is not mainstream thinking, but archetypal sectarian behaviour.

Their attitude to Gentiles must therefore be read against this quite specific background. From the point of view of the Dead Sea community, 'godless' Gentiles occupied the holy city of Jerusalem but apparently enjoyed the support of the equally godless Jewish opposition (the Sadducees?). Xenophobia is certainly rife in these writings: they are critical of temple priests for accepting sacrifices from impure and immoral Gentiles; they are fearful of the threatening hordes siding with the wicked in the forthcoming eschatological wars; and they are clear that the destiny of the nations is to be utterly destroyed by God.[26] Yet to be fair, the Qumran community takes an equally dim view of all outsiders, Jews as well as Gentiles. They imposed a strict discipline on themselves, and called down curses on any member who failed to keep the rules or left the community. Of course they were hostile to the Gentiles. But they were equally hostile to anyone who did not share their point of view.

Evidence of other Jewish literature hostile to Gentiles must similarly be plotted against a background of conflict and tension. The *Psalms of Solomon*, for example, date from around the middle of the first century BCE, and seem to come from a group connected with the Pharisees. Several of these psalms yearn for a time when God will forgive his people and destroy the arrogance of the Gentiles (e.g. *Psalms of Solomon* 2). He will call back the Jews from the Diaspora (*Psalms of Solomon* 11), and renew the Davidic monarchy (*Psalms of Solomon* 17 and 18 – two of the few references outside the New Testament to a Jewish Messiah). The destruction of the Gentiles, therefore, is simply another product of fear, this time in the shape of the advancing Roman army *c.* 66 BCE.[27]

Much the same could be said about other literature of the period. Following the destruction of the temple in Jerusalem 70 CE, 2 Baruch, 4 Ezra and the *Apocalypse of Abraham* contain bitter denunciations of the Gentiles for the apparent victory they have gained over Israel, and seek to explain God's failure to defend his people. The answer given is that defeat is the result of Israel's sin. The solution is simple – repentance, seen in terms of a rigorous enforcement of the Torah. Only then will God punish the wicked (Gentiles), and restore Israel to her former glory.[28]

It is clear that some Jews were bitterly critical of the Gentiles – sometimes.[29] Nevertheless, although these texts reflect a certain sense of ethnic superiority (in the same way that some of the Roman literature of the period reflects a similar racial prejudice), all of it needs to be read against a background of conflict and hostility. These are social, as well as religious, responses to real political crises. They are not the product of rational reflection, and must be carefully evaluated alongside alternative attitudes which could be far more open and positive.

Favourable Jewish attitudes to Gentiles
Most Jews were in day-to-day contact with Gentiles, and there is little evidence that this caused any lasting conflict. In the Diaspora, Jewish minority groups depended on the local social infrastructure for survival. Even in Palestine, the spread of Hellenistic cities, plus the political and military control exercised by pagan authorities, meant that Jews regularly came into contact with Gentiles. So, in the Gospels, Jesus meets Gentiles (e.g. Mark 5.1–34) just as any other Jew living in an area peppered with Hellenistic settlements might meet Gentiles, and the chief priests meet freely with the Roman military authorities (e.g. Mark 15.1ff). Josephus writes for Gentile patrons, and Philo praises Gentile philosophers. The extent to which Judaism was hostile to Gentiles should not be exaggerated. Even if some Jews were plainly uncomfortable, others were quite content to live in peace with their neighbours, and welcomed their support and friendship.

Thus, a remarkably positive view of the Gentiles could be taken by the Sibylline Oracles, a collection of Jewish prophecies, probably from Egypt. Although they were probably not completed in their present form until the fifth century CE, they contain earlier material from around the second century BCE, and give an interesting insight into an alternative Jewish viewpoint.

The oracles purport to come from the 'Sibyl', a mysterious woman seer associated with Erythrae in Ionia. Over the centuries, this venerable and productive person 'authored' a huge volume of literature, as pagans, Jews and Christians alike cashed in on the popularity of the genre to put forward their view of reality.[30] Of particular interest is Book 3 of the Jewish Sibylline collection. This book laments the sins of idolatry and immorality ingrained in the Gentiles, and the central core of three prophecies sets out gloomy predictions based on the experience of the immediate past. According to Nickelsburg, however, amidst this sorry litany of disaster and sin:

> Book 3 shows a remarkable openness to the Gentiles and may well
> have been written to be read by them. It employs Greek literary
> forms and draws on motifs from Greek mythology. More
> important, its attacks on Gentile idolatry and immorality are
> balanced by exhortations that the Gentiles repent of these evils in
> order to escape divine judgement and obtain the blessings of the
> one true God.[31]

On this view, however sinful they may be, Gentiles are clearly not beyond redemption.

Even more positive is the *Letter of Aristeas*, written towards the end of the second century BCE. This purports to be a letter from an Egyptian courtier named Aristeas to a certain Philocrates (a name which means something like 'strong friend'), but it is generally recognized to be the thinly disguised work of a Jewish scribe. It gives a detailed account of the translation of the Hebrew Scriptures into Greek (the Septuagint), and recalls how a miracle enabled seventy-two independent translators to reach identical translations simultaneously. One of the most remarkable features of the book, however, is the way in which differences between Jew and Gentile are reduced to an absolute minimum. For this author at least, it was possible to conceive of good and honest Gentiles, and to write warmly about them.[32]

So alongside the literature which is undoubtedly hostile, it is also possible to produce an impressive list of texts which are far more positive towards the Gentiles.[33] Philo and Josephus are again obvious examples, but even some of the rabbis could come up with favourable comments. E. P. Sanders concludes: 'The general impression is that the Rabbis were not ungenerous except when special circumstances moved them to view the Gentiles with bitterness.'[34]

The obvious conclusion, therefore, is that Jewish attitudes towards the Gentiles were formed largely on an ad hoc basis. Local circumstances influenced attitudes dramatically: Gentile generosity was received generously, whereas Gentile threats were treated with understandable fear and denunciation. In the normal course of life, Gentiles could share in worship, were welcomed and acknowledged as patrons of the local community, could even offer sacrifice in the temple in Jerusalem (though not in the inner courtyard in person). Inscription evidence points to noble examples of friendship and co-operation, and there are even examples of intermarriage between Jewish and Gentile families. Clearly, not all Gentiles were bad, and the boundary lines between the communities may have been more fluid than some have been led to believe.[35]

Conversion to Judaism

Those who wanted to participate fully as members of the synagogue, however, did have to convert to Judaism. Towards the end of the *Antiquities*, Josephus provides an important – but surprisingly rare – example of the process in action.

This is the story of Izates, king of Adiabene, an area in northern Mesopotamia. In a lengthy account, Josephus tells how Izates and his mother Helena had been independently converted through the teaching of Jewish merchants. Izates debates with his mother whether or not he ought to be circumcised, but Helena advises him against what she believes would be an unwise political move.[36] Eventually, however, Izates meets a rabbi from Galilee called Eleazar. According to Josephus, he had a reputation for being extremely strict, and he convinces Izates that he needs to be circumcised. Izates consents, and to Helena's lasting relief, no harm is done – either to the king, or to the kingdom.

This example is important for a number of reasons. Firstly, because it emphasizes the political nature of what might nowadays be thought to be a purely religious activity. It is a reminder that the modern distinction between religion and politics was not widely recognized in the ancient world. Religious conversion had clear political overtones: it was, in the words of Helena, to take on 'strange and foreign' customs.

Secondly, the argument about circumcision is curious. By and large, circumcision was seen as one of the most commonly recognized markers of Judaism. In an earlier account in the *Antiquities*, Josephus tells how the high priest John Hyrcanus added to the territory of Judah by invading neighbouring Idumea (from whence came the later King Herod) but 'permitted the Idumeans to remain in their country so long as they had themselves circumcised and were willing to observe the laws of the Jews'.[37] Hence, in 1 Maccabees 1.14f, one of the signs of apostasy was that those promoting Hellenistic culture 'removed the marks of circumcision and abandoned the holy covenant'. Yet, according to Josephus, it was apparently a matter of discussion whether or not Izates had to be circumcised.

Thirdly, the rabbi who finally persuaded Izates to go ahead with the circumcision came from Galilee – a district geographically remote from Jerusalem, and on the frontier between Palestine and the Gentile world. This may indicate nothing more than a case of provincial conservatism,[38] but the psychological significance of boundaries can be enormous, pushing some towards openness and tolerance, and others in the direction of the cultural barricades.[39] The rabbi from Galilee may have been well aware of the danger of creeping compromise, and was therefore anxious to end the ambiguity. But either way, the story illustrates that even the significance of circumcision was open to debate.

Fourthly, the person responsible for introducing Izates to Judaism is said to be a merchant. This provides an important clue to the way most conversions probably occurred – through personal contact, over an extended period of time. Izates was not brought into Judaism by an officially sponsored Jewish missionary, but by an opportunistic trader.

Finally, it is worth noting that, despite the attention given to this story by later Christian scholarship, it is one of the few conversion stories Josephus can produce. Although he is keen to promote a positive account of Jewish–Gentile relations, even Josephus is unable, or unwilling, to provide too many examples of converts. He seems to take it for granted that conversion was actually something of a rarity.

What Josephus does offer, however, are a number of generalized comments about the power of Judaism to attract supporters. Thus, he can say:

> The masses have long since shown a keen desire to adopt our religious observances; and there is not one city, Greek or barbarian, nor a single nation, to which our custom of abstaining from work on the seventh day has not spread [...] and, as God permeates the universe, so the Law has found its way among all mankind. [...] Indeed, were not we ourselves aware of the excellence of our laws, assuredly we should have been impelled to pride ourselves upon them by the multitude of their admirers.[40]

'Admirers', however, are not converts. And in any case, Josephus has a reputation for exaggeration.

The process of becoming a proselyte

Only a handful of Gentile admirers took the final step of becoming proselytes. The formal requirements for this are set out in the Mishnah, though whether this second-century code applied in New Testament times is difficult to determine. The Mishnaic regulations are set out in some detail, suggesting that the subject had perhaps been controversial and therefore required careful legislation. In the present form, the Mishnah describes three steps which a proselyte had to undertake: circumcision (obviously irrelevant for females – which is probably why rather more of them converted!), baptism (a rite of purification) and sacrifice in the temple.[41]

It is possible these Mishnaic rules describe not what actually happened but what later Jewish teachers thought ought to happen. The process of conversion may have been less regulated in earlier times.[42] For example, *Joseph and Asenath*, a Jewish book written around the turn of the first century CE, is the story of how the patriarch Joseph and the daughter of an Egyptian priest fell in love.

Joseph, as a devout Jew, would have nothing to do with her so long as she remained a pagan. But after prayer and some anxious discussion, Asenath is persuaded through the means of a heavenly vision to convert. She repents of her idolatrous past, and thus becomes the model proselyte.[43]

Admittedly, as a woman, Asenath did not need to undergo circumcision, so that is not an issue. Nevertheless, it is interesting that the heart of the matter for this author is the need only to shun idolatry and repent of immorality in order to convert. Asenath is not even baptized. She simply repents and takes up a new role as a member of the community of Israel.

It may be worth noting one further point: do the Mishnaic rules govern the means of conversion, or are they simply a description of the outcome? Circumcision, purification and sacrifice are required of every Jew under the Torah. Therefore, a convert who took on the 'yoke of the Law' was necessarily bound to carry out these requirements in exactly the same way as any other Jew. He would be circumcised, baptized and offer sacrifice not in order to become a Jew, but simply as a Jew.

It is unwise, therefore, to be dogmatic about the procedures adopted when would-be proselytes were accepted into first-century Judaism.[44] It is possible that different opinions prevailed in different places, and that the only absolute sign of conversion was acceptance by the receiving Jewish community.

Jews and Proselytes: Judaism and 'Mission'

Transfer from one religious community to another always has significant social consequences: it involves leaving behind a network of relationships and the acceptance of new responsibilities. It has important consequences for the families of converts, who may have to decide between loyalty to the convert and loyalty to their religious tradition. Even the receiving community has to accept a risk – not least, the risk of being betrayed by the new convert.[45] Many Jewish communities obviously welcomed the support of new members; but some rabbis were sceptical about the motives of converts,[46] and a few were reluctant to accept proselytes at all. These teachers apparently felt that Jews should be Jews, and Gentiles Gentile.[47]

Thus, it is highly unlikely that Jewish communities were uniformly keen to persuade interested Gentile sympathizers to convert. First-century Judaism tolerated various levels of adherence, ranging from the fully fledged proselyte through to sympathetic 'hanger-on'. These different levels of membership would have been recognized not only by Jews themselves, but almost certainly by the surrounding pagan community as well.

Levels of adherence

Those most fully integrated members of the Jewish community were, of course, those born into Jewish families. Next came the proselytes who (in theory) were considered to be equal, but in practice tended to remain a little apart – as shown, for example, in the rule that convert families could not marry 'true' Jews until the third generation after conversion.[48] In practice, it is likely that some members of a community will be 'more equal' than others.

Beyond native-born Jews and proselytes, there was almost certainly a third recognizable category called the God-fearers. Although the existence of this category of Gentile sympathizers has been hotly debated for decades (and still is by some), the discovery of an inscription in a theatre in the ancient city of Aphrodisias has done much to settle the argument. This inscription gives a list of the local Jewish community, and attaches the label 'God-fearer' to some of the names. Although the inscription is not unambiguous, it appears to describe the kind of 'associate-membership' of the Jewish community which had so long been suspected.[49]

McKnight suggests that there may have been even more categories of Gentile adherents, although it is unlikely these were worked out formally. Some rabbinic sources speak of the *gēr tōshāv* or 'resident alien' – any man (*sic*) 'who takes upon himself the seven precepts accepted by the sons of Noah'. This may define the 'righteous Gentile' some scholars suspect lies behind the wording of the so-called 'Apostolic decree' in Acts 15.19ff. Again, there is no direct evidence that this category actually existed, and it may be that comments cited by McKnight say more about the idealists within the later rabbinic community than about historical reality.

Even so, these social groups show that the boundaries between Jew and Gentile were less rigid than is often imagined. A number of

Jewish communities could identify informal 'friends of the synagogue', sympathetic supporters who did not want to get too closely
involved, but whose financial support was acknowledged.[50]

Jewish 'missionary' practices
But even allowing for this, the concept of mission is still missing
from all the evidence. There is little to suggest that Jewish
communities set out to engage in organized proselytizing activity.
All the indications are that, with the possible exception of a few
isolated individuals, potential converts took the initiative and
presented themselves to the local synagogue without waiting to be
persuaded by missionary teaching. The mere presence of a Jewish
community was enough to attract attention and start the process of
affiliation. Basically, Judaism made little effort to recruit new
converts, and expected interested parties to make the running. In
first-century Judaism, mission was an alien concept.[51]

❋ 3 ❋
The Historical Jesus 1: Jesus and the Concept of Universal Mission

Jesus lived in a community where a certain amount of movement across the social divide was normal. On the Jewish side, day-to-day contact with individual Gentiles could be open and friendly, but communal passions tended to rise during times of tension when the Gentiles might be roundly condemned as the enemies of God. On the Gentile side, attitudes ranged from the glowing respect for the ethical and religious rigour of Judaism, to the contempt shown for circumcision, Sabbath and the food laws. Different levels of adherence to Judaism were accepted, but only a handful of Gentiles took the exceptional step of full integration into the synagogue. Conversion from one community to another was generally not an issue. It is difficult, therefore, to find any antecedent in Judaism for later Christian mission. As Martin Goodman points out, the Christian concept of a universal mission was a shocking novelty in the ancient world.[1]

Some Christians will not be unduly taken aback by this result: the lack of a precedent for Christian evangelism is only to be expected because Jesus was unique, and as such, put together for the first time the theological framework needed for mission. Such a view, however, places Jesus well outside the range of normal Jewish attitudes attested in the first century. So it would be necessary to demonstrate that he gave explicit instructions to his followers in order to explain his novel ideas – otherwise, whatever he thought, no one else could have understood his teaching. This chapter will attempt to explore this possibility: to what extent do the gospels suggest Jesus had such a strikingly different attitude to the Gentiles?

The Socio-Religious Setting of Jesus' Ministry

Jesus was brought up in Galilee, a densely populated area by first century standards, and deeply penetrated by a network of Hellenistic cities. The capital of the region was Sepphoris, a Hellenistic city barely four miles from Nazareth, within view of the village and certainly within easy walking distance. Although Jesus probably spoke Aramaic as his first language, it is likely that as a tradesman (a carpenter) he had commercial contacts in the city, and therefore acquired a smattering of Greek. To use modern jargon, Jesus lived in a multicultural environment. It is surprising just how little this is reflected in the gospels.

Part of the reason may be that Galilee was on the margins of Judaism. It has already been noted that discrete social groups living on the boundaries tend to react in one of two ways to external cultural pressure – either by absorbing aspects of the alien culture through assimilation (acculturation), or by retreating behind self-imposed barriers into a social ghetto. Sometimes, they do both: they present a determined front against creeping social compromise at the same time as absorbing aspects of the external culture. It is not difficult to cite modern examples of the process – it is not unknown for people to resist the all-pervasive attraction of North American culture by putting up the cultural barricades and drinking North American soft drinks while they do it. The first-century equivalent was entirely possible in Galilee: assimilation was quite capable of living alongside resistance.[2]

Galilee had a reputation for provincialism. The local dialect was treated as a joke (Matthew 26.74), the religion was more charismatic, and the established religious leaders in Judea tended to look down their noses at some of their remote Galilean colleagues.[3] Political unrest was common, and the region was known as an area of political turbulence. The Maccabean rebels used Galilee as a centre for their guerrilla operations (1 Maccabees 5.14–23); a revolt against Roman rule was started by Judas the Galilean *c.* 6 CE (i.e. during the childhood of Jesus).[4] This was soon crushed by the Romans, but forty years later the family kept the rebellious spirit alive: two of Judas' sons were executed for seditious behaviour (*c.* 46 CE), and another was in the forefront of the fighting at the outbreak of the Jewish War. Jesus lived in turbulent times.

Geza Vermes presents a fascinating portrait of religious life in the area through the eyes of two Galilean teachers who were roughly contemporary with Jesus.[5] One was Honi the Circle-drawer, a charismatic figure from around 65 BCE. Apparently, he got the name from his habit of drawing a circle in the ground to set aside an area for prayer. He was a widely respected religious leader who held a well-earned reputation as a holy man and miracle-worker. His prayer life apparently bordered on the impertinent: he argued with God, and once refused to budge until his prayers had been answered.[6] His somewhat cavalier attitude to the Almighty may explain the suspicion shown towards him in the later Mishnah. At the time, however, he was known as an impressive figure, well remembered in the later tradition.

The other character sketched by Vermes is Hanina ben Dosa. The precise date of his ministry is uncertain, but he was probably around during the middle of the first century CE – that is, immediately after Jesus, roughly contemporary with Paul. Hanina was another Galilean charismatic miracle-worker – just like Honi and Jesus. Some of the parallels are striking. It seems at least a strong probability that all three came from the same stream of popular Galilean Jewish piety.

For example, Vermes convincingly refutes the oft-repeated argument that Jesus was unique in his readiness to call God *abba*, Father. If Jesus did speak about God in this way (and there are no serious grounds for doubting it: see Mark 14.36; Romans 8.15 etc.), he was in good company. So did other Galilean Jewish teachers at the time, using remarkably similar expressions. Even Jesus' spirituality was probably representative of his Galilean background.[7]

It seems likely, therefore, that other Galileans (like Peter, James and John) would have seen in Jesus another charismatic teacher in the same league as Honi and Hanina. They would have seen, perhaps, a slightly eccentric yet powerful holy man – a *hasid*. Jesus lived in a world where such people were not uncommon, and miracles were expected. It was a world where religion and politics fed each another, and 'mainstream' Judaism was apt to frown at the lunatic fringe. In socio-religious terms, Jesus was a first-century Galilean Jew.

The location of Galilee on the borders of Palestine places it precisely where most people might be expected to have regular contact with non-Jews. It also explains why the Jewish population could become intensely defensive in certain circumstances. The unstable political situation was contained effectively most of the time, but was liable to erupt into violence at the slightest provocation. The 'normal' response that might be expected of a first-century Galilean Jew like Jesus, therefore, would be that he should regard daily contact with Gentiles largely as a matter of indifference unless he felt his Jewish identity was being challenged. To what extent does this match the picture presented in the gospels?

Jesus and the Concept of a Mission to the Gentiles: Key Texts in the Gospels

The Great Commission

Perhaps the most obvious place to test the historical evidence relating to Jesus' attitude towards the Gentiles is with the classic mission text, the (so-called) Great Commission. This is a command from Jesus to preach the gospel to 'all the nations', and is found in variant forms in each of the four canonical gospels.[8]

All of the gospels agree this is a command of the risen Lord – that is, a post-Easter statement. This itself raises a host of difficult empirical questions:[9] in what sense are narratives relating to post-mortem conversations based on reliable historical data, given that death is normally the termination of verifiable human experience? In what sense is a 'resurrected person' the same as the person who lived before – and how would you know? The resurrection stories (and indeed Paul in 1 Corinthians 15 and 2 Corinthians 5.11–21) insist that the Jesus who rose from the dead was identical with the man who had been crucified, except that he was now completely different. How different? The texts are ambiguous. On the one hand, the evangelists are anxious to show Jesus after the resurrection as a real person with genuine physical needs (e.g. Luke 24.13–31; John 20.26–7): he could speak to the disciples, eat breakfast with them, teach them. On the other hand, the narratives also point out that Jesus was able to appear and disappear at will (Luke 24.32), walk through closed doors (John 20.19f), and was not keen to be touched (John 20.17). He apparently represents a wholly new category of experience.

The post-Easter narratives, therefore, belong to a unique category of literature. This in itself makes it difficult enough to evaluate them, but the problem is compounded by the conflicting evidence provided by the gospels. On closer inspection, it turns out that although the evangelists agree Jesus said something to his disciples about mission after his resurrection, that is about the limit of their agreement. They do not agree about what he said, when he said it, where he said it, or even to whom he said it. Further, after he has given the command, the evidence in Acts suggests the disciples completely ignored it. There is a prima facie argument to answer, therefore: where does the Great Commission come from – Jesus or the later church?

THE GREAT COMMISSION IN MATTHEW

Probably the best known form of the Great Commission is Matthew 28.18ff. For many, this is the missionary text par excellence,[10] familiar from baptism and other forms of worship. On the surface, it is compelling. As Dick France writes in his commentary on Matthew, 'Jesus' universal Lordship now demands a universal mission.'[11]

France goes on to acknowledge the tension between this passage in Matthew and the activity of the church shown in Acts, but he attempts to resolve the problem by suggesting the hesitancy in Acts was not related to the basic issue of preaching to the Gentiles, but to the conditions under which Gentiles might be admitted into the church. Like other Jews, the first Christians were happy to accept Gentiles who converted first to Judaism; the debate in Acts is therefore simply over the terms of admission for those who had not already become full Jewish proselytes.

This may be part of the answer: many Jews did indeed welcome Gentile converts. But it misses the point by glossing over the problem in Acts. The saying in Matthew 28.19f is not focused on the small number of Gentiles who converted to Judaism. There is therefore a major discrepancy between the sharp disagreement in

41

Acts over the status of the Gentiles and the unambiguous instruction in Matthew 28.19f to preach to the nations. The community in Acts does not behave like a church which agrees in principle with the Gentile mission and simply has a problem over the tactics. They behave like a community which has not really thought about the Gentiles at all.

Similarly, Paul shows little awareness of the Great Commission. Several of his letters betray a highly defensive attitude towards the Gentile mission (e.g. Galatians 1—2). If he had known about a command from Jesus, he would surely have leapt on it like manna from heaven. But he does not. On the contrary, he gives every impression he thought his understanding of mission was unique, an innovation in need of defence.

But, as C. H. Scobie points out,[12] Matthew 28.19f begins to look even more uncertain when it is put alongside two earlier sayings found in the same gospel. In Matthew 10, Jesus is reported as saying:

'Go nowhere among the Gentiles, and enter no town of the Samaritans, but go rather to the lost sheep of the house of Israel.' (Matthew 10.5f)

'When they persecute you *[when, not if]* in one town, flee to the next; for truly I tell you, you will not have gone through all the towns of Israel before the Son of Man comes.' (Matthew 10.23)

A similar point is made in Matthew 15.24, where Jesus says: 'I was sent only to the lost sheep of the house of Israel.'

So even Matthew does not think the historical Jesus extended his mission to the Gentiles. On the contrary, Matthew knows Jesus limited his interest to the Jews, and that a change in attitudes was possible only after the crucifixion, which is precisely why the Great Commission is given a post-Easter setting. It is a new development and demands a changing Christian perspective.

Secondly, though this is more contentious,[13] there are good reasons for suspecting that Matthew 28.19f has been significantly reshaped by the Matthean redactor. The christological focus of the text, for example, and the emphasis on obedience to the commands of Jesus are both distinctive themes within the Gospel (e.g. Matthew 5.17–48). In fact, Matthew 28.19f reads like an excellent summary of

Matthean priorities. Then, apart from this one passage, there is precious little evidence Jesus expected his disciples to practise baptism (except, perhaps, the slightly obscure reference in John 3.22 which is in turn balanced by John 4.2), though this became the norm in the later church (e.g. Romans 6.1–4). However, the real question mark over the passage concerns the use of a trinitarian formula. Early Christian practice seems to have been to baptize in the name of Jesus (e.g. Acts 10.48), not the Trinity. For many scholars, these clues are highly suggestive of early Christian redactional activity.

The form of the Great Commission as it now stands is also highly compressed, and does not begin to make clear how the mission is supposed to operate. There is a magnificent generality about the whole thing. For example, which commands are the disciples supposed to teach? In Matthew 5.17–20, Jesus has forcefully re-asserted the continuing authority of the Torah. So, are the Gentiles to be taught to be circumcised, keep Sabbath, observe the kosher food laws, and offer sacrifice in the temple? That would seem unlikely: despite his insistence in Matthew 5.17ff, Matthew is well aware that Torah observance has been dramatically relativized by the authoritative teaching of Jesus.[14] It would seem the disciples are no longer expected to teach an exclusively Jewish Law, but rather a reduced Jewish-Christian one.

Then, to which nations are the disciples to preach? On the surface, it would seem to be all of them. But in Matthew 21.43 Israel has been specifically excluded from the kingdom. So, are the disciples to preach to everyone except the Jews? Nor, as Martin Goodman points out, is there any indication of the method of preaching or of the expected result – are the new converts to join a church or not?[15] In short, Matthew 28.19f has far too many gaps to be a new instruction. Matthew assumes the reader already understands what is implied without it being spelt out. The readers know, because they already share Matthew's insider knowledge of how Gentile mission works. They do not need to be told by Jesus.

In brief, it is difficult to avoid the conclusion that Matthew 28.19f is a later saying which crept into the tradition after the first mission to the Gentiles was already under way. It is extremely doubtful whether the Great Commission in Matthew can be accepted as a new instruction from the risen Lord. It seems to say more about Matthew than the historical Jesus.

THE GREAT COMMISSION IN MARK

The Marcan version of the Great Commission can be discussed quite briefly. It is found in two forms, neither of which belongs to the original Gospel.

The ending of Mark has been hotly debated for well over a century. But as C. Cranfield notes, the language of the first extended ending (printed after Mark 16.8 in the NRSV) makes it 'clear that it cannot have been written by Mark'.[16] Morna Hooker agrees: 'This brief ending was clearly written by a subsequent writer in an attempt to round off Mark's gospel. It is found in a few late Greek MSS and a few of the versions.'[17] This alternative ending is nothing more than a subsequent attempt to tidy up the story.

Another alternative ending is found in Mark 16.9–20. There are significant variations within this textual tradition, however, and a number of features tell against their authenticity. Thus, in a rare consensus, few modern English translations accept either ending as original. Mark's Gospel finished abruptly at Mark 16.8. There is no Great Commission in Mark.

THE GREAT COMMISSION IN LUKE

The Lucan version reads: 'Thus it is written that the Messiah is to suffer and to rise from the dead on the third day, and that repentance and forgiveness of sins is to be proclaimed in his name to all nations' (Luke 24.47). On the face of it, this is rather more promising. It is short – usually a good sign of early tradition – and lacks many of the tell-tale signs of later redaction found in Matthew, such as the trinitarian formula. It merely speaks about repentance in 'his name'.

Alas, however, this text also has problems. Even these few words betray the hand of the evangelist[18] as Luke adapts the tradition to illustrate his particular brand of salvation-history. Luke has gone to some length in his Gospel to make it clear that everything happens according to God's foreordained plan laid out in Scripture.[19] He has a keen interest in the idea of fulfilment; and he is also one of the (surprisingly) few authors in the New Testament to stress the importance of repentance and forgiveness. The upshot of this analysis is that it is a very Lucan Jesus who speaks to the disciples. From his detailed study of the pericope, J. Fitzmeyer concludes 'The scene is thus largely a Lucan embellishment' of the 'Word of Command' that Luke 'shares [. . .] with the Marcan appendix and the Matthean finale [. . .]'.[20]

In short, all that may be deduced from the Great Commission tradition in the Synoptics is that Mark did not use it, and Matthew and Luke both independently adapt a late tradition to reflect their own distinctive views. They may ultimately draw on a similar underlying tradition, perhaps from 'Q', but it would be unwise to try and deduce what this might have said. It is difficult to conclude anything more positive from the Great Commission, therefore, than that two of the three Synoptic Gospels testify to an early Christian belief in the post-Easter mission to the Gentiles.

THE GREAT COMMISSION IN JOHN

As might be expected, John has a completely different vision again. This time, the disciples are locked in an upper room (the same upper room as the Last Supper?) 'for fear of the Jews' (as always, John presumably means the Jewish leadership). Jesus appears and says: 'Peace be with you. As the Father has sent me, so I send you' (John 20.21). As with the Synoptics, this short text betrays the hand of the evangelist. It conveys the characteristic concerns of the Gospel: sending and being sent, the authority of Jesus, the relationship between Jesus and the Father.[21] As Raymond Brown suggests, the idea of the Father sending Son as the model for Christian outreach is 'the special Johannine contribution to the theology of mission'.[22] For John, mission becomes possible only after Jesus has breathed on the disciples and given them the Holy Spirit. John 20.21 is the 'Johannine Pentecost'.[23] This may be an example of a curious series of Johannine and Lucan overlaps:[24] both evangelists link the development of post-Easter mission to receipt of the Holy Spirit. But apart from that, the Johannine version has little in common with the other gospels. The time, the place and the context are all very different.

But despite this apparent independence, the Great Commission in John broadly reflects the same understanding of mission as that found in the other gospels. If the later Marcan version is included, all four versions have just one thing in common – the idea that the commission to preach to the Gentiles is a command of the risen Lord. They recognize that universal mission was a new stage in the development of the church. Two of them link it to Pentecost, the coming of the Holy Spirit.

But the differences in the four versions of the Great Commission are so great that it is impossible to know what, if anything, lay behind the gospel traditions. It is clear from 1 Corinthians 12—14 that prophecy was a common feature of the early church, and perhaps this supplies the missing clue. Revelation 1.17–20 and 22.12–21 show there was at least one Christian prophet who was not afraid to speak in the name of the risen Lord. Perhaps that is how the Great Commission tradition developed: an early prophet spoke in the name of the risen Lord: 'Jesus says, go to all the nations and proclaim my name.' That would explain why it was a saying unknown to Paul and the tradition behind Acts, but was later so firmly embedded in the gospel tradition. But, whatever the origin, the versions now in the gospels reflect the interests of the evangelists or their editors. The Great Commission is evidence of the beliefs of the post-Easter church, not the historical Jesus.

The Commissioning of the disciples

Leaving the Great Commission aside, therefore, the suggestion that the concept of universal Christian mission grew out of the teaching of Jesus must be tested against the stronger evidence of the pre-Easter narrative. However, sayings on mission from this phase of Jesus' ministry turn out to be rather few and far between. Apart from a considerable number of comments about the nature of Jesus' own mission (mostly in John's Gospel) the relevant material appears in a few isolated sayings. The biggest block of teaching is the commissioning of the disciples, found in two sections in Mark (3.13–19 and 6.8–11), a single section in Matthew (9.35—10.23), and three sections in Luke (6.12–16; 9.1–6 and 10.1–12: see Throckmorton, Section 58[25]). John has no equivalent tradition.

The idea that Jesus chose twelve disciples is firmly rooted in the gospels. There are no valid reasons for doubting it. The tradition is found not only in the Synoptic Gospels, but also in 1 Corinthians 15.5 and Revelation 21.14, so it has multiple attestation.[26] Further, the team of apostles quickly disappears from the scene, so it is unlikely they were a hagiographic invention of the later church. On the other hand, twelve was a significant number in Jewish tradition, so it is entirely plausible that Jesus would choose twelve assistants to represent the tribes of Israel. Indeed, this connection with Israel is made clear in Matthew 19.28, which happens to be a strong contender for authenticity on the grounds that the early church was unlikely to create a saying containing an unfulfilled promise (the twelve have not – yet! – judged Israel). There are powerful arguments, therefore, for accepting that Jesus appointed the twelve. And if Matthew 19.28 really is authentic, the eschatological emphasis in the saying points to the purpose of the commissioning: the twelve are called for the specific task of judging Israel in the last days.[27]

The Matthean and Lucan versions of the commissioning provide a number of details not found in Mark, so the tradition may belong to the category of Mark/'Q' overlaps.[28] However, other explanations are possible – that Luke used Matthew, for example, or that both evangelists used a slightly different edition of Mark. Further, a closer look at the supposed 'Q' version suggests it could not have been vastly different from the parallel form in Mark.[29] Assuming Marcan priority, therefore, the strongest form of the commissioning story would appear to be Mark 3.13–19 and 6.6b–13.

The text of Mark 3.13–19 is confused. Among the significant variants found in this pericope, some manuscripts add the words 'whom he called apostles' in v.14, but the editors of N-A26 felt unable to decide whether these words actually formed part of the original text. Hooker thinks they were added by a later scribe who was operating on autopilot and added the phrase from memory. If so, Mark simply wrote Jesus called twelve people 'to be with him'.[30] On the other hand, the word 'apostle' appears in Mark 6.30, so Mark was apparently aware of the title, even if he sometimes thought of the group as simply 'the twelve' (e.g. Mark 6.7).

If the title is used in 3.14, it hints at the purpose behind the commissioning. The word 'apostle' comes from the same Greek root as the verb *apostellō* (send) used in Mark 3.14. The cognate noun *apostolos* therefore has the sense of a person who is 'sent' out as a commissioned agent. The twelve apostles were called by Jesus to work as his deputies, acting under his authority and representing his interests.

The terms of their commissioning are set out in Mark 6.6b–13. They are to go to unspecified villages to preach and cast out demons – to proclaim the 'good news' of the imminent arrival of the Kingdom of God, and demonstrate the power of the Kingdom by overcoming Satan. No geographical location is specified, but the last place mentioned in Mark 6.1 is 'his hometown', presumably Nazareth. The whole episode is certainly set in Galilee, because one of the consequences of the disciples' activity is that Herod the Tetrarch starts to feel distinctly nervous (Mark 6.14–29). They are sent to villages, however – not the Hellenistic cities in the region, but the smaller rural Jewish settlements. So the disciples were called by Jesus to act as his agents in a mission to Israel, not to the Gentiles.

The urgency of the task is spelt out in Mark 6.6–13. Jesus sends the twelve, two by two, giving them authority to act as exorcists. They are to take nothing with them for the journey:

> except a staff; no bread, no bag, no money in their belts; but to
> wear sandals and not to put on two tunics. He said to them,
> 'Wherever you enter a house, stay there until you leave the place.
> If any place will not welcome you and they refuse to hear you, as
> you leave, shake off the dust that is on your feet as a testimony
> against them.' (Mark 6.8ff)

There has been a lively debate about the significance of these regulations, but the underlying intention is clear. As Cranfield says in his commentary, 'the rigour of these prohibitions implies that the mission was extremely urgent'.[31] This is not the time for theological reflection. The twelve are to get on with it.

Matthew also emphasizes the eschatological urgency in his reworked version of the incident. He consolidates the two existing Marcan units to form the second of his five discourse blocks (Matthew 9.35—10.16). His new unit is introduced by Matthew 9.35ff, which is a routine summary from the evangelist using language reminiscent of Numbers 27.17 and 1 Kings 22.17 to stress the compassion of Jesus towards the 'crowds'. But this 'crowd' turns out to be quite interesting. According to some scholars, Matthew introduces the notion of a 'crowd' as a narrative device to describe the response of the uncommitted element in the audience. They are kept carefully apart from the disciples (the 'good guys') and the hostile Jewish leadership (the 'bad guys') until forced to come off the fence during the passion narrative. At this point, they make up their minds and decide to follow the Jewish authorities, thus sealing the fate of Jesus (Matthew 27.20ff).[32]

Back in Matthew 9.35ff, however, they are still open to persuasion. This is the task given to the twelve: they are to persuade the crowd to accept Jesus' teaching. Only when this attempt to win the 'crowd' finally fails (at the crucifixion) are the terms of the mission subsequently changed by the risen Lord. By that time, the neutral Jewish crowd has decisively rejected Jesus, and the post-resurrection prophecy of Matthew 28.18ff shows that conditions set out in Matthew 10.5 no longer apply. Matthew even underlines the importance of this rejection by transferring a unit from the Marcan apocalypse (Mark 13.9–13) into the middle of his mission discourse (Matthew 10.16–23). In so doing, he tames Mark's eschatology by transforming the disciples' commission into a preaching tour directed at unrepentant Israel. The disciples are under orders to be quick in order to give the 'crowd' the maximum opportunity to make up their minds before Jesus is put on trial. The net result is that this is no longer eschatological time for Matthew, but decision-making time for Israel. The purpose of the mission in Matthew 10 is simply to persuade Israel to choose. It decides against Jesus, so that he withdraws from them to spend an increasingly lengthy period alone with the disciples.[33]

Luke also reworks the Marcan story. Perhaps the most significant feature of his version is that (unlike Matthew) he keeps the two units of the Marcan narrative apart, but (unlike Mark) breaks the commissioning pericope into two. Luke's first section, as in Matthew, is a sending out of the twelve to Israel (Luke 9.1–6). But this is followed by a further commissioning of 70 (or 72) other disciples. The manuscripts are again quite confused about the number, but for once the confusion is probably rather helpful. There are enough hints in Jewish literature to suggest that the numbers 70 or 72 were understood as symbolically representing the Gentiles.[34] This, then, is the message Luke probably wants to convey through his second commissioning. He knows the twelve were sent out only to Israel, so he created a further narrative to show Jesus responding to the needs of the Gentiles. He is laying the foundations for his later programmatic approach set out in Acts: Jesus, like Paul, preaches to the Jews first, then to the Gentiles (e.g. Acts 13.46f).

The strange thing is, though, that Luke ends up limiting even this symbolic mission to the Jews. The 70 or 72 are sent out after Jesus has left Galilee for Jerusalem (Luke 9.51ff). This would seem to locate the group in Palestine, though Luke's geography may be a little shaky (the last specific location mentioned was 'a village of the Samaritans' in Luke 9.52; Luke may have thought Samaria was outside Israel, which, of course, it is not). Even so, Luke knows that Samaritans are not the same as Gentiles: they are fringe members of Judaism. At best, therefore, even allowing for his confused geography, the mission of the 70 or 72 foreshadows the mission of Philip in Acts 8.4–25: it is a mission to the margins of Judaism, not a universal mission as such.

Incidentally, it may be worth noting one other feature of the commissioning story in the Synoptics. Mark allows the disciples to take a staff, sandals and one tunic only, but no bread, bag, or copper money (that is, loose change). Matthew does not allow the sandals or the staff, and increases the cash limits to exclude gold and silver. So, he is more rigorous than Mark, but seems to assume a more upmarket community where disciples actually have gold and silver to worry about. Luke is quiet about the sandals as far as the twelve are concerned, agrees with Matthew in excluding the staff, and uses a different word for money, though his word means mainly silver coins. Where this positions the twelve on his social scale is difficult to tell! The 70 or 72 in Luke 10.1–12, however, are given a briefer list of restrictions: no purse, no bag, no sandals, as well as no time to stop and greet people on the road. Nothing is said about money, hinting, perhaps, at the changed conditions facing those who operated further afield outside the Jewish community – they needed the money to pay for their upkeep. This perhaps confirms the Lucan trend reflected in Luke 22.35ff, where the earlier rules governing the conditions of mission are specifically relaxed. What does this amount to? Not much, perhaps, except that the different restrictions found in these traditions hint at changing social circumstances. Luke, like Matthew, knows that the first Christians had different needs from the concerns of the historical Jesus.

All three versions of the synoptic tradition agree on the urgency of the task. The comment made on Luke 9.3 by C. F. Evans could apply to them all: 'Perhaps what is meant by all [the prohibitions] [...] is that the missionaries are to embody in themselves the extreme simplicity and detachment from the world that their eschatological message of the kingdom is to bring about.'[35] So this is apparently one of the purposes of the narrative: to set the boundaries between the values of the church and the social values of the rest of the world by projecting group goals and listing the required behaviour patterns. The commissioning reflects the process of group definition as the requirements for a distinctive self-identity are evaluated and described.[36]

All versions of the commissioning narrative, therefore, reflect the conditions of mission in the later church. In as much as they build on a plausible historical foundation, it was that Jesus appointed twelve disciples to act as agents in the proclamation of an eschatological message to the people of Israel. There is no evidence from any of this that Jesus expected his apostles to minister to Gentiles.

In summary, the two central blocks of teaching in the gospels on mission are the Great Commission and the Commissioning of the Twelve. Both traditions have been significantly reshaped by the evangelists, and reflect the theological priorities of the post-Easter church. The original basis for the Great Commission is too difficult to determine, but perhaps rests on the inspired word of an early Christian prophet. The Commissioning of the Twelve is probably rooted in an authentic Jesus tradition, but has been extensively modified in the light of later Christian experience. Stripped of these redactional elements, the underlying tradition does little to support the view that Jesus taught his followers to adopt a unique understanding of the Gentiles. Matthew 10.5 and 10.23 point in a similar direction: Jesus felt called to minister only to 'the lost sheep of the house of Israel'. The historical Jesus did not expect his disciples to preach to the nations.

❖ 4 ❖

The Historical Jesus 2:
Jesus and the Gentiles

Apart from the Great Commission and the Commissioning of the Twelve, there are a number of other pericopes in the gospels which may provide indirect evidence of a pre-resurrection mission to the Gentiles. These do not suggest a systematic programme of outreach, but they do show Jesus dealing with individual Gentiles on an occasional basis. Although this kind of contact was probably inevitable in a multi-ethnic environment such as Galilee, it is possible these traditions hold a greater significance in relation to the overall picture. In addition, there are a few isolated sayings about the Gentiles in general, and these 'off the cuff' remarks could also be highly significant for understanding Jesus' perception of those outside the people of Israel. On the evidence of this material, therefore, can it be argued that Jesus laid the foundations for a later systematic programme of mission to the Gentiles?

Contact with Individual Gentiles

Mark

Mark has two extended sections in which Jesus comes into contact with Gentiles. These are the healing of the Gadarene/Gergesene (another variant!) demoniac in Mark 5.1–20, and a collection of stories in Mark 7.24—8.21.

The healing of the Gadarene/Gergesene demoniac is a fascinating unit. In his study *Binding the Strong Man*,[1] Ched Myers offers a convincing analysis of the pericope from a social and political perspective. He highlights the hostility to the occupying Roman army which underlies the text, and sees the unit as an acted-out parable of the cleansing of the land from pagan impurity. The unclean animals are driven over the cliff into the sea.

Geography is crucially important in this section of Mark. From Mark 4.35 to Mark 8.21, Jesus makes a total of four crossings over the Sea of Galilee, from the Jewish side to the Gentile. As Kelber says, 'These boat trips combine into a purposeful itinerary which gives logic and unity to the section 4.35—8.21.'[2] Jesus then travels on to the northern limit of Palestine, into an area governed by Philip the Tetrarch and heavily compromised by Hellenistic culture. This provides the setting for Peter's confession of faith at Caesarea Philippi, on the borders of Judaism and paganism (8.27ff).[3] Travelling is an essential part of Mark's narrative strategy, allowing Jesus to reclaim both Jewish and Gentile territory for the Kingdom.

The healing of the demoniac takes place in this context. It is a major episode during Jesus' first excursion into a Gentile area on the 'other side' of the Lake. His first task is to clean up the pagan impurity symbolized by the presence of demons and the pigs. The message is clear: Gentiles are unclean.

The Marcan version of this story is longer than Luke's, and considerably longer than Matthew's. It was clearly of great importance for the evangelist, therefore, and reaches its climax with the instruction from Jesus to the healed demoniac: ' "Go home to your friends, and tell them how much the Lord has done for you, and what mercy he has shown you." And he [the cured man] went away and began to proclaim in the Decapolis how much Jesus had done for him; and everyone was amazed' (5.19f).

This conclusion is notable in two respects: firstly, because it is a good example of how rarely Jesus invited someone he had healed to become a member of his inner circle; the man is sent back to his own (Gentile) community. In fact, at no point in the Gospel does Jesus acquire any Gentile disciples. But, secondly, this is an obvious exception to the so-called 'Messianic secret' in Mark.[4] Instead of the usual command for silence, the Marcan Jesus instructs the man to tell everyone 'how much the Lord has done for him' (v.19). The cured demoniac is sent home to become the first Christian preacher in Gentile territory. He has no church or community to join or support him, of course.

The highly crafted nature of the narrative points strongly towards Mark as the guiding hand behind the present shape of the pericope:[5] he has reworked his source material into a powerful symbolic statement about the nature of Jesus' ministry. The roots of the incident in the ministry of Jesus are harder to determine, though it may be based on a genuine historical event.[6] But whatever lies behind the tradition, the narrative as it now stands has been moulded into a statement by Mark about the changed status of the Gentiles: their uncleanness has been exorcised by Jesus and driven over the cliff. Now they are able to proclaim the good news.

Mark's concern to emphasize Jesus' contact with the Gentiles is taken a step further in the section of material from 7.24—8.21. In 7.1–23, Mark embarks on a major offensive against *kasruth*, the food regulations prescribed by the Torah which kept Jews apart from the Gentiles. The contents of 7.1–23 are confused and confusing, but the issue is clarified in an editorial comment in 7.19: 'Thus he declared all foods clean.' This was news to Matthew, of course, who knew that far from being settled by Jesus, the kosher food controversy rumbled on for some considerable time in the life of the early church. He therefore drops Mark's unlikely comment in his parallel passage (Matthew 15.16ff). Luke, who has a particularly sharp awareness of the rules of table etiquette, drops the incident entirely.[7] But for Mark this is a crucially important turning point: Jesus removed the purity laws and so enabled Jews and Gentiles to eat together for the first time as equals in the Christian community.

This is followed in Mark 7.24ff by the moving story of the healing of a Gentile woman. Even Mark cannot disguise the fact that the woman is initially rebuffed by Jesus: 'It is not fair to take the children's food and throw it to the dogs' (7.27). Despite desperate attempts by some commentators to prove otherwise,[8] most scholars accept that the tradition records a thinly veiled insult. So much so that some 'historical Jesus' researchers doubt the authenticity of the incident.[9] The Gentile woman is a dog. Only a swift and witty response turns the rebuff around to her advantage: Jesus enjoys the joke, and grants her request. The woman is healed in this story not because she is a Gentile, but despite the fact she is a Gentile. This puts the incident, if it is an accurate historical memory, well within the range of normal first-century Jewish attitudes to the Gentiles. Jesus did not seek the woman out, she came to him. He is persuaded to respond. But the whole point of the story is that this is an exception, not the rule.

Next comes the healing of a deaf and dumb man (Mark 7.31–7). Jesus has come from the region of Tyre by an extremely unlikely route designed to keep him within Gentile territory. It is not clear from the text whether the man is a Gentile or not, and Hooker believes this to be irrelevant.[10] The careful narrative structure of the passage suggests to Myers, however, that Mark deliberately wove the incident into a framework which would suggest the man was a Gentile. The point would then be to show how someone who had previously been deaf to the word of God, and therefore speechless to proclaim it, was rendered capable of sharing the good news. Those excluded from the benefits of the Covenant with Israel – the Gentiles – are (for Mark) now able to hear Jesus. The result is astonishment (Mark 7.37).

This leads into the feeding of the four thousand. This is so closely related to the feeding of the five thousand (Mark 6.35–44) that most scholars believe it to be a duplicate of the same incident. If so, the differences between the versions are significant. This feeding now takes place on Gentile territory, and the numbers are changed: seven loaves, no fish, four thousand people, and seven baskets of leftovers. It is difficult to track down precisely the symbolism implied by these numbers, but some sort of representation of the Gentiles seems to be intended.[11] Only after the Gentiles have been fed as well as Jews is Jesus allowed to return to Jewish territory, having rebuked the (Jewish) Pharisees, who mysteriously appear out of nowhere.

It is at this point, close to the structural midpoint of the book, that an apparently bizarre dialogue about loaves takes place in the boat (that is between Jewish and Gentile territory). The disciples are hungry and not unreasonably concerned about what to eat. This provokes an unexpected outburst from Jesus about 'the yeast of the Pharisees and the yeast of Herod'. Not surprisingly, the disciples try to make sense of this cryptic dialogue, yet their intervention makes Jesus even more irritable. The anxiety Mark feels in this narrative is almost tangible. An exasperated Jesus demands 'Can you not see what is going on?' The answer, as you might expect from Marcan disciples, is frankly no.

So what is the point Mark is concerned to drive home? It obviously has something to do with the feeding miracles, which Jesus relates to the 'yeast' of the Pharisees and Herod, prominent representatives of the Jewish national community. The point would seem to be, therefore, that the ministry of Jesus radically undermines the traditional ethnic divide: Jesus can miraculously feed both Jews and Gentiles.

This heavy underlining sets the scene for the central discipleship section which lies the heart of this Gospel (Mark 8.22—10.52). Mark uses his 'sandwiching' technique to place two stories of blind men who have been healed either side of an intervening narrative on 'true discipleship'. The first miracle is remarkable as the only example in the gospels of an (initially) unsuccessful healing (Mark 8.22-6): Jesus has to have two attempts before the man's sight is finally restored. The second miracle (Mark 10.46-52) is also remarkable as the only example in Mark of a person who is said to follow Jesus on 'the Way' – that is, the way to the cross in Jerusalem. Unlike the disciples, who do not see the point about the forthcoming passion and have to be 'cured' for their lack of insight over and over again (8.31ff, 9.30ff and 10.33), Bartimaeus quite literally 'sees' the point and becomes the only person to follow Jesus as a true disciple along the way of the cross.[12]

In other words, these closely related incidents interpret each other: they form their own narrative commentary. The climax is reached in Mark 8.27ff, where Peter perceives the true significance of Jesus for first time and then loses it: he reverts to type immediately and becomes 'Satan', failing to understand the full implications of Jesus' ministry. First the Jewish purity laws were transformed by his teaching, now Jewish expectations have also been transformed. The ethnic divide between Jew and Gentile is rendered redundant. The problem is that apparently the early church in the form of Peter and the other disciples did not 'see' it.

In order to achieve his powerful account of transformed Judaism, Mark has to work hard on the received tradition, working isolated incidents and minor traditions into a new narrative framework in order to build them up into a systematic statement of the significance of Jesus. He offers one socio-political comment in the account of the Gadarene/Gergesene demoniac, and another in the block 7.1—8.33. The implications are spelt out in Mark 8.34—10.52: Jesus healed the ethnic division in the new community between Jew and Gentile, and casts off the curse of social division through his suffering on the cross. The barriers of the Torah which kept the Jews and Gentiles apart were torn in two by the death of Jesus, like the curtain in the temple (Mark 15.38). But this is perceived only by a Gentile centurion, in contrast to the Jewish disciples who were nowhere to be seen. Mark ruthlessly drives the point home: the Christian community has begun a new era in mission, yet the disciples apparently do not even realize it.

Jesus and the Gentiles in Matthew and Luke

Assuming Marcan priority, Matthew and Luke inherited the material on the Gentiles found in Mark and adapted this to suit their changing priorities. However, they also added a few extra elements not found in Mark. These must come from their alternative sources, perhaps 'Q', or in some cases from their own independent tradition.

One of the new features of Matthew is the genealogy at the start of his Gospel (1.2–17). Although this has the primary function of locating Jesus within the context of first-century Judaism – he is the 'son of Abraham, the Son of David' – there are some features which are surprising. Manasseh is named, for example, the notorious monarch who did 'much evil in the sight of the Lord' (2 Kings 21.9). But also noteworthy are the four women included in the list: most biblical genealogies give only the male line. These names are missing from the parallel in Luke, but then neither Matthew nor Luke set out to provide an accurate pedigree: both genealogies are theological symbols, not tables of actual ancestors.[13]

The four women listed by Matthew are Tamar, Rahab, Ruth and Bathsheba (the wife of Uriah the Hittite – 2 Samuel 11.1—12.25). All four had a reputation in the biblical tradition for sexual irregularity of one kind or another, so perhaps they are named to prepare the reader for the unusual circumstances of the virginal conception. They make the point that God, in his providence, can use even the most unlikely situations.

However, there is another tradition which makes all four women Gentiles. Rahab and Ruth certainly were; Tamar and Bathsheba were arguably so. If this is Matthew's intention, not only is the line of the Messiah traced through a wicked king and a number of irregular sexual unions, but also through Gentile women. Matthew is presenting a preview of his Gospel: Jesus is 'God with us' (Matthew 1.23), the one who saves not only Jews but Gentiles as well.

Matthew 4.14f is another insertion into the Marcan narrative, and provides one of the 'formula quotes' characteristic of this Gospel.[14] The quotation drives home the same point made by the genealogy: Jesus is the light for all who sit in darkness, Jew and Gentile alike.

More significant, perhaps, is the story of the healing of the centurion's servant in Matthew 8.5–13 (parallel Luke 7.1–10: Throckmorton, Section 46). Matthew does not actually say the centurion was a Gentile, but Jews did not serve in the regular Roman army. The pericope may thus be compared to the story of the Syrophoenician woman in Mark 7.24ff. In both cases, the person in search of a cure is a Gentile; they are both praised for their persistence and rewarded with the desired cure; and in both cases the healing takes place at a distance. But in both stories it is also the Gentile who takes the initiative: Jesus does not seek them, they seek Jesus.[15]

Matthew's Jesus abstracts a general principle from the incident of the centurion's servant, however. He comments: 'I tell you, many will come from east and west and will eat with Abraham and Isaac and Jacob in the kingdom of heaven' (Matthew 8.11). In the present context, this is the clearest statement that Jesus expected Gentiles to share in the coming Kingdom of God: more than that, they will displace 'the heirs of the kingdom of heaven', the Jews.

Luke also has this saying, but his version is embedded in a totally different context which throws the Matthean account into question. In Luke, the saying forms part of a dialogue between Jesus and an unspecified group of people discussing salvation along the road to Jerusalem (Luke 13.22–30). This different setting has the effect of turning the unit into a comment on Jewish perceptions: 'You [will] see Abraham and Isaac and Jacob and all the prophets in the kingdom of God, and you yourselves will be cast out. Then people will come from east and west, from north and south, and will eat in the kingdom of God. Indeed, some are last who will be first, and some are first who will be last' (Luke 13.28–30).

The Jewish nature of the audience is confirmed by the arrival of the Pharisees in Luke 13.31, who, incidentally, present at this point the only positive picture of the Pharisees in the entire New Testament: they come to warn Jesus to avoid Herod. This is a thoroughly Jewish context, therefore. In Luke the saying about people coming from east and west, north and south is not about Gentiles flooding into the Kingdom, but about Jews from the Diaspora returning to Zion.

The evidence thus suggests two possibilities: either Luke moved the saying and broke up the unit as it is now found in Matthew; or he was more faithful to the original setting in 'Q', and it was Matthew who reworked the tradition. Given that elsewhere Luke shows a keen interest in the Gentiles, it would be difficult to explain why he should want to modify a perfectly good story if that were in the sources in front of him. The other alternative is therefore more likely: Matthew took a saying about Jewish followers and turned it into a saying about the Gentiles. The underlying 'Q tradition used by both of them spoke only of an eschatological ingathering of 'many [Jews] from the east and west [of the Diaspora]'.

The next incident in Matthew involving the Gentiles, but without a Marcan parallel, occurs in Matthew 12.15–21. This is another Matthean summary, and concludes with a 'formula quote' from Deutero-Isaiah. This is simply a Matthean construction.[16]

It would seem from this review of Matthean additions to Mark, therefore, that the additional material relating to the Gentiles can largely be assigned to the editorial interests of the evangelist. When this is put to one side, a significantly different picture begins to emerge.

The fact that Matthew reports a specific instruction to limit mission to the people of Israel has already been noted (Matthew 10.5 and 10.23). This is locked into the tradition, and confirmed by the statement added by Matthew to the story of the Syrophoenician woman: Jesus is 'sent only to the lost sheep of the house of Israel' (Matthew 15.24). Further, it goes 'against the grain' of Matthean redaction and of later Christian activity, and so passes the authenticity test as an embarrassment to the gospel. It shows that the historical Jesus had no interest in a Gentile mission.

Also noteworthy, however, are the asides found in Matthew which are either dismissive of the Gentiles or positively hostile towards them. Examples include Matthew 5.47, 6.7, 6.32 and 18.17. When his guard is down, Matthew shows the historical Jesus had the same reaction to Gentiles as most of his Jewish contemporaries: some may be acceptable (individually), but as a whole, Gentiles are definitely not like 'us'.

Luke's treatment of the Gentiles is slightly more involved, and his Gospel needs to be considered alongside the companion volume in Acts. But perhaps one example of the Lucan perspective may suffice for the moment. In Luke 17.11–19, there is a pericope found only in this Gospel, meaning it is either from his special source ('L') or from the pen of the evangelist himself. It tells the story of the healing of ten lepers, of whom only one returns to thank Jesus. Malina makes the interesting observation that from the perspective of social anthropology, the function of thanksgiving in the first-century honour-shame culture was apparently to terminate the obligation between the parties involved. Arguably, therefore, the people who behave properly in the story are the Jews who stayed away and remained under an obligation to Jesus![17]

In Luke, however, Jesus asks 'Was none of [the ten] found to return and give praise to God except this foreigner?' (17.18). If this is the authentic voice of Jesus,[18] it serves only to confirm the pattern already observed. Jesus does not go out of his way to contact non-Jews (here, a Samaritan or mixed-race Jew), but he is prepared to accept them if they come to him first. He does not take the initiative, they do; and when they respond, he is mildly surprised – only a mere foreigner has bothered to come back?

Jesus and the Gentiles in John

An encounter with a Samaritan also provides the background for another snippet of indirect evidence about Jesus' attitude to foreigners. John 4.1–26 presents the second of his extended discourses, and touches on the relationship between Jews and Samaritans. Lindars notes the remarkably accurate picture of Samaritan life presented in the text, but points out this is a fragile basis on which to make claims for the historical Jesus. Presumably, plenty of Jews (including John the Evangelist?) were familiar with the problems of Jewish–Samaritan relationships. So,

> The one thing which strains the credulity is the suggestion of a mission to the Samaritans, or at least the conversion of a whole village, in the course of the public ministry of Jesus. The Samaritans are expressly excluded from his mission charge (Matthew 10.5f) [...] Much more to the point is the fact that [Luke] records a very successful mission to the Samaritans in the early days of the church (Acts 8.4–25) [...] successful work among the Samaritans gives a good basis for some Christians to be well informed about them. This is sufficient to account for John's knowledge, without entailing a full-scale tradition stemming from the ministry of Jesus himself.[19]

The high proportion of Johannine words and motifs points in the same direction: this is a Johannine construction. As Raymond Brown argues,[20] the story reflects the experience of the later Johannine community. It is theological reflection, not historical memory.

What the story does show, however, is that an internal debate continued for some time within the Christian community about the mission to non-Jews. John is sufficiently Jewish (despite his hostile comments about the 'Jews') to know that 'salvation is from the Jews' (4.22). But his Jesus supersedes the older categories. Worship is no longer to be in either Jerusalem or Mount Gerizim (the Samaritan holy place), for 'God is Spirit, and those who worship him must worship in spirit and truth' (4.24). This proposition provides the context for an evaluation of the Samaritan mission, which concludes that (now) Jesus is 'the Saviour of the world' (John 4.42).

In between the proposition and the conclusion lies the saying about Labourers and the Harvest (John 4.35ff). The theme of agricultural labourers is well attested in the Synoptics (e.g. Mark 12.1–12; Matthew 20.1–16), and could suggest that John is basing this part of his discourse on authentic Jesus material. However, as a free-floating pericope, the underlying tradition could just as easily refer to a Jewish harvest as to a Samaritan one.[21] It was Christian reflection on the meaning of Jesus' 'food', said in John 4.33 to be his activity (doing 'the will of the one who sent me'), which allowed the connection to be made: the (mission) 'fields are [now] ripe for harvesting' (John 4.35). John has woven these elements together to make the point: Jesus brought in a new era in which mission moved beyond the limits of Judaism.

This is the point confirmed in John 12.20–6, where certain 'Greeks' (are they Gentiles or Hellenistic Jews from the Diaspora?) ask Philip if they may see Jesus. Philip relays their request, which receives the cryptic response: 'Unless a grain of wheat falls into the earth and dies, it remains just a single grain; but if it dies, it bears much fruit' (John 12.23). This presumably means 'no'; the Greeks, whoever they are, never get to see Jesus. He is not available to them until after his death.

This Johannine picture fits in well with the evidence from Acts and the Epistles, both of which show that the highly controversial subject of mission was resolved only by later Christian reflection on the significance of Jesus' resurrection. Mission to the Samaritans or to the Gentiles is not possible before the appropriate 'hour' of Jesus' death on the cross.

The only other significant encounter between Jesus and a Gentile in John's Gospel occurs immediately after the episode with the Samaritan woman. This is the version of the healing of the centurion's servant in John 4.46–54. This has such obvious similarities with the Matthean parallel (Matthew 8.5–13) that it is likely to be dependent on a similar tradition. Therefore, the comments on the Matthean version apply equally well to this one. The link with the 'first' miracle at Cana in Galilee, however, is noteworthy. These are the only two signs in a numbered sequence which John never completes. This prompted Bultmann, followed by Fortna,[22] to suggest that the evangelist had access to an earlier source document containing synoptic-type material called 'the Book of Signs'. Although Fortna's thesis is disputed – and certainly exaggerated – it is an interesting theory, and could easily account for some of the 'overlaps' between John and the Synoptics. If so, the story of the healing of the servant has a strong claim to belong to the authentic Jesus tradition on the grounds of multiple attestation. But even then, all it shows is that Jesus was sometimes ready to go to the aid of a worthy individual Gentile – but only when asked to do so.

But John was as happy as the other evangelists to use his source traditions creatively. In his version of the story, the man is a 'royal official' rather than a centurion – perhaps a civil servant attached to the court of King Herod. So there is actually nothing in John's text to suggest he was a Gentile. Unlike Matthew, John does not allow the official to argue with Jesus, for that would not fit the image of Jesus as the Son of God who is always in command. Instead, the man pleads with Jesus for the boy (or servant) and Jesus remains in charge. John, like the other evangelists, has moulded the tradition to reflect his own interests.

By and large, then, John has little to contribute to the reconstruction of Jesus' attitude to Gentiles. If any conclusion is to be drawn, it is that John has remarkably little interest in the subject, and probably thought that mission outside the Christian community was a secondary issue, possible only after Jesus' death (John 12.20ff). Like the other evangelists, he knows that universal mission was a concept which belonged to a new order of salvation (John 4.19–26).

Isolated Sayings on the Gentiles

Mark 11.15–19 and parallels
The sequence of events surrounding the entry of Jesus into Jerusalem ('Palm Sunday') is gloriously muddled in Mark. He has a terrific build up as Jesus takes the city by storm, accompanied by shouts from an eager crowd (Mark 11.1–10). Having entered the city, he goes straight to the temple; but then, right at the climax of the story, Mark has Jesus simply go away again because 'it was already late' (v.11).

The reason for this limp anticlimax lies with Marcan intercalation. This 'sandwich' technique allows Mark to frame the incident of the Cleansing of the Temple with the Cursing of the Fig Tree, so that they mutually interpret each other. Matthew and Luke both found this sequence unsettling, because they independently change it (see Throckmorton, Section 199): Matthew abbreviates it, omitting the offending comment about the figs 'out of season', and Luke drops the entire unit altogether. But for Mark the story is crucial. The narrative subtext set up by the juxtaposition of the two incidents moves something like this: Jesus comes to claim the temple as a place of encounter with God for all people, including the Gentiles (Mark

11.17). But the Jewish leaders reject him and take counsel against him (Mark 11.18) – they are 'out of [God's eschatological] season'. Their plot to kill Jesus brings down a curse on their leadership, and triggers the final sequence leading to the cross (Mark 15.33–41), but the death of Jesus enables a Roman centurion to recognize the significance of events symbolized by the tearing down of the temple curtain which kept the Jewish God safely apart from the Gentiles (the Greek used in Mark 15.38 to describe the tearing of the curtain is especially vivid). As Jesus dies, God comes storming out of the restricted zone. By resisting Jesus, the chief priests bring about the demise of Jewish exclusivity: like the fig tree, the temple is doomed to wither.[23]

In his study of the historical Jesus, E. P. Sanders draws on this incident to support his argument that Jesus was a Jewish restoration prophet – that is, a prophet who felt called by God to 'purify' Israel in preparation for the imminent arrival of his Messianic kingdom. Sanders argues convincingly that the temple incident was probably related to this self-understanding – it makes perfect sense as a symbolic action in the prophetic tradition (e.g. Jeremiah 32.6–44 or Ezekiel 4.1–8) intended to warn Israel of God's impending judgement. That is what Jesus' contemporaries would have seen: an action symbolizing God's judgement. It was this which caused offence and led to his arrest by the temple authorities – the chief priests.[24] Jesus was condemned like the prophets before him because he announced God's sentence against Israel.

Although Sanders' reconstruction has not passed unchallenged, it makes excellent sense. If he is right, the original temple incident had absolutely nothing whatsoever to do with claiming the temple for 'the nations'. Mark alone turns the story that way by using the quotation from Jeremiah 7.11. The cleansing of the temple does not prove Jesus was concerned about Gentiles. On the contrary, it almost certainly confirms he was first and foremost concerned about unrepentant Israel.

Mark 13.10 and parallels

Another isolated saying about 'the nations' appears in Mark 13.10 and parallels (Throckmorton, Section 215). The setting is once again in the temple, but this time during a discourse in which Jesus instructs his disciples about the coming end-time. It should be noted that at least one element of this discourse appears to belong to the authentic Jesus tradition – the admission in Mark 13.32 that not even Jesus knew the time or the final hour. Nevertheless, there are signs of a composite structure underlying the present form of the narrative, not the least of which is the rather obvious aside in Mark 13.14: 'let the reader understand'. This is hardly likely to be a comment from Jesus speaking to the disciples about the temple!

A number of scholars suggest that behind the present text lies an earlier Jewish–Christian apocalypse. This is largely an argument from silence, and cannot be either proved or disproved. It is probably safer to say Mark has based this passage on an earlier source.[25] As a cautious scholar like Cranfield says:

> Our tentative conclusion is that xiii 5–37 does give substantially
> our Lord's teaching. That does not mean that we can be certain
> that throughout the discourse we have his exact words. It is
> intrinsically likely that his words have suffered some modification
> in the course of transmission here as elsewhere in the gospels. Nor
> is it implied that it was uttered as a single discourse. That it is
> composite [...] seems likely from the fact that some of the sayings
> in it occur in Matthew and Luke in other contexts.[26]

But that does not rule out the possibility that some of the material belongs to the authentic tradition, so each of the sayings must be considered independently. What, then, of the claims to authenticity in Mark 13.10?

Cranfield first notes the difficulties over the punctuation of the Greek text. Since the original manuscripts had no punctuation this had to be added later. In this case, some interpreters punctuate the verse so that the reference to the nations is taken with the preceding verse. It then reads 'and you will stand before rulers and kings for my sake in order to testify before them and to the nations. But first, the gospel must be preached' (author's translation). This has the effect of making 'the testimony to the nations' not a mission but a defence the disciples have to offer when accused in the courts. Nor are they necessarily foreign courts – Jesus could just as easily mean the local courts in Palestine managed by the Gentile forces of occupation.

However, both Cranfield and Hooker feel the most natural sense of the Greek is to take the phrase 'to the nations' with v.10. Hooker goes on to note, though, that v.10 interrupts the flow of the argument, which otherwise flows naturally from v.9 to v.11. Both Matthew and Luke drop the phrase in their parallel passages (Matthew 10.17–21 and Luke 21.12–19): Matthew has a general comment about 'bearing witness before the nations' (v.18, author's translation) and Luke has 'and it will result in you giving testimony' (v.13, author's translation). Hooker concludes that the phrase is an editorial comment, but assumes it was inserted by the evangelist to prepare the ground for his teaching on the later Gentile mission.

Thus, according to Cranfield, Mark 13.10 is an isolated, possibly authentic, saying of Jesus from an unknown context – a dislocated fragment which could have been about anything under the sun. Alternatively, according to Hooker, it is an editorial comment from the hand of Mark. Either way, it seems flimsy evidence for a theory of dominical teaching on a Gentile mission. It is about somebody testifying in some unspecified situation to Gentile authorities, possibly under conditions of persecution. By itself, it establishes very little. It raises a lot of interesting questions, though.

Mark 14.9 and parallels

At the beginning of the passion narrative, after Mark has noted the progress of the plot against Jesus, an incident in which an unnamed woman anoints Jesus[27] takes place in the house of Simon the leper. This provokes an argument between Jesus and his disciples about the appropriateness of the action. Jesus says that the woman's action is prophetic, foreshadowing his death and burial: her deed will be proclaimed wherever the gospel is preached (Mark 14.9).

And indeed, it has been – though possibly not in the way Mark envisaged. His version of events became subsequently inextricably fused with the similar (but different) story in Luke 7.36–50. The incident occurs in Luke at an earlier stage in Jesus' ministry, when a woman, represented as a repentant sinner, anoints his feet, not his head as in Mark. For Luke, this is all about forgiveness. There is no mention of this in Mark, however; for him, the focus is on a concern about wastefulness.

The first issue, then, is the relationship between two stories.[28] Luke has a much noticed interest in 'sub-themes' throughout his

Gospel, two of which concern the role of women and the need for repentance.[29] To find both of these sub-themes together in one incident, therefore, cautions against ready acceptance of the Lucan account. However, Luke's version is in fact so different in the details that many scholars doubt whether it is really a report about the same incident.

On the other hand, this is one of the few incidents over which there is near agreement in all four Gospels. John also has a version of the story in John 12.1–8. Unless his Gospel is directly dependent on one or other of the Synoptics, as some scholars continue to argue[30] (though many feel this is unlikely[31]), then this is an independent tradition. This makes the broad outline of the incident a serious contender for authenticity on the grounds of multiple attestation. The question then becomes, did the original underlying incident include a reference to the good news to be proclaimed throughout the world? Hooker thinks not: 'These words introduce what seems to be yet another addition – a saying about the world-wide mission of the Church already referred to in 13.10.'[32] This is a post-Easter editorial comment on the woman's action. After all, it is a strange memorial in which even the woman's name is forgotten.

Thus, this sampling of the three 'nations' sayings in Mark – the temple cleansing (11.17), the Little Apocalypse (13.10) and the anointing for burial (14.9) – point roughly in the same direction: the universal element in the sayings was almost certainly added by the evangelist, or by his sources. They were not part of the authentic tradition about Jesus.

John 3.16

John 3.16 is said to be the most widely quoted verse in the whole New Testament: 'For God so loved the world that he gave his only Son, so that everyone who believes in him may not perish but may have eternal life.' This comes towards the end of the Johannine discourse between Jesus and Nicodemus, a Jewish leader who, not insignificantly, comes to Jesus 'by night'.

Given that Jesus is 'the light of the world' (John 8.12), Nicodemus almost certainly represents those elements of the Jewish leadership who are sympathetic to Jesus but who remain in 'darkness'.[33] It is noteworthy that by the end of the Gospel all Nicodemus has done is give Jesus a decent burial (John 20.39f). This man honours Jesus, but he is not a disciple.

One of the more remarkable features of John 3.1–21, however, is the abrupt change of audience. Throughout vv.3–10, John uses second-person-singular forms of the personal pronoun – 'thee' and 'thou' in English. Suddenly, without warning, he switches to the second-person-plural forms 'you' from v.11 onwards. This is entirely lost in modern English, but signals in Greek an important change of direction. Jesus is no longer addressing a potential Jewish disciple. He is addressing everyone.

This is picked up in the language of John 3.16. This is no longer part of the conversation between Jesus and Nicodemus, but part of the more generalized teaching to every reader. It is unlikely to have been part of the original conversation.[34]

An analysis of John 3.16 confirms this. The Greek uses several obvious Johannine terms, including *agapaō*, one of several Greek verbs meaning 'love', but one which has a special significance for John (see, for example, the Farewell Discourses in John 13—17). Another example is *kosmos*, 'the world', a word which often has a hostile sense in John (see especially 17.15ff), though it can be morally neutral. The latter sense is probably in view here in John 3.16, where it provides a kind of literary flashback to the Prologue (John 1.1–18).

There is one feature of John 3.16 which is slightly out of character for this Gospel: the text says God *gave* his Son in contrast to the more familiar Johannine language which would say God *sent* the Son. Lindars notes the echo of Romans 8.32 ('He [God] did not withhold his own Son, but gave him up for all of us') in this verse,[35] which begins to make it sound like an early credal formula.

If so, John picked up a familiar Christian statement similar to Romans 8.32, and reworked it using his own characteristic language in order to summarize the significance of Jesus as the 'light of the world'. Nicodemus plays the role of the counterfoil, a representative of those who walk in darkness. The odds on this classic verse being an authentic word of Jesus are not high.

PART TWO

The Development of Universal Christian Mission

❖ 5 ❖

The First Christian Communities: Controversy over the Law

The story so far goes something like this. There is little in the Hebrew Scriptures to account for the later development of a Christian mission to the Gentiles. There is even less evidence of proselytizing activity by Jews in the first century. The portrait of the historical Jesus which emerges from a close reading of the gospels suggests that he fell well within range of the normal attitudes that might be expected in a first-century Palestinian Jew: he was not particularly hostile to Gentiles, but neither was he particularly interested in them. Jesus did not set out to build up contacts. He responded to Gentiles on an individual basis, and took no initiative to go out and meet them. Jesus intended to limit his mission to the people of Israel.

On the other hand, the gospels presuppose a strong sense of commitment to universal mission, as witnessed not only by the Great Commission but also by the number of incidents concerning Gentiles reported within the developing Jesus tradition. By the second half of the first century, the evangelists took it for granted that Christian believers were commissioned to 'preach to the nations'. Obviously, therefore, something happened to change attitudes during a remarkably short period between the death of Jesus and the writing of the gospels.[1] The task of the second half of this book is to try and work out what that 'something' might have been.

The difficulty is that an acute shortage of reliable data makes it almost impossible to account for the dramatic change. The only significant source of information comes from the Book of Acts, and therein lies the problem. From a scholarly point of view, Acts is fraught with difficulty, and the reliability of Luke's account is hotly disputed. Indeed, Acts has been likened to an impressionist painting:[2] everything appears clear from a distance, but becomes more and more blurred on closer inspection. Acts can only be used as a basis for historical reconstruction with the utmost caution.

History and Interpretation in Acts

Like the gospels, Acts circulated until the middle of the second century without a title. Eventually, it came to be known as the Acts of the Apostles, but this name is really misleading: Luke is quite specific about his definition of an apostle -- he believes the term only applies to a limited group of twelve people who accompanied Jesus 'from the baptism of John until the day when he was taken up from us' (Acts 1.21f). On this basis, Acts has very little to say about the apostles, and confines itself largely to the activities of Peter and John in the first part of the book. Attention is then switched to other characters such as Stephen, Philip and Barnabas, before the real hero emerges in the shape of Paul. This towering figure dominates roughly 50 per cent of Acts, approximately a quarter of Luke-Acts combined. The irony is that on Luke's terms Paul was not even an apostle.

Paul would not have agreed with this, however (cf. 1 Corinthians 9.1 etc.), and the picture of Paul which emerges in Luke-Acts is considerably at variance with what the man says about himself. Luke, for example, never mentions the one fact which is known by almost everyone else – that Paul wrote letters. Curiously, Luke suggests Paul was a powerful speaker (e.g. Acts 17.22–31) whereas Paul thought otherwise (1 Corinthians 2.3f; 2 Corinthians 10.1–11). Key elements in Pauline theology are missing in the speeches attributed to him, and so on. The question eventually becomes unavoidable: how much did Luke really know about Paul? The evidence is not encouraging.

For a start, trying to work through the relationship between the sequence of events outlined in the autobiographical section of Galatians 1.11—2.14 and (presumably?) the same events in Acts 9— 16 is a sure recipe for a headache.[3] Tracing Luke's itinerary of Paul's movements around the Mediterranean is another nightmare – did Paul go out on specific 'missionary journeys' from a 'home base' in

Jerusalem? If so, how many times? Where did he go? When? But perhaps the most unlikely part of Luke's account is Acts 16.3, which has Paul take Timothy and have 'him circumcised because of the Jews who were in those places, for they all knew that his father was a Greek'. Is this really the same person who wrote that circumcision is nothing and those who insist on it should 'castrate themselves' (Galatians 5.6–12)?

A number of recent studies have helped to clear away some of these difficulties by demonstrating that Luke almost certainly re-edited his material to reflect matters of more immediate concern to his readers. Some modern readers may find this disturbing, but it is important to remember that Luke-Acts is a first-century text, not a twentieth-century one. Authors had different expectations: they might write to inform or entertain, but above all they wrote to persuade. So Luke presents his history the way he believed things ought to be, not necessarily the way they were.[4] In particular, he glosses over conflict in order to present a more harmonious picture of early Christian history. The concept of objective reporting was not widespread in the ancient world.

But this is not the same as saying that Luke invented his whole account. Parts of Acts (for example the material on Corinth in Acts 18) fit in well with the snippets of information provided by Paul, as well as with the limited external archaeological data.[5] Some of Luke's material may well be based on accurate information, therefore. The problem is sifting out the wheat from the chaff, distinguishing the historical material from the editorial composition.

Fortunately, it is possible to gain something of an idea of Luke's literary style by studying his Gospel alongside the equivalent material in Mark or Matthew. Such a comparison suggests that Luke was generally quite conservative: he was prepared to summarize or 'improve' the grammar, and was ready to augment his sources, where he felt it was necessary, with supplementary material. But there is little to suggest he manufactured stories *ex nihilo*. Luke – like many authors – simply felt free to adapt (perhaps massage) his source material in order to make it fit his view of reality.

Luke obviously had access to source material when he composed his Gospel, but whether he also had sources for Acts is far from clear.[6] But assuming he had access to some basic information,[7] it would seem likely that he continued his practice of editing, summarizing and augmenting, but rarely creating a narrative entirely from scratch.

Because it is so difficult to unravel Acts, a number of scholars despair of the attempt and give up.[8] But there is so little other information about the early church that it is almost impossible to ignore Luke-Acts, and sooner or later even the most sceptical commentators are driven back to the book. This is no excuse for swinging from one extreme to the other, however, and naively assuming Luke's narrative can be read as a straightforward historical account.[9] It is not that. Each part of the text must be assessed independently for its historical reliability.

In order to do this, it is necessary to establish a baseline against which the evidence can be evaluated. One way to do this is to consider the purpose of Luke-Acts, on the grounds that this would provide an insight into the interests which helped to shape the author's thinking. So why did Luke write an account of Christian origins in two volumes – the first telling the story of Jesus, the second the story of the early church? After all, none of the other evangelists felt compelled to supplement their gospels in this way.

One suggestion is that Luke was interested in evangelism. Thus, in his first volume he sets out the basis of the good news (Luke 2.10) in the story of the life and death of Jesus. Then, in volume two, he shows how that good news spread 'from Jerusalem [. . .] to the ends of the earth' (Acts 1.8). Against this view, however, is the fact that Luke-Acts is unlikely to persuade potential converts who are not already committed – it requires a considerable commitment to plough through 52 lengthy chapters! In any case, the preface to the two volumes assumes a working knowledge of Christianity (Luke 1.1–4). On top of that, it has an untidy ending (was Paul convicted or released?), and this is hardly likely to impress doubters. Luke-Acts simply does not read like a missionary tract.

So another possibility is that Luke was a historian and intended to write a history of the early church. This has greater merit, and there are a number of interesting parallels between Luke-Acts and other examples of the historical genre found around the same period. None of these books would qualify as histories in the modern sense: there is no attempt to give an unbiased and objective account of events.[10] But on the other hand, there are important differences in style and content between Luke-Acts and these proposed parallels. Acts may be history (in the first-century sense), but is clearly more than that.

Other scholars point to parallels with the ancient genres of biography and romantic fiction. But again, despite attractive points of contact with each of these classical forms, Luke-Acts fits neither of them comfortably. All roads lead in the same direction: history, biography and fiction – none of these proposed genres offers a fully adequate explanation of Luke's purpose.

Luke sets his own parameters in the preface in Luke 1.1–4.[11] This is especially noteworthy for the strong emphasis it places on the 'orderly account' based on the evidence of 'eyewitnesses' (in the ancient sense) which Luke has been 'investigating [. . .] carefully' so that the reader may 'know the truth [. . .] about which you have been instructed'. Luke apparently knows of many alternative accounts (*diēgēsis*) which he is anxious to correct in some way. He assumes the reader has received basic Christian instruction (*katēchēthēs*), but wants to supplement this with accurate (*akribōs*) information so that they might have a greater degree of certainty (*asphaleia*). This adds up to a subtle statement of intent: the purpose of Luke-Acts, apparently, is to correct other versions of Christian history which Luke feels are misleading in some way.[12] In other words, he wants to correct what he feels is a distorted view of Christianity.

A look at the issues raised in the two volumes suggests that two themes dominate his attention: the relationship between Christianity and Judaism, and the relationship between the church and the wider secular society.[13] These, therefore, were presumably the cause of the anxiety felt by Luke.

Luke deals with the relationship between Christianity and Judaism by setting out an orderly progression from the Hebrew Scriptures (Zechariah in the temple in Luke 1.15ff) to the new world of Christianity at the heart of the Empire (Paul in Rome in Acts 28.30f). Changes in Jewish practice had undoubtedly occurred, but these were not the result of casual human innovation but were part of a preordained plan carefully prepared by God. Everything is necessary, or according to plan – *dei*, to use the Greek verb.

The second issue concerning Luke was the question of how Christians should relate to the wider pagan society. This is addressed by showing that although Christianity was a new movement based on the teachings of a man executed by the government, Christians are neither subversive nor a threat to the established social order. Jesus was crucified as a criminal, Stephen was likewise executed by a lynch mob, and Paul was arrested for disturbing the peace, but the centurion supervising the crucifixion recognized that 'this man was innocent' (Luke 22.47), and all the authorities concerned could see that Paul meant no harm (Acts 26.30ff).

Weaving these elements together, Luke tries to reassure his readers of several things at once. Firstly, he reassures the Jewish Christians in his community that the drift towards the Gentiles did not mean that the church had abandoned the God of Israel. By the same token, the emphasis on God's control over events is designed to reassure Gentile readers that they have gained a place in the (previously exclusive) people of God. Finally, by emphasizing the power of the supernatural, the works of charity and the piety of the early Christians, Luke is able to produce an argument which Jews and Gentiles alike would find persuasive. Everyone could see from Luke-Acts that Christianity was not a threat to decent society.[14]

In order to achieve these objectives, however, Luke is compelled to bend history to bring it into line with his ideas. He smoothes over the conflict of transition from Judaism to Christianity by shaping an orderly progression from the Old Testament world of Luke 1—2 through to Paul (the immediate predecessor of Lucan Christianity?). His main characters link together like a chain, or like runners in a relay: each plays their part and then hands on the baton to the next person. In short, in the words of one of the leading commentators, Acts is Luke's reply to 'the theological problem posed by the mission to the Gentiles without the law', and his solution is 'a simplification of the course of history'.[15] Any study of early Christianity which makes use of Acts must take this obvious Lucan tendency into account.

Piecing Together the Evidence

Returning to the theme of the Gentile mission, there are perhaps two widely held theories about the development which draw heavily on Acts. One is eloquently presented in an influential book by David Bosch. According to this, although Luke knew Christian mission to the Gentiles had been a controversial innovation (Acts 15), he believed the move was compelling because Jesus had set a precedent by preaching to those on the fringes of society, especially outcasts, sinners and the poor. Thus, the apostles were already living on the boundaries of Judaism and were ready to be pushed out towards the Gentiles once they had thought through the implications of their post-Easter experience.[16]

But there is a clear weakness in this argument: the people on the fringes of respectability in the gospels are Jews, and therefore do not provide an obvious precedent for extending the constituency of Israel. Jesus' ministry speaks about renewal, not about a radical change of membership.[17] It is by no means obvious – except to those who want to make the connection on other grounds – that his concern for Jewish outcasts opened the door to those who never belonged to Israel in the first place.

The alternative explanation of the origins of Christian mission is a composite argument and has to be built up in stages. It tends to go something like this:[18]

- There was a widespread belief in first-century Judaism that God was about to intervene decisively in history to vindicate Israel.

- According to the prophets, on the 'day of the Lord' the Gentiles would come flooding into Zion in pilgrimage. Stage one in the argument is thus established: the Scriptures supply a crucial link between eschatology and the Gentiles.

- Next, the early Christians believed the eschatological age had already arrived: Jesus was 'the first fruits of those who have died' (1 Corinthians 15.20) so that 'if anyone is in Christ, there is a new creation: everything old has passed away; see, everything has become new!' (2 Corinthians 5.17). This supplies the necessary shift in perspective.

- The final stage is to fuse these elements together. Because the eschatological promises of Scripture had been fulfilled in Jesus, the Gentiles were now entitled to share in the community of God alongside the people of Israel.

- QED: the first Christians felt compelled by Scripture and their post-resurrection perspective to go out to the Gentiles and engage in a universal mission.

All this is nonsense, of course. Apart from the fact that it did not occur to non-Christian Jews to look for an eschatological mission to the Gentiles on the basis of Scripture, there is a basic logical flaw in this Christianized version of the argument: the movement in Acts is completely the wrong way round. According to Luke, the first Christians moved *from* Jerusalem *to* the Gentiles, whereas the Scriptures predict a movement *from* the Gentiles *towards* Zion. It is centrifugal, not centripetal. Further, the eschatological influx predicted by the prophets was to be driven by God and did not require missionaries to go out and preach. And in any case, the Gentiles were coming to submit, not to join the people of God as equal partners. In short, the composite argument simply will not work.[19]

The novelty of the idea of a mission to the Gentiles is well reflected in Acts, which shows that the first Christians were deeply split over the issue (Acts 15.1–35). Most Jews – including Christian Jews – welcomed individual converts, but the conversion of large numbers of Gentiles became a threat to Jewish identity. This is the real concern in Acts: was the Jewish-Christian movement to remain a minority sect within Judaism, albeit one that attracted a few Gentile adherents (as in many other synagogues); or was it to become detached as a fully fledged independent community which took no account of the covenant with Israel and required all members, Jews and Gentiles alike, to opt into the movement on precisely the same terms? The heat generated by this argument is a powerful indicator of the lack of precedent. Those opposed to the open policy towards the Gentiles did not debate with their colleagues about the eschatological significance of mission. They simply said no.

This is presumably why only a tiny handful of Christians actually engage in mission in Acts: Philip, Peter and a few other lone individuals attract a following, but only Paul and Barnabas become involved in a systematic mission. Even they fell out (Acts 15.39). The later New Testament texts such as the Pastoral Epistles suggest a similar lack of interest: these letters are far more concerned about church structures and individual Christian behaviour than outreach to non-believers. And the indifference to missionary activity apparently continued well beyond the New Testament period. In the *Didache*, hospitality rules for wandering 'missionaries and charismatics' show that itinerant preachers are to be 'welcomed as the Lord', but should not 'stay more than a day, or two days if it is really necessary'. This is because if they stay any longer, they are clearly scroungers and not genuine missionaries.[20] This description presupposes that only a handful of Christians are actually on the move: mission is a specialist ministry involving designated individuals (see 1 Corinthians 12.28). Further, such itinerant preachers as exist are engaged in a church-based activity revolving around the existing congregation. There is no mention of evangelism.

In short, many early Christian texts give the impression that mission was scarcely a priority. Neither the Hebrew Scriptures nor existing Jewish practice provided a conceptual framework for evangelism, and the development caused deep controversy within the earliest Christian communities. So, why did it develop?

The Dispute between the Hellenists and Hebraists

According to Acts 8.1, the first mission to non-Jews was a consequence not of conscious outreach but of inter-group conflict. One group of believers (but not others) was persecuted by another group of Jewish extremists (represented by Saul/Paul), and this resulted in the relocation of some Christians (but not the apostles) throughout Judea and Samaria. This presented the exiles with an opportunity to preach to people on the outer boundaries of Judaism (Samaritans and God-fearers in Acts 8, but not yet Gentiles), although a theological rationale for the ad hoc move was not provided until after the process had already started (Acts 10—11). The situation was not fully regularized until even later (Acts 15).

The narrative sequence leading up to this begins with an abrupt announcement that there had been a bitter dispute between the 'Hellenists' and 'Hebraists' (Acts 6.1ff). This controversy erupts out of nowhere, for up to this point Luke has been at pains to emphasize the overwhelming sense of harmony in the early church. The constituency of the two groups concerned is also unclear.[21] Perhaps the most likely explanation is that they refer to different linguistic groups: the Hellenists are Greek-speaking Jews, originally from the Diaspora but now resident in Jerusalem and perhaps connected with the synagogue of the Freedmen (Acts 6.9), whereas the Hebraists are perhaps Aramaic-speaking Palestinian Jews.

Luke says the argument was over the neglect of the Hellenist 'widows [...] in the daily distribution of food' (Acts 6.1). The apostles resolve the problem by appointing seven assistants from the Hellenists 'to wait on tables' so that the twelve might devote themselves more fully 'to prayer and to serving the word' (Acts 6.2–6). Curiously, five of the seven disappear almost immediately – rather like Matthias the apostle in Acts 1.23f – whilst Stephen and Philip neither care for the widows nor wait at table. Not another word is said about the distribution of food. Instead, Stephen next appears in trouble in the Hellenistic Jewish synagogue (Acts 6.8ff), whereas Philip reappears engaging in the very activity supposedly reserved for the twelve – preaching the word (Acts 8.4–40). In other words, the narrative is inconsistent. Both Stephen and Philip look more like leaders than welfare assistants.

This suggests that behind Luke's account there lies an earlier tradition that spoke about a controversy between two Christian groups in Jerusalem: both were Jewish, but one was associated with the seven and related to the Hellenist Jewish synagogue, whilst the other was headed by the Hebraist (Palestinian) apostles.[22] The Christian movement was thus already split into different strands, and even a generous reading of the New Testament makes it unlikely that the church ever existed as a single unit.[23]

But this was to be expected. According to Acts 2.5–13, the audience at Pentecost consisted of a cross-section of 'devout Jews from every nation under heaven'. Of course, Luke's narrative displays his characteristic ambiguity – for example, were the apostles speaking foreign languages, or were they just incoherent (Acts 2.13)? The speech that follows (Acts 2.14–36) is unmistakably Lucan.[24] But even Luke does not say the three thousand or so people baptized that day joined a church, only that they were instructed to 'repent and be baptized' (Acts 2.38). This fits in with Acts 2.46, where Christian meetings are held in addition to regular Jewish worship in the temple. The Pentecost believers did not leave Judaism but went back to their synagogues as 'followers of the Way' in the same way that other members of their group might be Pharisees or followers of another Jewish movement. This is a point worth stressing, because Craig Hill rightly criticizes scholars for over-simplifying the Hellenist–Hebraist dispute in Acts 6: he properly points out that it can be too easily assumed that the Hebraists were 'conservative' and the Hellenists 'radical'.[25] All that the evidence suggests is that the groups came from different communities, both of which almost certainly had their fair share of traditionalists and liberals alike.

A significant feature of Acts 6—8 is the comparatively minor role played by the Hebraists. The focus quickly switches from the dispute over the distribution of food to Stephen and the 'synagogue of the Freedmen [...] Cyrenians, Alexandrians, and others of those from Cilicia and Asia' (Acts 6.9). These are Hellenistic Jews one and all. Thus, the events leading up to the death of Stephen and the expulsion of some Jewish Christians from Jerusalem was not the unfortunate outcome of a division between Hebraist and Hellenist Christians, but purely an internal affair within the Hellenist synagogue of which Stephen was a member. That is why the Hebraist Jewish Christians led by the apostles were left untouched by the controversy (Acts 8.1ff): it did not concern them.[26]

Turning to Acts 6.13, the charge against Stephen is that he said 'things against this place [the temple] and the law'. This is strange, because in his extremely long speech, Stephen appears to say little about either. As he rehearsed the chain of events from the patriarchs to Jesus without saying much in his defence about the law or the temple, it is difficult to understand why the judges did not tell him to stick to the point!

L. D. Hurst believes he may be able to identify in part how Luke saw a logical connection between this speech and the charges against Stephen. The link turns on the interesting parallel between Acts 7 and Hebrews 7—10.[27] In Hebrews, a sharp contrast is drawn between the sacrifices for atonement laid down by the Old Testament law and the new cult inaugurated by Jesus. The author's critique rehearses the story of Abraham and Melchizedek from patriarchal history (Hebrews 7) in much the same way as does Acts 7, and the point drawn from this in Hebrews is that Jesus was invested with a form of priesthood which was infinitely superior to the Levitical priesthood servicing the temple in Jerusalem. The old Covenant was inadequate and provisional (Hebrews 8.13), based on 'the blood of bulls and goats' (Hebrews 9.11–14) sacrificed in a 'sanctuary made by human hands, a mere copy of the true one' (Hebrews 9.24). The tabernacle in

Jerusalem was merely a rough draft of God's intention, but this had now been definitively disclosed in the sacrifice of Jesus, who offered himself once and for all in the heavenly sanctuary before God.

Surprisingly, the temple building is never mentioned in Hebrews: the comparison is always between two types of tent (e.g. Hebrews 9.1). This omission has led some commentators to speculate that the author of Hebrews had never been to Jerusalem and was arguing on the basis of textbook theory. But according to Hurst it is equally possible that the careful words in Hebrews reflect an implied criticism of the Jerusalem cult: in Exodus 24—25, God instructed the people of Israel to construct a moveable tent, not a massive stone building. In which case, the sacrifices in the temple were not only inadequate, they were carried out in direct contravention of a divine command.

A number of similar themes appear in Stephen's speech in Acts: following the rehearsal of God's saving relationship with Israel through the patriarchs, Solomon is criticized for building a temple on the grounds that God does not dwell in a building made 'with human hands' (Acts 7.48). Having conspired to disobey God's Law, therefore, the temple authorities were unable to recognize the new cult established through Jesus, and they had proved their intransigence by killing God's appointed servant (Acts 7.51-3). Stephen's defence, then, is to turn the tables on his accusers: it is they who are guilty of breaking the Torah, because the temple building had never been part of God's plan. Which is why, perhaps, the judges 'became enraged and gnashed their teeth' (Acts 7.54).

The author of Hebrews wrote in fluent Greek, used forms of Greek rhetoric and quoted the Scriptures in Greek. Presumably, therefore, he was a Hellenistic Jew.[28] Stephen belonged to the Hellenistic Jewish synagogue. Both traditions, therefore, bear witness to similar forms of Hellenist Jewish Christianity which were sharply critical of the existing cult. But they were not alone. Philo, a Hellenistic Jew roughly contemporary with Paul, also felt compelled to spiritualize the temple: it was not the butchery of animals that was important, but the sacrifice of human obedience it symbolized. Here at least was one other Hellenist Jew who was uncomfortable with the blood of animals splattered around the altar.[29]

Nor is it implausible that other Diaspora Jews resident in

Jerusalem held similar views. They had travelled long distances to be in the city, so it is reasonable to assume that most of them had a strong commitment to their religious heritage. For some, arrival in the promised land would be like a homecoming: but for others, the reality of life in Jerusalem might prove rather disappointing. Instead of the devout holiness they had anticipated, they encountered the sight, smell and noise of hundreds of animals packed together in a small courtyard waiting to be slaughtered. It would not need a late twentieth-century animal activist to argue that the process of butchering the victims was too much: Hosea had long before said that God desires 'steadfast love, not sacrifice' (Hosea 6.6), and the Psalmist had written of God as saying 'If I were hungry, I would not tell you, for the world and all that is in it is mine. Do I eat the flesh of bulls, or drink the blood of goats? Offer to God a sacrifice of thanksgiving, and pay your vows to the Most High' (Psalm 50.12–14). Such people were going to find the temple more an embarrassment than a thrilling cultural centrepiece or a focal point for devotion.

But such dissent was unlikely to prove popular. Apart from the fact that the temple was a highly significant symbol of national identity, Josephus estimates that over 18,000 men were employed in building projects connected with the temple,[30] to say nothing of the regular staff – priests, Levites, singers, guards and so on. Even allowing for Josephus' tendency to exaggerate, it is not unreasonable to assume that a major part of the economy of Jerusalem revolved around the temple, especially if local traders and suppliers are added in. At a quite elementary level, opposition to the cult was a serious threat to the economic survival of the city.

Behind the present account of the bitter dispute in Acts 6, therefore, lies a tradition which shows that two completely different streams of Jewish Christianity existed at an early stage in Jerusalem. One was centred around a group of Aramaic-speaking Palestinian Jewish Christians who remained faithful to the temple (Acts 2.46). This community was led by the apostles, observed the Torah, and kept its distance from dangerous radicals like Stephen. The other community was based on the Greek-speaking Hellenist synagogue. Led by Stephen and other members of the seven, some of these Jewish Christians shared the radical critique of the temple espoused by other Hellenist Jews. Other more conservative members of their synagogue apparently took a dim view of this challenge to the ethnic and religious values of Judaism, and as a result Stephen was killed and his colleagues expelled.

These radical members of 'the Way' (Acts 9.2) took into exile their critique of conservative Hellenist Judaism. 'Scattered throughout the countryside of Judea and Samaria' (Acts 8.1) they found themselves meeting isolated individuals on the fringes of Judaism who spoke the same (Hellenist) language. Enter Philip – first with the Samaritans (Acts 8.4–13) and then with the Ethiopian eunuch. The Samaritans had a well established but ambivalent relationship with Judaism: as a neighbouring and recognized 'half-Jewish' community they were accepted for some purposes and rejected for others. They are right on the margins of tolerance for first-century Judaism.[31] The Ethiopian eunuch is in a similar position. He is enough of a 'God-fearer' to be reading Isaiah on his way home from a pilgrimage to Jerusalem. A Gentile adherent to the synagogue is thus the first recorded convert. Even now, Philip is not preaching to complete pagans.

Luke offers no explanation for this expansion in missionary horizons – his only comment is that it was effective (Acts 8.13–17). But perhaps the Hellenistic Jewish Christian group expelled from Jerusalem was open to potential sympathizers on purely pragmatic grounds – they needed new supporters to help rebuild their broken community. The bonus for Samaritan and Gentile God-fearers was that 'the [Christian] Way' offered acceptance by the Jewish God without the trauma of rejecting their own culture or assuming the nationalistic implications of proselyte conversion. The result was a steady trickle of outsiders who joined the first Jewish Christian group to accept them without prior proselyte conversion. It was on these casual foundations that the concept of universal mission was later to build.

The Argument from Experience

Luke glosses over the tension between these different Christian movements because he is anxious to reassure his readers. In particular, he needs to show the Jewish members of his community that the decision to preach to the nations did not evolve casually out of the death of a dangerous radical, but was worked out in full accord with God's preordained plan.

So, in order to drive the point home, he gives Peter – a prominent Palestinian Jewish leader – the honour of converting the first Gentile. Peter is called to minister to Cornelius, a 'devout man who feared God', that is to say a God-fearer like the Ethiopian eunuch, a fringe member of the synagogue. But still Peter does not take the initiative alone – he has to be persuaded by means of a heavenly vision that the distinction between Jew and Gentile has finally been abolished. Luke tells the story twice to make sure the reader gets the point: this was a new move, one which had to be authorized directly by God (Acts 10.9–16 and 11.5–17).[32]

But even Luke has to admit that early Christianity continued to be divided over the issue (Acts 15.1–5). The Palestinian (Aramaic-speaking) community had not been involved in the disruption following the death of Stephen and therefore saw no reason for change. They shared the perspective of most other Jews, for whom mission to the Gentiles was not an issue. On the other hand, the expulsion from the Hellenistic synagogue into a predominantly Gentile environment gave the group around Philip a wider vision. Inter-group rivalry about the development of Christianity erupted between the two movements, and Acts 15.6–29 shows that diplomatic relations were only possible after a definitive compromise had been worked out.[33]

The letters of Paul suggest that the controversy continued to stir up passions for some while after (see Romans and Galatians). It is worth noting that according to Acts, it was through the radical Hellenistic Jewish group that Paul first came into contact with Christianity. He makes his first appearance holding the coats at the stoning of Stephen (Acts 7.58; and see 1 Corinthians 15.9; Galatians 1.13; Philippians 3.6). He then obtains authority to travel to Damascus, a Hellenist city outside Palestine, in order to root out Hellenistic Jewish Christian subversion (Acts 9.1ff – though Luke fails to explain how Paul might persecute people outside the jurisdiction of the Jewish authorities). En route, he encounters the risen Christ (Acts 9.3–9), and on arrival in Damascus he is initiated into the Hellenist Jewish Christian community (Acts 9.10–22). The whole episode of Paul's 'conversion'[34] takes place within the context of Hellenistic Jewish Christianity.

In his letters, Paul claims a direct revelation from God as the basis for his authority to preach to the Gentiles (e.g. Galatians 1.1, 15–17) and insists on his independence of the Jerusalem community (with a more conservative view of the Gentiles?). There are grounds, however, for arguing that although Paul came into Christianity through a group which was already more open to the Gentiles, he continued to develop his missionary thinking in the light of experience. The evidence is indirect, all the same, and has to be put together piece by piece.

In Galatians 1.18—2.1, Paul says that after he became a Christian he ministered for fourteen years in the regions of Syria and Cilicia. This is an area on the borders of Palestine where Jewish influence was still relatively strong, but contact with Gentiles was inevitable. Paul does not say that he preached exclusively to Jews during this period, but neither does he say he preached to Gentiles. Actually, Acts 13.46 suggests he adopted a policy of preaching to Jews first and Gentiles later, and this is backed up by passages such as Romans 1.16. Further, the famous statement in 1 Corinthians 9.19ff is notoriously difficult to interpret, but one way of reading it is to see it as chronological sequence ('first, I became as a Jew [. . .] then later to those outside the law I became as one outside the law [. . .]').[35] It would seem possible, then, that in the early stages of his ministry Paul followed established Christian custom by preaching exclusively to the circuit of Jewish congregations in the Syrian and Cilician Diaspora.

But this would have been enough to bring him into contact with a Gentile audience – not only because he was moving in a predominantly pagan environment, but because most of the synagogues he visited would have had a small but significant number of Gentile adherents. In preaching to Jews, therefore, Paul automatically preached to God-fearers as well. He only needed to attract a handful of these (over a considerable period of time – fourteen years according to Galatians 2.1) for the ethnic balance within the new movement to change. Eventually, Paul decided to check out the position with the 'acknowledged leaders' of the Palestinian movement in Jerusalem (Galatians 2.2f), and he was reassured by them that no harm was done in preaching to pro-Jewish Gentile sympathizers. But in his home congregation back in Antioch, some of the more conservative Jewish Christians directly affected by the impact of the shifting ethnic balance took exception to Paul's success. Apart from threatening the identity of the movement, the growing number of Gentiles sharing meals with Jewish Christians (the Eucharist) undermined adherence to the biblical purity laws. The dispute within the Antioch church had the effect of polarizing opinion, and both parties were forced to take increasingly committed positions to defend themselves. When matters were forced to a head, Peter and Barnabas attempted a compromise, but this was characteristically rejected by Paul, who accused them both of hypocrisy (Galatians 1—2).

Paul never finishes the story in Galatians. He accepts the 'right hand of fellowship' (Galatians 2.9), which would have signalled the temporary cessation of hostilities.[36] But assuming this is the same disagreement with Barnabas represented in Acts 15.37ff, Paul began to operate as an independent agent from that point on. Like the Hellenist Jewish Christians before him, Paul's ministry grew out of an experience of conflict over the admission of Gentiles into membership of the Jewish-Christian movement.

And so the evidence continues to mount up. When Peter was persuaded to baptize Cornelius, he appealed to the experience of a vision to justify what he recognized as an innovation – the conversion of a Gentile (Acts 10—11). When Paul later needed to defend his authority to engage in mission to the Gentiles, he appealed to his experience of a direct commissioning by God (e.g. Romans 1.1-6). Neither of them appeal to established theological principle, because there was none. Both Acts and the letters of Paul acknowledge the novelty of a situation in which Gentiles were received into full membership of a Christian community without prior conversion to Judaism. It was an innovation based on experience and interpreted as a new development authorized by God. The theology followed afterwards.

✤ 6 ✤

Christianity in a Pagan World

The Hellenist Jewish Christians 'scattered because of the persecution [...] travelled as far as Phoenicia, Cyprus and Antioch' (Acts 11.19). Or to put it another way, they went home – back to the comparatively safe territory outside the jurisdiction of the Jerusalem authorities, in the familiar Hellenistic environment from whence they came. But they kept exclusively to Jewish circles: 'they spoke the word to no one except Jews'.

Or did they? Not for the first time, Luke muddies the waters and creates a more complicated picture. Apparently, 'some men of Cyprus and Cyrene [...] on coming to Antioch, spoke to the Hellenists also, proclaiming the Lord Jesus' (Acts 11.20). But who were these Hellenists? Were they the same sort of Hellenists as those mentioned in 6.1f, that is to say Greek-speaking Jews? If so, Luke is simply repeating himself – he has already said in v.19 that the believers spoke only to Jews. The tone of v.20 implies an intended contrast, however: the two verses might even be paraphrased 'although the group as a whole spoke only to Jews, a few of their number preached to non-Jews as well'. But if that is what Luke meant to say, he has shifted the meaning of 'Hellenist' so that it now refers to Greek-speaking Gentiles. This would be clearer if the variant reading 'Greeks' is accepted, though the manuscript support for this is far from certain.[1] Still, at the very least the variant tradition shows a number of early scribes saw the difficulty and thought this must be Luke's intention. Assuming, then, that the Hellenists in Acts 11.20 are Gentiles, Luke is describing a new development. A few head-strong believers had broken ranks with Jewish Christianity, with the result that the Jesus movement spread throughout the city. The outcome was 'it was in Antioch that the disciples were first called

Christians' (Acts 11.26). A new name is needed for a new status: Christianity was starting to attract attention as a distinctive religion, not simply as variant form of Judaism.

Why would these believers suddenly choose to preach to the Gentiles? Perhaps for the same pragmatic reasons Philip and Paul turned to Gentile sympathizers – opportunism in a multicultural environment. But from Luke's point of view (perhaps exaggerating the success a little), 'the hand of the Lord was upon them, and a great number became believers and turned to the Lord' (v.21).

Whatever the explanation, news of the initiative filtered back to the Hellenist Jewish Christian community in Jerusalem (Acts 11.22). They decided to send an embassy in the person of Barnabas: as a Hellenist Jew from Cyprus attached to the Jerusalem community (Acts 4.36) he was an ideal candidate for the job. On arrival in Antioch, he was immediately impressed by the quality of the Gentile Christian adherents (Paul thought he was 'easily led' in the less sympathetic report presented in Galatians 2.12), and he was persuaded to see the new development as the work of God. Consequently, he invited another Hellenist Jewish Christian colleague to join him in a new missionary alliance. Enter Paul.

In launching this new missionary drive, the fledgling group in Antioch was moving out into uncharted waters. So long as Christianity remained a reformist movement within Judaism, it enjoyed a degree of protection from external social pressure. The Jews, of course, had always been vulnerable to communal disapproval because of their exclusive attitude to outsiders, their refusal to conform to normal patterns of behaviour (such as eating normal food or working seven days a week), and disrespect for the local pagan gods. But they were generally tolerated because they had the advantage of ancient ancestral custom. Christians could claim no such thing. By insisting on withdrawal from the surrounding pagan culture and simultaneously offending Jewish sensitivities, Christians antagonized both groups at once. They were in an extremely weak position. It may not be coincidental that reports of persecution in the New Testament begin to surface at precisely this stage.[2]

The letters of Paul reflect the manoeuvring this changing situation demanded. In Romans, for example, Paul attempts to redraw the socio-religious boundaries around Judaism, Christianity and the

Gentile world. He thus has to argue for Jewish and Gentile Christian unity within the group (Romans 14) whilst at the same time moving to quell unease over the changes in process – especially the theological shift away from the centrality of the Jewish Torah (Romans 3—8) and the consequent re-evaluation of Judaism this required (Romans 9—11). He also has to allay fears about the perceived social threat often associated with new religious movements (Romans 13.1–10).[3]

Another direct consequence of the shifting membership was that Paul could no longer assume his readers would routinely understand the basic tenets of Judaism. Thus, in Galatians 5.2f he has to spell out the implications of Torah observance, whilst in 1 Corinthians 10.14 he has to exhort Christians to 'flee from the worship of idols'. Paul is being forced to spell out the outline of a Jewish belief structure to a Gentile audience which has not yet been able to internalize a code alien to their upbringing.

The arrival of Gentiles into the Hellenist Jewish Christian community in Antioch thus had far-reaching consequences. A shift in the ethnic make-up of the movement was pushing the theological argument beyond the limits of Jewish tolerance. It was in this social context of what might now be called interfaith dialogue between Jewish, Christian and Greek religious beliefs that the concept of universal mission was forged.

The Greek Cultural Environment

The world into which Christianity had moved was the predominantly urban environment of the Hellenistic city. An extensive network of cities throughout the eastern Mediterranean had grown out of the Macedonian conquests under Alexander the Great. Immediately after his death, the Empire had been divided up between rival generals, some of whom embarked on aggressive programmes of Hellenization to strengthen their political grip and social control; one of the casualties of this policy had been Israel at the time of the Maccabeans. Old settlements were revamped along Hellenistic lines and new ones founded.[4] The lingua franca of the region became *koinē* Greek, a form of classical Greek modified through everyday speech in a multilingual context. It is one measure of the success of the infant church in adapting to this environment that the Christian Scriptures were written in Greek rather than the Aramaic/Hebrew dialects of Palestine.

The network of ancient urban settlements around the eastern Mediterranean was based on the pattern of the pre-industrial city, not the familiar conurbations of the modern world.[5] Such cities operated within clearly defined physical boundaries. Enclosed by fortifications, they often had internal walls or markers to designate the areas open to the general population. Very few people could move freely across all the boundaries – perhaps only priests, actors, singers, town-criers and the like. By and large, the layout of a city reflected the local social structure. The focal point of power would be roughly in the centre, inhabited by the élite. Next to that would be an area controlled by guilds of tradesmen and the other recognized professionals needed to support the economic life of the settlement. Further out were the quarters of the lower classes, and right on the outskirts – literally on the fringes of society – were the areas where prostitutes, beggars, tanners and outcasts were located. Outside the city itself there would be a further network of tightly controlled dependent settlements which kept the urban population supplied. There was an obvious symbiotic relationship between the two – the village looked to the town as a political and cultural centre, the nodal town looked to the villages for supplies of food, labour and services. A similar pattern would be reflected further up the social scale – provincial towns were linked to metropolitan centres, which in turn looked to regional centres, and so on. Position in the urban network was a socio-political statement, and mobility within a settlement, or from one town to another, conveyed coded social messages which represented interactions within the local social hierarchy.

The relationships symbolized by this system were fixed rigidly. Although social hierarchy is familiar enough in the modern world,[6] it is important to recognize a major difference in the way hierarchy operated in ancient Mediterranean society. In most contemporary western societies it is assumed that in the right circumstances upward social mobility is a real possibility. Personal preferences play a significant role in colouring social behaviour, and most individuals expect to take a degree of responsibility for their own destiny. Such expectations were rarely possible in the ancient world. In the Graeco-Roman world, social location was generally unambiguous and structured in such a way that everyone knew their place.

Social anthropology describes this kind of system as one supported by dyadic relationships. This is a series of interlocking relationships where people are located within an established pecking order which generates a sense of mutual obligation towards those immediately above or below. These dependency relationships provide the framework for protection as well as the resources needed for survival. In the patriarchal society of the Graeco-Roman city, the dominant role was that of patron and client. But this was rooted in the more familiar model of the father–son or mother–daughter relationships. It was the primary duty of the paterfamilias to support the household, whereas other subordinate members owed a duty of obedience to the (male) head of the family. So powerful was this sense of mutual responsibility that in certain circumstances the paterfamilias could hold even the power of life and death.

Other dyadic relationships included slave–master, soldier–commander, friend–friend, craftsman–customer, benefactor–recipient, and so on. All of these contributed to a fixed position in the local hierarchy and brought with them recognized social obligations. Many of these relationships were further embedded within other levels of authority, so that the paterfamlias had obligations to the local aristocracy, who also had obligations to the governor, who in turn had obligations to the emperor. Each tier positioned the individual precisely in the sequence, and most people knew exactly what was expected of them.[7]

Room for personal initiative was thus severely restricted – especially towards the lower end of the social scale. Given the general lack of welfare and the ever present danger of sickness, violence or accident, most people had little control over their daily lives, which is why so many of them felt like victims of circumstance (*tychē* or fate). Destiny could never be controlled, but the damage might (literally, with luck) be contained through appropriate forms of behaviour – sacrifice to the gods to appease their capricious anger or perhaps a little magic to give fate a helping hand. Superstition was rife, as most people tried to keep one step ahead of disaster by consulting the immensely popular oracles at Delphi or Claros, resorting to astrology and divination, or turning to the gods for healing and protection.[8]

By and large, patterns of religious piety reflected the same outlook – which is why it was so unusual for belief to be considered a matter of personal choice. It was not even something most people thought about often, but was merely another aspect of the social fabric. Just as ordinary mortals were in a position of obligation to their superiors, so the community was obliged to respect the governing powers who controlled destiny. Organized religion was an extension of civic responsibility.

The one aspect of life where some people might expect to exercise a limited degree of choice concerned membership of the innumerable clubs or guilds which flourished throughout the Roman Empire. These had often been established for purely practical purposes – such as the funeral clubs which, like twentieth-century co-operative societies, gave the poor an opportunity to save up for a decent burial. Other clubs were trade or business associations. Normally they met in private houses during the evenings (after a long day at work), shared a meal and provided members with a sense of privileged belonging. Proceedings quite often included an element of formal religion – a bit like prayers at school or before a local council meeting. Given the widespread popularity of such groups, outsiders who saw Christians meeting in a private house for a cultic meal were almost certain to see just one more voluntary association among many.[9]

These guilds tended to mirror local social institutions. This meant they usually had a clear hierarchy imposed through an accepted code of conduct. They normally reflected the same pattern of patronage – those with cash and status were expected to use it to support the less fortunate. Those on the receiving end were expected to be grateful and recognize the superior status of the benefactor. The only difference from the world outside was that clubs offered a greater chance of promotion – the opportunity to take a stake in the running of the group. In the social microcosm of the guild, the individual gained a sense of belonging and perhaps experienced for the first time the possibility of upward mobility within the group. The slave might not be able to change the master, but they could aspire to be the treasurer, or maybe even the president of the local club.

One product of this pattern of behaviour is the honour-shame culture of the eastern Mediterranean world. This is a relatively easy mechanism to understand, though it is of huge importance for understanding the New Testament texts. Honour in this context means the esteem experienced by an individual within society. It is a limited commodity, and can be increased or diminished only through social feedback. If an individual behaved in a way approved by the social unit they gained in reputation, whereas the reverse would be true if behaviour was perceived to be worthless or discreditable. Honour was thus linked to the expectations and obligations imposed by society.

Shame, on the other hand, was not the disgrace felt in modern society by a person guilty of misbehaviour. In this context, it means the protection of honour. To be 'shameless' is to engage in reckless activity, to be 'shameful' is to defend honour as a fragile and expendable commodity. If honour is the acquisition or loss of social prestige, shame is the protection of the accumulated social credit.

Honour and shame operated as partners in the same framework and were closely linked to male and female roles: by and large, men were expected to acquire honour, women to protect it. Thus, men could seek opportunities to enhance the family reputation by engaging in activities perceived to be socially valuable, whilst at the same time they would have to take care to avoid situations which might threaten their standing. On the other hand, since women were in the dyadic relationship of 'belonging' to men either as daughters or wives, they had the primary obligation of protecting family honour by avoiding irresponsible behaviour which could ruin their reputation. The woman's role was to protect her 'man' (be it husband or father) through 'proper' conduct. If she misbehaved, she brought 'shame' on everyone.

This unspoken code was constructed to protect or enhance honour without incurring loss. Every encounter with another person (friend or foe) could be damaging to personal reputation, so every move or gesture had to be carefully considered as a potential challenge. Invitations to social functions were thus a minefield – would acceptance or refusal be more costly in terms of personal prestige? Gifts were another difficult exchange: to accept one was to acknowledge dependence and a debt of honour to the donor, but rejection was a clear insult, unless the gift was offered by someone who was manifestly inferior. The only honourable course was to reciprocate to near equals with an equivalent gesture of equal magnitude. Obviously, this reversed the process so that the original donor was placed under an obligation and faced a similar challenge to respond. And so on; the possibilities were endless, and the game could go on and on for many rounds until (quite literally) honour was satisfied.

The parable of the Wedding Guests in Luke 14.7–14 is almost certainly a tale about such honour-shame calculations. Words in the gospels or epistles such as honour, blamelessness, repute, fame, disgrace, dishonour, despair, revile, reproach and anger are all related to the honour-shame code.[10] Honour challenges are frequent: Jesus, for example, is tested, entrapped, mocked, rebuked. Even one of the key words in New Testament Christology is straight out of the code – *doxa* or glory refers to the exalted reputation associated with God (see especially John 12.20–43).

This pattern of behaviour operates powerfully within the Pauline Epistles. Paul's need for hospitality placed him in a position of dependence on patrons (reduced honour). This required an appropriate response to minimize the obligation and restore the balance – hence his assertion of independence and self-sufficiency, as well as his attempt to claim the debt had been repaid through his teaching (see especially 1 Corinthians 9.8–18). In the 'thankless thank you' of Philippians 4.10ff, Paul is less than gracious about a gift he has received from the Philippians precisely because their charity represented a challenge. So he replies by insisting they should be grateful to him for the opportunity he has granted them to show generosity towards their spiritual patron.

The honour-shame code was almost certainly one factor operating behind the crucial incident at Antioch (Galatians 2.11–14): Paul lost face in the argument with Peter and Barnabas, and the fact that the 'right hand of fellowship' was extended to him clearly placed him in a position of inferiority. He needed to restore his reputation – hence the aggressive tone. He attempts to do this in two ways – first, by establishing his independent authority as an apostle of equal status appointed by God, and then by relativizing the Jerusalem 'pillars' who were held in high esteem by others. He wanted to be seen among the élite.

The interlocking nature of dyadic relationships meant that the honour of the whole family, clan, village, town or city was dependent on the behaviour of each individual: the shameless behaviour of one person might bring dishonour on all the rest. In such circumstances, there is no possibility of private morality, only a public awareness of performance. All behaviour is carefully observed, and the group may be expected to react sharply when necessary to enforce compliance – even in the church (see 1 Corinthians 5.1–9).

The complex hierarchy of the Graeco-Roman world was shaped like a pyramid. At the bottom were the outcasts, criminals and beggars. Next came slaves, followed by peasants and day-labourers who enjoyed a status only marginally superior. Then came the traders and craftsmen, then the more substantial merchants and landowners, then the local aristocracy, and finally the tiny minority of the all-powerful Roman élite.

Sub-hierarchies existed within each of these bands. Gang slaves were rock bottom, and normally lived a miserable existence. Household slaves, however, had a higher status and often enjoyed a reasonable lifestyle. Well-educated slaves might be in positions of considerable influence as teachers, doctors and local civil servants. Gang slaves might be expected to be worked to death under concentration camp conditions, but other slaves could reasonably hope to be released after about twenty years of adult service. Some preferred to remain slaves, however (see 1 Corinthians 7.21f) – after all, it gave them a high degree of security in an otherwise uncertain world.[11]

There was no middle class as such, but the nearest equivalent would be the tradesmen. Above them were the aristocracy, rising through the three estates – the Roman senators, equestrians ('knights') and decurians who controlled local councils and acted as magistrates. Together these orders probably amounted to no more than 100,000 or so of the approximately 50 to 80 million people in the Empire, or less than 0.5 per cent of the total population. They controlled most of the wealth and power, leaving the remaining 99.5 per cent of the *plebs urbana* and the low status *plebs rustica* in a position where they could only look on and dream.[12]

Social location generally rested on three factors: birth, wealth and past achievement. This meant the dice were always loaded against the low-born, and there was little they could do about it. Those born into the élite might lose status through careless behaviour, but others could never expect to rise to their level simply on merit. Acquired wealth could help status – though it was by no means as significant as in modern society, partly because it went with status anyway, and partly because the acquired wealth of the nouveau riche was considered less 'worthy' than inherited wealth. Carefully used, however, money could buy enhanced status through the patronage of the arts, sport or other civic amenities.

As they moved into the Gentile world, the first Christians interacted at every level with each of these social systems. So when Paul claims in Romans 15.19 'that from Jerusalem and as far round as Illyricum I have fully proclaimed the good news of Christ' he does not mean he literally visited (on foot) all the thousands of settlements in the designated area; he means he has identified the nodal points in the regional network of cities, established missions in those places and relied on the normal communication system to spread the word to the dependent communities beyond. When he talks about slaves, he simply takes the institution for granted, neither arguing for nor against the practice (which was probably just as well, given the extent to which the Empire was dependent on slavery). He was happy to take on the role of patron when asked to help ameliorate the conditions faced by an individual client (Onesimus in the Letter to Philemon) and takes for granted the inferior status of women. Changing Christian ideals modified his values, as might be expected in any dynamic system of beliefs. But it did not obliterate them.

Thus, in 1 Corinthians 11.1–16 Paul has to struggle to work out what happens when Christian values conflict with social expectations: Christian idealism insists that women have the right to contribute to worship (Galatians 3.27f), but his first-century social values rise to keep women in their 'proper' place. Paul desperately tries to justify his position, but is driven to exasperation (1 Corinthians 11.16). 1 Corinthians 8 and 10 are also about a clash of values – in this case, what to do with dinner invitations, both to private and to civic functions. 1 Corinthians 11.17–34 is about patronage at house Eucharists: the homeowners of the Christian community in Corinth functioned as normal patrons, keeping a 'top table' for themselves and graciously allowing the lower orders to enjoy their benevolence. Paul's response was not to challenge the benefactors, but to insist the wealthy should not add insult to injury by reminding the less well off of their dependence. Both sides are to compromise by sharing the food eaten at church meetings, but the wealthy are still allowed to indulge themselves privately (1 Corinthians 11.34).[13] Gerd Theissen calls this love patriarchalism,[14] which he defines as the mechanism which permits social inequality to continue but mitigates the impact by calling on both sides (the 'strong' and the 'weak' in Paul's terms) to respect the sensitivities and status of the other.

Edwin Judge has shown convincingly that the Pauline communities drew people from all levels of society.[15] Thus, when Paul says in 1 Corinthians 1.26ff 'Not many of you were wise by human standards, not many were powerful, not many were of noble birth', he implies that some were. He has a pointed reference to the 'household of Stephanus', indicating a person of rank and status, and the argument of 1 Corinthians 8, 10 and 11 presupposes the presence of the relatively wealthy homeowners. Finally, there is near certainty that Crispus and Gaius were people of substance. The church in Corinth reflected a cross-section of society in general.

Paul's own status is an interesting question.[16] If Acts is correct, he had dual citizenship of both Rome and Tarsus, which would give him relatively high social standing. As the centurion in Acts 22.25–9 recognizes, Roman citizenship was a rare honour at this time, and Paul had acquired it by birth, unlike the centurion who had had to buy it. On the other hand, the apostle claims to work for a living (1 Corinthians 9.6). He never says what his business was, but if Acts 18.3 is reliable, he was merely a tradesman, and (even worse) a leatherworker (an unclean trade). If so, Paul was likely to receive very mixed social feedback. Nevertheless, his position had certain advantages: his high standing as a Roman citizen gave him access to the relatively powerful people like Crispus and Gaius (the only ones, he thanks God, he baptized himself – 1 Corinthians 1.14f), whilst his low professional status opened out the opportunity for contact with colleagues in the trade (Acts 18.3).

The Religious Environment

Gentile converts had to abandon their inherited religious loyalties when they became Christians, with all the social disapproval this generated in the tightly knit framework of first-century dyadic relationships. Converts were expected to adopt a modified form of Jewish monotheism which was experienced by many pagans as pure atheism – refusal to honour the gods.

Social conformity also meant that most people had little opportunity to shop around in a market place to sample new religious movements.[17] This was one of the startling features of Christianity: in order to become established, the church had to overcome not only the barrier of social resistance but also demonstrate that it had the answer to questions most people were not even asking. The wonder is not that Christianity was an insignificant minority throughout the first century, but that it attracted any interest at all. It could only succeed if it was literally in the right place at the right time.

To explain how Christianity achieved this remarkable feat, it is often suggested that the Jesus movement arrived just as paganism was in terminal decline. This is most unlikely.[18] Paganism thrived well into the fifth century, and although local cults ebbed and flowed, there is little evidence of widespread disillusionment with the standard religious diet on offer.

Local pagan cults

Hellenistic religion was not based on a single set of beliefs, but consisted of innumerable independent cults dedicated to countless gods. The term paganism is thus potentially misleading because it suggests a systematic religion. Like the term 'Buddhism' in the nineteenth century, paganism is a Christian label, a way of defining something other than Christianity: it is not what so-called pagans in the ancient world called themselves. The word comes from *pagani*, meaning perhaps either 'civilian' or 'rustic', though even this definition is disputed.[19]

Although the origin of Hellenistic religion is shrouded in myth, many religious shrines were located in areas of great natural beauty. Springs, mountains and trees in particular were seen as gateways to the supernatural, places of encounter with the divine.[20] Each place had its own god, and what became known as the Olympic pantheon only emerged gradually as local deities were identified with Zeus, Hermes, Aphrodite, Pan and so on. Eventually, all of the gods came to fall broadly into one of four categories – the Mother goddess (Atargatis, Artemis, Diana etc.), Zeus, the Sun god (especially in Roman colonies), and Fortune or Fate (*Tychē*). Some intellectuals took the process further, and began to argue that all of the local gods were basically different manifestations of the one great god Zeus. A functional henotheism, in other words, was beginning to emerge.[21]

This does not mean that paganism was preparing the ground for Judaeo-Christian monotheism, however. Far from it. At a popular level, the cult of the individual gods was unquestioned, and even intellectuals accepted the reality of the different manifestations. Generally, such religious debate was not a live issue. Piety was more about reinforcing the sense of belonging to a social community protected by the local gods than about personal devotion. Homes might have shrines or religious artefacts to provide a focus for devotion, but these were used primarily to seek divine protection for the household. Greek culture discouraged individualism in all matters, including religion, and emphasized the need for proper observance of social norms.[22]

It was this social dimension which almost certainly led to the evolution of the emperor cult. This was a comparatively late development in antiquity, and only became significant during the first century. The deeper roots of the cult lay in the tradition of sacral kingship, but Augustus introduced a new dimension when in 27 BCE he allowed a decree to be published 'that he may be deified as much as possible'. He was a sensible man, however, and aware of his limitations: reluctant to allow an excessive cult during his lifetime, he encouraged the idea of worshipping his genius or guardian spirit. Officially, he only became a god after his death in 14 CE.[23]

Sane emperors thereafter followed suit. Other emperors such as Gaius Caligula, Nero and Domitian pushed the process along. The development of the cult was pursued with the greatest vigour in the Roman province of Asia (modern Turkey), which had long been a productive area for the growth of specialist cults. Gratitude to Rome for support after a series of disasters prompted a number of cities in the province to compete for the honour of being styled *neōkoros* or temple-warden – an official centre of the emperor cult. Several cities listed among the seven churches of the Book of Revelation (Revelation 2—3) fall into this category – Pergamum, Smyrna and Ephesus all tried to outdo each other in their enthusiasm for Rome. It is perhaps worth registering that this was precisely the area where Christianity found fertile ground for mission.

The emperor cult symbolized dramatically the link between religion and social obligation: to offer cult to the gods was to cement the bond of social stability. This was the real threat presented by Christian exclusivity. No one was likely to be challenged for having personal religious preferences: many people had them, and one more god, even one like Jesus, was no great problem. The difficulty was that Christians, like Jews, refused to pay honour to the other local gods as well. No one else refused. Visitors to a community usually found it prudent to pay their respects to the god just as they might greet the head of the household. Christians and Jews alone held aloof from this obligation to honour the gods who embodied the well-being of the community. They were clearly anti-social.

Mystery religions

Christianity arrived in the Hellenistic cities at almost the same time as a growing number of mystery cults. This was no coincidence: social change within the Roman Empire had started to make religious innovation possible. Given that religious and secular power were intimately connected in ancient thought, defeat by a superior force meant religious humiliation – the local gods had been defeated as well. The Roman Empire thus established a new religious environment as part of their new political reality. Although the Romans were broadly tolerant of most local religions, their military victories put old religious loyalties under strain. It is in this sense that Christianity was in the right place at the right time.

Among the mystery cults which competed with Christianity for attention were that of Cybele, the great Mother goddess worshipped mainly by women, and Mithras, the rather macho counterpart worshipped mainly by soldiers. Dionysus or Bacchus was also widely worshipped, as were Hermes Trismegistos and Asclepius.[24] Head and shoulders above them all, however, was Sarapis-Isis, the great goddess from Egypt. In a fascinating paper, Tran tam Tinh sets out the parallels between this immensely popular cult and Hellenist Christianity: both were based on a henotheistic theology, were universalist in outlook, depended on the initiative of charismatic leaders and often founded new worship centres in response to divine revelation. They also similarly appealed to the cognitive, evaluative and socio-emotional interests that were the product of the same social context. Tran tam Tinh concludes that 'Christianity was born into a spiritual milieu permeated with a new religiousness to which the cult of Isis and Sarapis made an important – perhaps funda-mental – contribution. Everywhere the devotees of Isis preceded the missionaries of Jesus.'[25]

What set the mystery religions apart from local cults was their optional status – people had to choose to seek admission before they could participate. In order to attract adherents, therefore, the cults had to offer something over and above the benefits of routine religious practice. It is difficult to say precisely what those extra benefits might have been, partly perhaps because it varied from individual to individual. But probably it was a combination of things like perceived mystical power coupled with a sense of privileged belonging. Further, unlike the local cults they had a theology – beliefs about 'higher wisdom', life after death and so on. But the real attraction was perhaps their ability to consolidate a group around a shared set of values. This was facilitated by the various rituals which bonded the group together.

Because no one belonged to these cults by right of birth, the first significant ritual was initiation – the process of selection and indoctrination which marked the transition into membership. There is a considerable body of evidence to suggest that rigorous and demanding initiation rites result in a significantly stronger bond between the individual and the group:[26] it is almost as if the more humiliating and painful the ritual, the greater the perception of worth – 'if I had to go through all that, this group must be worth while'. Many modern organizations continue to trade on this belief – Freemasons, the army and a number of professional organizations, to name but a few. Perhaps the best-known initiation rite in the ancient world, however, was the practice of the *taurobolium*, often associated with Mithraism but actually more closely connected with the cult of Cybele.[27] In this ritual, the initiate was placed in a trench with a grid over the top. A bull was slaughtered over the trench so that the blood poured out on to the person underneath.

Presumably, this was meant to symbolize initiation into the power of the god. Group bonding thereafter was usually consolidated through cultic meals which only the initiated could share. This is perhaps one of the best-attested aspects of the mystery cults because of the number of papyri found in Egypt and elsewhere inviting guests 'to the table of Isis' or whichever god the host happened to acknowledge. These meals were occasions for learning, sharing and supporting – but above all, for reinforcing the sense of belonging to a privileged élite.

Baptism and the Eucharist, therefore, provided Christians with a recognizable point of contact with patterns of behaviour associated with the mystery cults. Here was another group which needed recruits since no one had yet become a member by birth. Here was a sect which required converts to undergo a period of rigorous training and indoctrination before entering into full membership. Here was a group with a demanding initiation ritual, which generated a sense of group-identity regularly consolidated through regular cultic meals. In the streets of Antioch or Corinth, these aspects of church life must have seemed familiar.[28]

Philosophical sects

The next nearest equivalent to the church after the synagogues, clubs, guilds and mystery cults was probably the looser movement of philosophical sects. These did not form a single recognizable group in any sense, but were distinguished by the presence of particular teachers and their followers. The great names of the classical period, Socrates, Plato and Aristotle, continued to provide a forum for the discussion and development of intellectual ideas, though during the first century three schools of thought attracted a wider degree of popular support: the Cynics, the Epicureans and the Stoics.[29]

Cynicism as a movement took its name from the reported lifestyle of one of the founding figures, Diogenes of Sinope (c. 350 BCE), who was said to have lived like a dog (kynarion in Greek). Cynics preached extreme scepticism about the normal values of life and idealized the concept of autarkeia or self-sufficiency (see 1 Corinthians 9.15–18 and Philippians 4.11). It was not a sect as such, but a category of charismatic individuals who travelled around like beggars and taught the need for detachment from power, wealth and ambition – 'preaching morality and acting demonstratively'.[30] As a number of commentators point out, these Cynics provide an interesting parallel with Jesus. In fact, as a wandering charismatic teacher with a small group of followers practising an alternative lifestyle and holding a critical attitude towards established values, Jesus would have looked and sounded to many people like a Cynic – especially when he preached the virtue of detachment (Matthew 6.25–34 and parallel in Luke 12.22–31).[31]

The Epicureans were another group with a sceptical view of normal social aspirations. Their movement grew out of the teaching of Epicurus, an Athenian philosopher from around 300 BCE. He held a deeply pessimistic view of life in general, and taught that the primary aim of life should be the pursuit of pleasure. The highest virtue was *ataraxia* or freedom from anxiety, which is to be achieved through the elimination of desire and fear – fear of the gods, and fear of death.

It is not quite true to say that the Epicureans were the self-indulgent hedonists they are often thought to be. Since the highest good for them was freedom from fear, they valued the self-control and discipline which placed an individual beyond pain and the threat of social constraint. Nor were they atheistic, as is sometimes assumed: they believed the gods were real enough, but they inhabited another realm and were therefore irrelevant to human concern most of the time. They certainly could not harm people. So the Epicureans were ruthlessly critical of conventional piety and popular superstition. Indeed, they have been likened in some respects to the Quietists of the Enlightenment or modern-day Quakers. Their blend of science and philosophical religion enabled the movement to thrive well into the fifth century CE and beyond.[32]

The third widely recognized philosophical movement of the period was Stoicism. Founded by Zeno *c.* 350 BCE, this movement generated interest at two levels of society: it was immensely popular in certain Graeco-Roman intellectual circles, and won its greatest admirer in the Roman Emperor Marcus Aurelius (161–181 CE). But a watered-down version of the philosophy was also extremely popular, and a number of stoical concepts became 'common-sense' beliefs in everyday discourse.

Stoics were basically pantheists who believed that all creation was an expression of the divine *logos*, or rational order behind nature. Since this power permeated creation, everything and everyone shared the presence of the divine. God may thus be called by many names – Zeus or Jupiter, Nature, Reason, Fire or Spirit, but these are simply alternative labels for the same awe-inspiring experience of creation. The parallels between this and the concept of *logos* in the Prologue to John's Gospel are, of course, well studied.[33] The good news for Stoics is that every person reflects the *logos* to the same degree – they are all products of the creative principle called god. The bad news is that because creation is an expression of a greater purpose in nature, nothing much could be changed – everything was fixed by the logic of the natural order. Hence the Stoics tended to preach resigned acceptance: there was little individuals could do to change the universe, so wisdom was to be found in recognizing the logic of the situation and living at peace with the greater purpose of creation. Again, it is not difficult to find modern parallels to this kind of poignant intellectual resignation.[34]

The Social Transition

The arrival of Christianity on the streets of the Hellenistic cities in Syria, Asia Minor and Greece sparked off a process of interaction with pagan culture. Although most people, believers and outsiders alike, continued to regard Christianity as a predominantly Jewish sect, the process of detaching itself from the synagogue and being transposed into the Graeco-Roman environment brought a subtle transformation in basic values. Small communities of believers unconsciously absorbed the outlook of their host culture, and this is reflected in the later writings of the New Testament.

Christianity, then, had to compete with many other social and religious dynamics within Graeco-Roman society. Various factors perhaps helped the new movement to gain a foothold. One was the small but significant number of Gentile adherents to the synagogues who provided a valuable point of contact. Another was the clubs and guilds which provided a model for the concept of a voluntary association. But the advent of the mystery cults and philosophical sects provided a crucial window of opportunity – an intellectual environment in which old loyalties could be relativized, personal choices made, religious questions asked and new forms of devotion expressed. Christianity still had some way to go, however, to overcome completely the resistance of social obligation.

Other factors helped. One was that Christianity rendered redundant the sacrificial cult of both Judaism and the pagan shrines. This was not without precedent, but was nevertheless remarkable in a world which took the ritual slaughter of animals for granted (see Hebrews 10.22). Another was that whilst challenging the ethnic boundaries of Judaism, Christianity appropriated a Jewish sense of religious exclusiveness: there could be no other God than the God of Jesus, the jealous God of Israel (Deuteronomy 5.9). There was a clear limit to the compromise infant Christianity was prepared to accept with paganism.

The result was, however, that Christianity became an exposed minority on the margins of Judaism and paganism with few friends and little influence. It had to make hard choices – either retreat, or gather new recruits in order to develop a new life which offered a sense of purpose and privilege to Jew and Greek alike.

❀ 7 ❀

The Social Mechanics of Early Christian Mission: Christianity in the Religious Market Place

I n order to compete in the emerging religious market place of the Graeco-Roman world, Christianity had to be seen to be attractive: it had to offer real benefits to the potential convert. Of course, the number of people who had even heard of Christianity should not be exaggerated, but some Gentiles manifestly found this Christian preaching persuasive. Those who joined the Christian community brought with them a cultural legacy which gave them a strong sense of mutual obligation rooted in the honour-shame code. They believed in the power of fate, longed for protection from uncertain fortune, and saw rescue from these unseen cosmic powers (salvation) as one of the most positive features of Christianity. As the steady trickle of Gentile converts increased, all of these Graeco-Roman attitudes were gradually absorbed into the Christian psyche and came to have a profound impact on the later texts of the New Testament.

But to make further headway outside the ranks of pro-Jewish God-fearers, Christianity had to overcome the inertia of a social system which made deviant religious behaviour extremely rare and unpopular. When followers of 'the Way' finally emerged as a recognizable religious group in Antioch, they found themselves an obvious target for abuse by their blatant anti-social behaviour against both Judaism and the local pagan cults. Disapproval would have been expressed through the usual mechanisms of social feedback: the signs, gestures and actions which make it clear to individuals that their behaviour is unacceptable.

Most communities tolerate a degree of deviance, and some even require dissent as a foil for established values.[1] Nevertheless, there is a point beyond which such behaviour becomes intolerable, and then groups will usually act swiftly to enforce conformity, along the scale from a quiet word through to the more formal systems of discipline. Ultimately, the group may remove an offender through expulsion or excommunication, or in certain circumstances they may even impose the death penalty. Those who continue to challenge established norms run the risk of provoking a sharp response.

There is some evidence that early Christians sought to overcome the barrier of social disapproval and attract a wider audience through the persuasive power of charismatic activity (e.g. Acts 14.3). New Testament authors simply assume that such phenomena are self-authenticating: Luke, for example, places a particularly high premium on demonstrations of spiritual power.[2] So also Paul. When he wants to remind the Galatians about their reasons for their conversion, he recalls the irrefutable evidence of the Holy Spirit (Galatians 3.1–5). Similarly, in Romans 8.15–27 he assumes that manifestations of the Spirit are an unmistakable sign of transformation. Indeed, it seems that one of the problems at Corinth was that some believers placed too much significance on charismatic activity (1 Corinthians 12.31—14.19).[3]

But the Corinthian correspondence also shows that the need for internal stability and good order sooner or later drives most groups – even those founded on charismatic leadership – towards an institutional form of life (e.g. 1 Corinthians 11.2–34; 14.20–40). At that point, the group processes of social psychology swing into action as the new community begins to take shape. Group formation is a complex process, but it operates within a framework of received cultural values and expectations, coloured by the hopes and aspirations of individual participants. These values may be challenged and modified in the formation process, but they provide an essential starting point.

As far as first-century Christians were concerned, the starting point was Judaism as experienced in the Diaspora – though a continuous dialogue between Jewish and Hellenistic values interacting with Christian experience had the effect of rapidly modifying perceptions as Christianity forged a new distinctive identity. In order to take root and grow, the movement had to build on this foundation and establish a recognizable base from which it could operate and attract new members. To do that, it had to meet four basic conditions:

1. The distinct identity of the movement had to be acknowledged not only by the membership but by outsiders as well.

2. A pool of people interested in a modified form of Judaism had to be available.

3. A system of initiation and support had to be in place to enable recruits to integrate fully into the new group.

4. A flexible programme of community maintenance had to be established to allow Christianity to adapt to the challenges of a changing membership as well as the normal day-to-day dynamic of intra-group processes.

In short, Christians had to signal to outsiders that their group was distinctive, available, open for business and of interest.

Key Stage One: Establishing a Group Identity

The first requirement for a successful mission, therefore, was a public presence. In fact, this may be broken down into two further sub-elements:

1. Simple awareness of the group – as Paul says in Romans 10.14, 'how are they to believe in one of whom they have never heard?' Christianity needed to 'spread the word', or more bluntly, to advertise. The evidence is that this was achieved by word of mouth using the communications system of the ancient city network. Thus Paul centred his preaching on the main nodal centres where he felt able to exploit his Jewish contacts (1 Corinthians 9.20 – and perhaps also 2 Corinthians 11.24?[4]) as well as his colleagues in the trade (Acts 18.2; see also Romans 16.3 and 1 Corinthians 16.19). Thereafter, he could rely on the local grapevine to do the rest.

2. A nucleus of like-minded enthusiasts who could form an embryo group. The crystallization of such a core group tends to occur informally as a small number of dedicated supporters meet for mutual encouragement and the exchange of information. This, in due course, often evolves into a more formal structure.

Society rarely ignores new groups, because their presence forces a realignment of other relationships within the wider community.[5] Often the response may be benign, usually because the group is not perceived to pose any direct threat to the established social order. New movements thought to support the status quo may even be encouraged, whereas groups thought to endanger the social fabric will provoke a sharp and often hostile reaction. A decision about the appropriate response often emerges informally through consensus, and this judgement is used to locate the group on the relevant social map. From that point on, both members and outsiders 'know' where they are and, like it or not, they absorb that perception into their own sense of self-identity.[6]

Drawing this social map requires information about three related factors. The first concerns the social categories to be used. Social categorization is the near universal phenomenon of lumping together people or things believed to have characteristics in common – it is probably an essential survival tactic designed to reduce the day-to-day barrage of data down to manageable proportions. It works by identifying a perceived recognition pattern – a stereotype of 'things like that'. This obviously saves an enormous amount of time and energy by rendering it unnecessary to produce discrete judgements about every isolated incident or person.

The formation of broad categories is usually straightforward – the category 'car', for example, is commonly thought to consist of four wheeled self-propelled vehicles capable of carrying passengers from one place to another. However, simple categories tend to blur quickly around the edges, and this renders them less useful: for example, is a three-wheeled vehicle capable of conveying passengers a 'car' or something different? This problem may be resolved by creating sub-categories: three-wheelers are different types of car, diesels are different again, and so on. These subdivisions must have sufficient in common to maintain the generic similarity, but they allow finer distinctions to be made. Occasionally, however, the differences between sub-groups will begin to overwhelm the under-lying category, and then the only solution is to create a new one.

But this cannot be a unilateral decision, because the purpose of social categories is to facilitate communication between different people within the community. They must all speak the same language. Thus, individuals may posit stereotypes, but unless other people accept them they have little significance. Categories are thus negotiated within a particular culture: different people in different places at different times use different categories to establish their stereotypes.

By the same token, believers could not unilaterally choose to be called Christians: that was a decision which had to be negotiated within society. So long as Christianity looked like Judaism, this was not a problem. But when Hellenist Jewish Christianity began to display characteristics not usually associated with the category 'Jew', a new stereotype was needed (Acts 11.26). The interesting question is at what point did this finally occur: when circumcision, the kosher food laws, and the temple cult were perceived by the general population to be undermined, or when mainstream Judaism publicly withdrew recognition of the Christians – or when?

Different Christian core groups probably reached this point at different times.[7] But the need to place people in appropriate categories almost certainly lies behind some of the fiercest rhetoric in the New Testament – were new converts to be placed in the Jewish group (and thus required to observe the circumcision command) or in a new Christian group (which requires Christian initiation, not Jewish)? Galatians gives Paul's answer, but suggests that his was not yet a common view.

In general, social categories are commonly defined in negative terms. Thus, the term 'Christian' means neither Jewish (Hellenist or Palestinian), nor 'pagan' (adherents of local traditional cults, followers of Isis or Cybele or whatever), nor a philosophy like the Stoics or Epicureans. Only after it has started to crystallize, when friend and foe alike need further information to locate the new group, does the community start to define itself more positively. This is precisely what happened when early Christians began to develop distinctive christologies to serve as group recognition signals.[8]

As new social categories are defined, individuals need to relocate themselves in relation to them: am I (still) a Jew, or an initiate of Mithras, or have I become a Christian? This process of self-identity is also a two-way dialogue, especially in the world of dyadic relationships: I may call myself a Jew, for example, but unless everyone else agrees (Jewish and non-Jewish) and treats me accordingly, I am deluded. Only social feedback allows me to know my place in life.

This was presumably the cause of the sharp exchange in Galatians 2.11ff – Peter, Barnabas and Paul initially thought that the existing social categories could survive despite the steady trickle of Gentiles adhering to Christianity. This was challenged through the negative feedback from Jewish Christians in Jerusalem, which had the effect of forcing a rethink (Galatians 2.12). Peter and Barnabas modified their behaviour accordingly and moved back within range of accepted Hellenist Jewish Christian stereotypes. Paul refused to conform, however, and insisted on redefining the categories. He was now on his own unless he could persuade others to accept his suggestion.

Once a new social category is broadly accepted, the final step for establishing a revised map of social groupings is the process of social comparison. This is another near universal phenomenon: groups and individuals routinely form judgements about the perceived value of their current status based on criteria perceived to be important within their culture: are they located in a good, bad or indifferent position? The conclusion reached may then trigger a competition to improve the perceived status.[9]

But the game has strict rules. The first is that the criteria used for social comparison must be thought to be reasonable – most people recognize wishful thinking when they see it. Rule two is that the factors chosen for comparison must be salient – that is, relevant to the interests of the people involved. Finally, the categories used must be thought to be fair: unfair definitions are likely to provoke a powerful response.

The emergence of Christianity as a distinctive group forced a new round of social comparison as founding members and outsiders alike had to decide whether it was a good thing or a bad thing to be Christian. The consensus probably varied from place to place, but potential converts had to calculate carefully within the terms of the honour-shame code. This would have been particularly tricky in the case of Christianity, because Christians emphasized criteria which were normally rated low on the honour scale: humility and service.[10]

But perhaps this was just another example of the well-established practice of trying to turn perceived disadvantage around by redefining the values used to make the comparison (e.g. black is beautiful): for the purposes of Christian group definition, poverty is wealth, and humility is really honour. Even so, in order to be convincing, the arguments mustered by Christians to establish social worth had to be very persuasive.

Key Stage Two: Identifying the Audience

Since only a handful of pagans converted, clearly most people did not find the gospel persuasive. Further, since conversion in this context amounted to cultural treason and involved the betrayal of key family relationships and obligations, Christianity had to work hard to find anyone ready to change.

Conversion of those with a comparatively high social standing was thus extremely rare: not impossible, but rare, because individuals in this category had the highest investment in the status quo. If they were attracted to Christianity at all, it was almost certainly because they wanted to reduce a sense of conflict between their social and their personal values. People lower down the scale were more likely to be attracted because they had less to lose: these were precisely the kind of people who might see conversion as a step towards self-enhancement.[11]

But it would be wrong to make a simplistic link between the perceived benefits of Christianity and the personal aspirations of potential converts. Interest in a group is dependent on a huge number of variables, and attraction operates at three different levels of experience: the cognitive level (I know this is where I ought to belong), the evaluative level (this is a good group to join) and the socio-emotional level (I like this group).[12] These three elements commonly combine to produce a kind of satisfaction index about the current set-up, and it is only when this is felt to be highly unsatisfactory that discontented people are likely to start looking for alternatives. In short, those with a high satisfaction rating are unlikely to be persuaded, however good the preacher; and even the most dissatisfied person must be convinced that the benefits of conversion outweigh the discomfort of change. As Eileen Barker says, 'it simply is not true that 'anyone' is susceptible [to conversion]'.[13] They must be ready for change.

Those with a high dissatisfaction rating have few options, and these can be summarized as the 'put up or shut up' scenario. 'Shutting up' means resigned acceptance – there is no realistic alternative. This is the normal reaction where the current situation is thought to be legitimate, or the powers that act to prevent change are felt to be too strong. Thus, in the case of slavery in the ancient world, few people wasted time trying to change things, and would not have achieved very much had they tried. Only after an extended period of social friction is the power of the established order likely to be weakened.

By contrast, 'putting up' with the cause of dissatisfaction presents two further possibilities. An individual may attempt to improve their lot through promotion within the existing group. This is the basis for a form of leadership struggle. Or alternatively, the person may decide to move off somewhere else perceived to be better. Not everyone is able to exercise this last option, however, because it requires access to considerable personal and practical resources. Only those willing and able to face the cost and upheaval of change are therefore available to an alternative group as potential recruits.

In terms of early Christian mission, this means that preachers had to identify people who were sufficiently dissatisfied with their current social location to want to move *and* had the freedom to do something about it. This is a quite specialized target audience.

It may be possible to be even more precise. Using Erikson's eight stages of life, it is possible to identify transition points in personal development which tend to generate psychological crises which demand a response.[14] Perhaps the best known of these is adolescence, when most young adults reorientate family and social relationships around their newly acquired status as independent people. But there are other crises later in life which focus on issues of intimacy, moral values and the recognition of human mortality.

Erikson's scheme is based on research which makes assumptions about modern cultural values which simply did not apply in the first-century context. It would be foolish, therefore, to transpose his scheme naively into the world of the first Christian converts. What his work does suggest, however, is that there may have been similar moments of social transition within Graeco-Roman culture which presented other conversion possibilities.[15] The two most obvious ones might be the change from youth to young adult when life-values are established, and from mature adult to older person when the realization of approaching death becomes unavoidable. At such points, ethical rigour and the promise of salvation would certainly feel attractive.

Gerd Theissen suggests one final factor which may influence the process. He argues that new religious movements serve an important social function by providing a harmless channel for unrest through the appropriation of recognized religious symbols.[16] They tame dissent by providing an acceptable alternative to violence or rebellion. This suggests that the kind of people likely to use religious means to deal with dissatisfaction are not those who reject established values entirely. If this is added to the personal profile of potential converts, the first Christians were looking for people in search of improvement, not radical change.

Even then, the preachers were far from home and dry. They still had to persuade the potential converts that membership of the church met their personal aspirations. This meant they had to engage the attention of the audience at each of three formatives levels of awareness which influence self-identity – the cognitive, the evaluative and the socio-emotional.

At the cognitive level, Christianity had to present a convincing matrix of beliefs which the potential convert might be expected to share – a plausibility structure. At first sight, this might seem like a odd proposition – if a belief is true, then, as many a politician has been heard to say, 'a fact is a fact'. But there is rarely anything simple about facts: they are nothing more than a snapshot of reality taken from a limited perspective and representing a clear set of interests. Thus, since the pioneering work of Peter Berger and Thomas Luckmann, it has been accepted that even 'knowledge' is the product of the normative values and assumptions operating within a given culture.[17] In order to know something, therefore, it is necessary to share the same matrix of attitudes and beliefs which selected the data in the first place. To take an obvious example, the system of beliefs which made it possible to know in the first century that exorcisms and miracles were a fact of life no longer operates in many sections of modern society. For many people, a different matrix of belief makes such knowledge quite implausible.

What, then, were the cultural factors which enabled potential converts to evaluate Christianity within the first-century Graeco-

Roman context? There were many: shared concepts of life, ethics, and even concepts of the divine to a limited extent. But one of the chief factors was the sense of helplessness which gripped the ancient world. Building on fragmentary Jewish beliefs, Christian preachers expanded the geography of hell, making it a thoroughly unpleasant place within which to spend eternity.[18] The plausibility structure adopted presented a stark choice between a powerful God who offered salvation from cosmic forces or eternal punishment in the fires of hell hereafter. In terms of the evaluative appeal to those who shared this plausibility structure, the church was certainly a better place to be.

At the socio-emotional level, Christianity had to be persuasive in two ways. First, it had to establish contact at a personal level. According to Weber, this is the role of the charismatic prophet, a person with a powerful magnetic personality who attracts a following and builds up a recognized spiritual authority, often based on visions, dreams and other revelatory phenomena.[19] Through their teaching, the prophet establishes a set of values which reflect the changing aspirations of a community and acts as a catalyst by providing the necessary focus for the redrawing of boundaries.

Paul was clearly such a person. He had the energy to attract and sustain the interest of a number of receptive individuals. He responded to the challenge of rejection at Antioch by redefining his status as the leader in a dissenting mission – the 'apostle to the Gentiles'. He thus took upon himself the role of a prophet in Weberian terms, and redefined the boundaries between the Jewish Christian and Pauline communities. The nature of his personal charisma needs to be carefully defined, though – he is, after all, quite dismissive about himself in 2 Corinthians 10.10f. But a prophet need not be an impressive performer: they need only be the magnetic personality which enables others to make better sense of life by accepting the alternative values they offer.

The role of the charismatic leader is to initiate contact. The second necessary component is socio-emotional relationships within the group: the new community must provide a support network which feels attractive. Christianity addressed this point by adopting the model of a household – the place where people belong and a very powerful image in the ancient patriarchal world. Family language is common throughout the New Testament: 'our Father' (Matthew 6.9); 'brothers and sisters' (*adelphoi* – e.g. James 1.2); 'love one another with mutual affection' (Romans 12.9); 'love the family of believers' (1 Peter 2.17) and so on. Christians share (family) meals and generally feel at home in the *ekklēsia*. And finally, the sense of sharing a privileged identity is reinforced (e.g. 1 Peter 2.9ff). Being a Christian feels good.

Therefore, a full profile of a potential convert in the first century context begins to look something like this. The early Christian communities needed people who were:

- in personal transition, perhaps in a process of reorientating their values;
- sufficiently dissatisfied with their current social location to want to seek some form of personal enhancement;
- in possession of the necessary personal resources to enable them to manage change effectively and cope with social disapproval;
- nevertheless sufficiently committed to society to want to stay in touch and register effectively little more than a protest;
- therefore attracted to the use of religious symbols as a means of enhancing self-esteem;
- open at a cognitive level to a form of modified Hellenistic Jewish beliefs, to whom the language and culture of the proselytizing group would make sense;
- attracted to the charismatic prophetic personality of early Christian leaders like Paul or Peter;
- able to feel at home in the web of developing Christian relationships.

The evidence presented has already identified one obvious category of people who meet these requirements – the collection of Gentile adherents to the synagogue who like the Ethiopian eunuch (Acts 8.27), Cornelius (Acts 10.1), or Sosthenes (Acts 18.7) had already been drifting towards Judaism. As it happens, the power of Christianity to attract such influential benefactors of the synagogue probably accounts for some of the hostility shown towards the church by continuing Judaism.

But among other potential targets were lone individuals experiencing what Wayne Meeks calls status inconsistency.[20] This may be defined as the sense of tension experienced when individuals receive mixed messages (like Paul) about their perceived worth within society. Social status is not dependent on a single fixed value – there are a number of factors, any one of which can be in conflict with another. For example, in the first-century world, former slaves who earned their liberty and became citizens achieved a relatively high social status. On the other hand, as freedmen they could never be as esteemed as freeborn citizens. Although they might be better educated, hold down significant positions of power and influence, and might even be richer than the rest of society, they could never be anything other than freedmen. There was a conflict between their achieved status and their acquired status. People can be high on one social scale, but simultaneously low on another.

So also a woman might be born into a prominent family, have an education, possess wealth and influence (high status), but in the Graeco-Roman world she could never be anything other than a woman (low status). Slaves might enjoy a comfortable standard of living, work in the professions, perhaps even have a limited degree of power over others and control their own personal finances (higher status). Nevertheless, they were still slaves (low status). All these people might feel a real sense of pride over their achievement, but could never be satisfied within a system which guaranteed their inferiority. Such ambivalence could easily make a new faith in which 'there is no longer Jew or Greek, slave or free, male or female' (Galatians 3.27f) look very attractive, especially when it expressed dissatisfaction with the present world order in a quite respectable way (Romans 13.1–7). As a derivative of an established ancient religion widely respected for its beliefs about God as well as a strict morality code, they were being offered enhanced status within a new family which made them feel good.

Meek's use of the status inconsistency thesis has been criticized as anachronistic and over-simplistic.[21] There is undoubtedly some truth in this, but it would be foolish to dismiss his work entirely: Meek's analysis is more likely to be inadequate than completely wrong. Research into conversion processes suggests that many converts are seeking to resolve an inner conflict of one kind or another, and something certainly persuaded a few people in the ancient world to convert when the overwhelming majority proved resistant. Dissatisfaction over social status in the honour-shame culture was almost certainly one factor which made some of these people available to the Christian missionaries.

Key Stage Three: The Successful Integration of New Recruits
Faith conversion may be defined as a religious response to a self-conscious predicament in which an individual chooses to relocate him- or herself in a different network of relationships, authoritative structures, beliefs and values, and attaches new significance to the symbols associated with that system.[22] Although Paul is often held up as the archetypal convert on the basis of Luke's account of his Damascus road experience,[23] conversion is rarely as dramatic as that, and more characteristically occurs over an extended period of time. Although converts often draw attention to a single event which they experience as a sudden change of lifestyle or a new burst of energy, this symbolic moment of conversion is typically preceded by a gradual build-up of interest as the potential recruit is drawn into the receiving community. One of the reasons the lengthier period is generally played down is that recruits learn to conform to a group stereotype of what it is felt ought to happen: the dramatic moment of final commitment marks a point of transition into a new set of social relationships which is literally life-changing.

Another common misunderstanding is that cognitive elements in conversion are central – the convert accepts that a given pattern of belief is 'correct' and this brings insight and liberation.[24] In fact, research suggests that the supposed truth of a religious belief is low on the list of factors which normally attract new members. More significant is the pastoral care shown to the individual before and after admission into the group, the emotional warmth which provides a sense of personal meaning in answer to a specific need.[25] Hence the feelings associated with initiation and subsequent aftercare are far more crucial to the bonding process than the correctness of any new package of belief.

Conversion is thus a complex reorientation around a new symbolic universe of social values, as new myths and symbols are internalized and used to undergird the perception of reality. At a social level, conversion requires a realignment of personal relationships and acknowledged authority structures – as many families discover when modern offspring choose to join a new religious cult. And finally, at a personal level conversion has an impact on feelings, actions and behaviour – most commonly reported as despair replaced by joy.[26]

Several different types of conversion experience have been identified, but among these perhaps only the categories of apostasy, affiliation, institutional transition and tradition transition are of immediate relevance to the first generation of Christian converts. Apostasy in this context means the conscious repudiation by an individual of previous socio-religious loyalties – as when a former pagan converts to Christianity. Affiliation refers to a looser form of attachment requiring only minimal commitment to the receiving group. This was certainly a possibility in the first-century world, though not perhaps a likely one, since in the earliest stages of group formation a strong level of commitment is required to see the group through the trauma of differentiation and social disapproval.

Institutional transition and tradition transition are processes of particular interest in relation to potential Jewish converts. Institutional transition refers to the perception that a convert has simply switched denomination. To use an illustration from modern Christian experience, this would occur when, say, a Methodist changes to a Baptist. Both are similar Protestant churches, but they have formed around different institutional values and structures. Tradition transition describes the situation where a convert feels they have carried over their previous commitments, but they have brought them into a new context by transferring allegiance to a different movement. In this case, there is a strong sense of both continuity with the past and discontinuity. Using these categories, how would a Jewish Christian convert view their conversion to Christianity? As an institutional switch (simply a different version of Judaism), or as a tradition switch (the fulfilment of Jewish hope)?

Although their work has been much criticized, Lofland and Skonovd propose seven motives which can trigger any of these conversion processes:[27] an intellectual quest for information, a mystical experience, an experimental attitude (trying out the options), affectional bonds (friendship), revivalism (a communal response to a charismatic personality) and coercion. First-century Christians were not in a position to coerce, and the experimental attitude of shopping around is essentially a twentieth-century phenomenon. Both of these motives may thus be eliminated from early Christianity. The philosophical quest for more convincing ideas tends to be attractive only to a limited number of people, and there is little evidence before the second century that Christianity was considered an intellectual heavyweight. Mystical experience certainly accounted for the initial Christian converts (the resurrection appearances), and may have contributed to the ongoing appeal of Christianity. However, the Pauline letters and Acts tend to suggest that converts experienced charismatic phenomena as a result of conversion, not the reverse. Revivalism presupposes a situation in which new life is breathed into a flagging faith – hardly an appropriate description of a fledgling movement. That leaves affectional bonding as the most likely motive for recruitment – friendship transmitted by word of mouth through personal contact.

Every conversion is a unique event, but Rambo suggests there are a seven phases within the actual transition process.[28] The starting point is the social context of the individual rooted in their experience, network of relationships, social location, education and so on. Within this framework the potential convert will experience a growing sense of dissatisfaction which renders them open to change. At this point, the group needs to act with a positive response and supply the outsider with information and insight into their predicament. This leads to a dialogue during which the partners will attempt to establish a degree of mutual assent. If this is achieved, personal factors become increasingly important: the warmth of the hosts, the level of care and the encouragement which is experienced – especially from the group leader who takes an interest. If these stages are negotiated successfully, the next phase is a move towards public commitment, often symbolized in the form of an initiation ritual and experienced as a 'surrender' or 'new life' (baptism[29]). This, though, is only the beginning of the process of assimilation into membership, which is completed only when the convert has successfully internalized the group norm and reconstructed their personal biography around the significance of membership. Only then will they finally arrive in the 'new world' – literally, because their symbolic universe has changed to centre on a new set of values and structures.

Throughout the process, there is a three-way adjustment as the convert is absorbed into the receiving community. There is a change in personal perceptions, a restructuring of social relationships with those outside the group, and – just as important – an acceptance of the new member by the group. The convert is literally changed – not only is euphoria widely reported, but more lasting, perhaps, is the sense of renewed commitment. But the group is also changed as it adapts to the new membership. And society is changed, as the balance between competing religious groups is subtly altered. To coin a phrase from the Anglican wedding service (a not totally unrelated transition ritual), this a way of life not to be undertaken carelessly, lightly or selfishly.

Even after the dust has settled, the process continues. Few converts succeed in internalizing new religious and ethical values completely, and thereafter they often display a fierce fanaticism and inflexibility as they force themselves to 'get it right'.[30] Although the convert is likely to insist they have 'found peace', there is a sense in which they have invested their entire future in a new and risky transition.

Key Stage Four: Group Maintenance

Thus, ongoing reaffirmation and encouragement continue to be important for all concerned. Internal group dynamics and external social pressure continue to exert an influence over the shape of the movement. Further, the initial enthusiasm following the successful launch of a new group usually evaporates in time, as does the similar euphoria experienced by new converts. Most group members are likely to encounter periods of self-doubt sooner or later. There is no point at which the certainty of intra-group cohesion can be assumed. This almost certainly accounts for the number of New Testament texts which seem designed to reduce anxiety – Luke-Acts has already been mentioned,[31] but the point probably applies to the Letter to the Hebrews[32] and perhaps 1 Peter as well.[33] Once established, early Christian communities had to continue to protect, support and encourage each other.

This required careful attention to the maintenance of group boundaries. Generally, this is done through the local leaders who police the membership, set the communal goals and motivate the group in action. But in addition to these up-front figures, there are often less obvious leaders who operate behind the scenes. These attend to the socio-emotional needs of the group by attending to the damage caused by the insensitivity of more assertive public leaders.[34]

These internal tensions mean that in time the initial enthusiasm of the group is likely to dissipate.[35] Following Weber, there is a recognizable pattern once this begins to happen. Groups which begin life in open rebellion to an established order (Hellenist Judaism in the case of Christianity) are generally regarded by the parent body in largely negative terms. At first, the anger and certainties of the new core group tend to camouflage the pain of this rejection, but as new members arrive and intra-group dissension begins to surface, some will almost certainly start to regret their decision to join. At this point, legitimation concerns rise to the surface.

Legitimation is the label given to the rhetoric used to attempt to convince members that their group perception is correct. It is only an issue where the legitimacy of a group is under question, either by outsiders, or by dissidents within the group itself. In general, three techniques are commonly used to dissipate anxiety: denunciation of opponents, use of sharp antitheses to set up a clear boundary between 'them' and 'us', and the reappropriation of a common heritage which is felt to be of significance.

Denunciation is the uncompromising condemnation of the opponents: 'they' have betrayed the cause because they are evil liars and deceivers. Antitheses reinforce this distinction by contrasting the false values of the parent body with the truth held by the new movement. The characteristic rhetoric includes terms like light/darkness, truth/falsehood, life/death, wisdom/deceit and so on. Everything is either good or bad with little room for compromise. 'We' are right (by definition) and 'they' are traitors. The reappropriation of tradition follows on from this: since 'we' alone know the truth, only 'we' can be the true heirs of the treasured tradition. It follows that 'we' have not changed at all – it is the opponents who have abandoned the cherished values. 'We' are merely doing what the founding fathers always intended.

A good example of such behaviour (for those who remember British politics of the eighties) was the formation of the Social Democratic Party (SDP).[36] The SDP (the sect) broke away from the Labour Party (the parent). The founder members issued the 'Lime-house Declaration' in which they denounced the Labour leadership for betraying democratic values, contrasted their policies with those of the Labour Party through a series of antitheses, and reclaimed the common tradition by declaring that they alone lived in the true spirit of social democracy which the Labour Party had betrayed. They had not left the Labour Party; the Labour Party had left them. In this way, the founders of the new party sought to legitimate their decision to form a rival organization.

A similar pattern can be detected behind a number of New Testament texts – classically in the writings of Paul. His developing sense of Christian self-identity allowed him to invite Gentile converts to join a Jewish Christian community without first becoming proselytes. This provoked a predictable response of hostility – first, from the Jewish leaders who were annoyed at his poaching of respected patrons from the synagogue, second, by other Hellenist Jewish Christian leaders who had developed a different sense of self-identity (see Galatians). Anger thus provided the standard trigger for the redefinition of social categories along sectarian lines. Paul now needed to engage in an opening round of legitimation, which he provides in Galatians: he denounces his opponents (e.g. Galatians 1.8; 5.12), sets up a series of antitheses (e.g. faith/works, circumcised/uncircumcised – most of Paul's proposi-tions, in fact, are either/or), and reappropriation of the tradition ('we', not 'they', are the true heirs of Abraham).[37] As it happens, most of Galatians 3—4 would leave the average Jewish reader gasping at the audacity of Paul's exegesis. But from his perspective, he is simply reclaiming ancestral tradition for his version of the sect, and denying access to his opponents. He hopes his argument will be persuasive and hold the group together as he wishes. The intensity of the rhetoric, however, suggests he realizes he is on unsure ground.

The Dynamics of Group Formation and Early Christian Mission

The concept of universal mission evolved during a period of social adjustment as Jewish, Greek and Christian groups interacted in the multi-layered processes of group formation which led to the recognition of Christianity as a new movement. This would have been a complex affair, and it is unlikely that every Christian group reached the same outcome at exactly the same time. This means that the broad category distinction posited between Palestinian and Hellenist Jewish Christianity is almost certainly an over-simplification. Not only is it unlikely there ever was a single united church, but the simple logic of group dynamics almost guarantees there were many variant subgroups, all of which had to compete to establish their own distinct identity.

This was certainly true during the second half of the first century when the New Testament texts were being written. There is not only the obvious conflict between Paul and the unnamed opponents in Galatia (Galatians 1.7), but also the evidence of other Hellenistic Jewish variants – Matthew has a subtly different vision of Christianity from Paul, for example,[38] whereas the Letter to the Hebrews is different again and the Letter of James almost certainly represents a relatively late attempt to halt the decline in the influence of Hellenist Jewish Christianity generally.[39] Interaction and conflict between groups, individuals and society fuelled the processes which brought the movement to the public attention and made mission a possibility.

John Gager has attempted to go beyond these normal group processes and suggest a more precise mechanism to account for the development of the later Gentile mission. Adapting the theory of cognitive dissonance first developed by Festinger during the 1950s,[40] Gager applies it to the behaviour of certain types of breakaway religious groups labelled 'millenarian sects' by Burridge[41] and Wilson.[42] These sects are defined as groups of people who hold a strong belief that the present social conditions are intolerable and that some sort of major structural upheaval is inevitable. Often rooted in protest, these movements are characterized by strong group bonds in which the membership is tied together in a tight and exclusive network.[43]

Gager argues that such groups tend to display five characteristics – the promise of an imminent arrival of heaven on earth, the subsequent overthrow of the present world order, a strong emotional environment, a limited lifespan (because the radical hopes of the group can rarely be sustained for any length of time), and a dominant leader who holds the group together. He then explores how these sects behave in conditions hostile to their survival when their core beliefs have become totally implausible: what happens if you believe in the end of the world and it does not arrive?

There are a number of possibilities, including resigned acceptance and the dissolution of the movement. In certain carefully defined circumstances, however, Gager suggests that certain types of sect will deal with the problem by engaging in aggressive missionary activity – as if, somehow, the idea that they can persuade others to share their belief means they were right all along, even when all the evidence points to the contrary. On this scenario, mission serves a crucial function by providing an alternative channel for the energy generated by disappointment.

Certainly eschatology was a major element in early Christian thinking. Indeed, disappointment over the delay in the parousia is already an issue in 1 Thessalonians 4—5, one of Paul's earliest letters. His sense of eschatological urgency is well summed up in Romans 13.11ff: 'Now is the moment to wake up from sleep. For salvation is nearer to us now than when we became believers; the night is far gone, the day is near [...].'[44] But caution is in order: Paul wrote these letters to encourage people who were already believers, and although he promotes his own Gentile mission, he does not exhort his readers to follow suit. Perhaps Romans 11.25–36 is nearest to Gager's model, but even here the fit is not exact. In this passage, Paul says that the function of the Gentile mission is to provoke the Jews to 'jealousy' – the idea seems to be that 'stubborn' Jews will be persuaded to accept salvation when they see themselves overtaken by the Gentiles (it is curious that Paul never quite says that these Jews must become Christian before they can be saved). He uses this argument as a way of legitimizing the apparent rejection of Christianity by Judaism and relates this to the mystery of God's providential dealing with Israel. What he does not do is use the rhetoric to promote new and more aggressive forms of missionary activity.

There is little doubt that Gager has overstated his case.[45] Theologians are notoriously good at jumping on bandwagons to try and support shaky speculation, but it is unlikely purely on sociological grounds that his theory can be sustained.[46] The roots of universal Christian mission lay in a complex interaction, as isolated Christian groups became detached from the synagogue at different times and in different contexts. They responded, therefore, to different social pressures. The only common factor was that in due course, all of them became increasingly vulnerable in a hostile world. But not all of them adopted a radical response. Millenarianism may have exercised an influence over some of these groups, but all of them needed to survive. To do that, they had to identify a target audience of people who might be open to the persuasive arguments of Christianity. Whatever their eschatological fervour, it was only when the necessary local social conditions and the aspirations of would-be converts converged that Christian mission became a realistic option.

❖ 8 ❖

The Birth of a Concept

Christianity did not leave the synagogue with a fully developed theology. Christian ideas continued to evolve over a period of time, initially within Judaism, thereafter in the independent Christian communities which sprang up in different places at different times. The debate centred on conflicting views over the role of Jesus in the providence of God. In the heat of the argument, all the interested parties were driven to increasingly committed positions, as Jews, Jewish Christians and Gentile converts responded to the pressure to justify their christological views more precisely. Theology on all sides was forged through continuing doctrinal controversy.

Developing Christian belief was thus a by-product of conflict. It is too simplistic to suggest that the competing groups split neatly around the perceived truth of fully fashioned ideas. Reality is more dynamic, and clearly formulated beliefs were usually the result of complex interaction between groups, ideas and individuals. More precisely, Christian belief is the product of core Jewish beliefs about the God of Israel modified in the light of Christian convictions about the life, death and resurrection of Jesus, further refined by the social dynamics operating within Hellenist Judaism, underwritten by the instinctive assumptions and values of Graeco-Roman culture, and shaped by charismatic personalities such as Peter, Stephen and Barnabas.

The crystallization of Christian groups out of Judaism was thus an enormously complicated process, whose outcome was dependent on a large number of variables. It is necessary, therefore, to sharpen the focus a little further and pay attention to the dynamics of social and theological interaction, in order to consider how these factors may have played a role in the birth of the concept of universal Christian mission.

Attitudes and Behaviour

In general, personal behaviour is closely related to attitude. This may be defined as the hierarchy of values, feelings and beliefs which make it possible for an individual to form judgements about the significance of external objects (people, things, ideas, events). Because such attitudes are routinely acquired during the course of childhood development, they reflect cultural perceptions as well as individual opinion. This is generally an inarticulate process, and most people would be hard pressed to explain why they favour one view over another. Attitudes are rarely static: an initial assessment of the value of something may be made on a rough and ready basis (the underlying heuristic model), but this will be constantly adjusted in the light of further experience and reflection. Acquired and modified attitudes thus colour behaviour by suggesting appropriate responses to each new encounter, ranging from warm enthusiasm (positive attitude) through to outright hostility (negative attitude) via sheer indifference.[1]

Apparently, attitude consists of three underlying components – cognition (what a person 'knows' or believes to be true), affection (what they like or dislike), and behaviour (defined in this context as the intention to act in a particular way).[2] Salience reappears as another crucial factor, so that individuals must be persuaded that a person, idea, thing or event has some relevance to their own personal situation. Usually, most people try to hold all these elements together in a coherent relationship. As D. C. Pennington writes, 'Cognitive consistency is such a powerful force in our social lives that its absence or opposite (inconsistency) is experienced as extremely uncomfortable [. . .] and people are motivated to reduce or avoid inconsistency whenever possible.'[3]

Balance theory is a simple model for studying this mechanism. It holds that attitudes are balanced when they are in harmony with each other, unbalanced when they do not form a coherent pattern, and that imbalance is an unstable state which normally leads to an adjustment in order to restore the preferred equilibrium.

So, for example, in a relationship between two people (Person A and Person B) concerning an idea, thing or person associated with one of them (an object), balance is said to exist when the attitudes generated by all three elements are either positive or any two of the attitudes are negative. This gives eight possible states (four balanced and four unbalanced), including those shown in Figure 1.

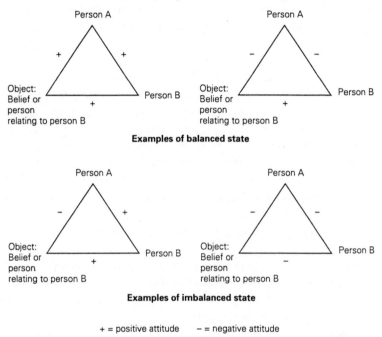

Examples of balanced state

Examples of imbalanced state

+ = positive attitude   − = negative attitude

Figure 1

The first pair of examples are balanced because the elements meet the conditions for equilibrium: in one case, all three attitudes are positive and therefore in balance, whereas in the other, two attitudes are negative and one positive. In the second pair of examples, however, the attitude taken by person A towards person B is out of step with the attitudes taken by both towards the object. In one case, person A likes person B, but dislikes the thing associated with person B; in the second case, person A dislikes both person B and the object, but person B was not very keen on the object in the first place. In both cases, a state of attitudinal imbalance may be said to exist.

Since changes in behaviour are closely linked to attitude, a modification in one will necessarily disturb the pattern and generate instability. As a result, one element or another in the relationship will need to be adjusted in order to restore balance, and this will have a further knock-on effect on both attitudes and patterns of behaviour.[4]

In the case of religious conversion, simple balance theory would predict a sequence of change something like this. The initial pattern expected would be broadly one of balance. In the potential convert, this condition would be represented by two negative attitudes and a positive, assuming the evangelist has a positive attitude towards the gospel and the potential convert has a generally negative attitude towards both Christian belief and the evangelist (otherwise they would already be on the way to changing their attitude). These initial negatives need not be hostile, but simply negative either in the sense of indifference (lack of salience) or sheer ignorance (negative cognition).

This is a stable condition, so before conversion can take place, a state of imbalance must be generated either in the attitude taken towards Christian belief (I find this idea convincing) or towards the evangelist (I like this person). This modified attitudinal position (now two positives and a negative) creates an imbalance, and the preferred state of equilibrium can only be restored when the potential convert revises their attitude towards the remaining element (all three elements positive). In diagrammatic form, the conversion process looks like Figure 2.

The first route presupposes sufficient data to enable the potential recruit to formulate a positive opinion about Christian belief. This might be labelled the cognitive route: Christianity is held to be intellectually satisfying. The second is relationship-orientated, and may be called the affective route: the relationship feels good.

As Weber predicted and as later research suggests, the affective route turns out to be the most common – converts tend to be attracted either by the membership of the receiving group or the activities of the group or both.[5] In fact, in the case of an emerging group, a charismatic leader is likely to be the first point of contact. On balance theory, therefore, it follows that the instability introduced by a positive change of attitude towards the evangelist

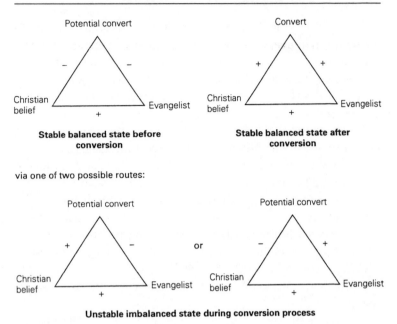

Figure 2

(this person sounds interesting) will force a modification in the attitude taken to belief as well. In other words, cognitive perceptions are not a necessary precondition for conversion. Intellectual agreement is just as likely to follow after interest has been generated on socio-emotional grounds.

However, this is obviously an elementary model in which attitudes are held to be either positive or negative. In the real world, attitudes may be held with varying degrees of strength, so a more sophisticated version of the theory is needed to take account of these variables. One such refinement is based on congruity theory. This is similar to balance theory in that three positives or two negatives and a positive are still required for stability, but the model now allows for degrees of change along the two axes controlled by the subject (in this case, the potential convert). A graded scale is used to measure the strength of each response ranging from strongly positive (+3) to strongly negative (-3). A change in terminology reflects this refinement, so attitudes are held to be either congruous or incongruous.

On this model, it has been found that a person persuaded to change the value of one attitude (from positive to negative or vice versa) is also likely to adjust the strength of their other attitudes as well. Those attitudes held most strongly at the outset are most resistant to change, whereas those held weakly adapt more easily.[6]

Applying this to conversion (and assuming again a scenario in which the evangelist is expected to hold a positive attitude towards Christian belief, and that there has been no significant 'past history' to distort the personal relationships), it is probable that a potential convert would start with a broad indifference towards the evangelist, but a stronger hostility towards the alien beliefs on offer. If the outsider (the evangelist) is able to establish the positive relationship expected of a powerful charismatic personality, the conversion process now looks like Figure 3.

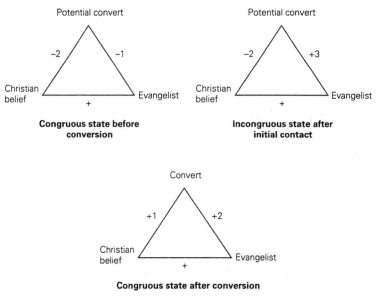

Figure 3

In this example, the magnetic attraction of a charismatic personality (the evangelist) has modified an initial weak negative attitude (–1 or lack of interest) into a strongly positive response (+3). This produces the incongruous state in which the attitudes in the total relationship are out of kilter – the potential convert likes the evangelist, but remains hostile to the gospel. The desired stable state can only be restored when the attitude towards Christian belief is also modified and congruity re-established. On this model, belief is found yet again to follow personal attraction.

The significant finding, however, is that the transaction in conversion incurs a cost to the evangelist's reputation. The convert at first feels a strong attraction to the charismatic leader, but as congruence is restored, some of the energy invested in the personal contact is displaced into cognitive understanding (Christian belief rises from -1 to $+1$; feelings towards the evangelist go down from $+3$ to $+2$). In other words, the convert comes to show less interest in the teacher and more in the message.

Because attitude/behaviour modification is a continuous and dynamic experience, the attitudinal relationship between personalities and beliefs is in a constant state of flux. In other words, attitudes, beliefs and behaviour are interrelated, consist of cognitive, affective and experiential elements, and combine with social factors, personal characteristics and learned responses to determine the actual behavioural pattern. Further complexity is added as the game is expanded and other players are brought on to the field: relationships are rarely limited to the charismatic leader and a lone convert, and other personalities in the group conspire to complicate the picture. In this dynamic situation, cognitive beliefs are only one variable among many, and they are just as likely to crystallize out of the interaction as to be the cause. In short, you may not know what you believe until after you have joined the group and stopped to think about it.

It is entirely possible that this kind of congruence exchange helps to explain the tension witnessed in the Corinthian correspondence. Paul initially attracted a following on the strength of his charismatic personality, but his converts traded personal affection for cognitive belief as they moved towards a new state of attitudinal congruence. Paul was thus forced on to the defensive as he recognized his declining influence and moved to protect his leadership status (e.g. 2 Corinthians 1.8—3.6; 10—13 etc.). The change of attitude on his part towards the Corinthians caused a response from them, and changes in the affectional relationship between both parties prompted further adjustments in their cognitive values. And so on. As the new recruits began to think for themselves, Paul discovered that there was a personal price to pay for expanding the community.

The Origins of Christian Mission

Attitudinal and behavioural exchanges between leaders, group members and potential converts are thus a significant factor to be considered in the development of mission, alongside the other more obvious theological or cultural components. This is perhaps the missing factor behind the incident at Antioch (Galatians 2.4–14). The effect of preaching Christ to Jews in this region of the Diaspora was to allow Gentile sympathizers to overhear the gospel. Some of these Gentiles were subsequently drawn into the Christian movement, and this gradually shifted the ethnic balance within the group. After a while, some of the founder members began to feel uneasy about waning Jewish influence, and changing attitudes drove behaviour: they responded in a typically atavistic mode. Peter and Barnabas were thrown into the middle of a first-century Hellenist Jewish Christian version of a 'back to basics' campaign.

These two leaders were opposed by Paul – a member of the group who felt that the growing number of Gentiles was not a threat but an opportunity. Although the point is disputed by some,[7] Paul's background[8] made him ideally suited to act as a go-between. Born in the Diaspora, but with strong Palestinian connections and perhaps brought up in Palestine from an early age,[9] he was immensely proud of his Jewishness (Galatians 1.13–15; 2 Corinthians 11.22; Romans 11.1f). He never rejected his upbringing,[10] though he does say that with the benefit of Christian hindsight he came to regard it as so much 'rubbish' (to use the delicate euphemism of the NRSV) by comparison with what he now has in Christ (Philippians 3.5–6). But in his thinking about God, righteousness and the Law, Paul remained thoroughly Jewish. He continued to insist on the strongest possible continuity between the Jewish God of Scripture and the Christian experience of God's action in Christ.

However, his extended contact with sympathetic Gentiles (perhaps the fourteen years of Galatians 2.1) resulted in a modification of his attitude towards the socio-religious markers which set Jews apart. During the course of the normal daily exchange between experience, attitudes and personal relationships, Paul was forced to re-evaluate his opinion, and his behaviour *and* beliefs followed suit. He felt called to preach to the Gentiles (Galatians 1.16).

This modification of cognitive attitude helps to explain the reasons behind the dispute with Peter and Barnabas in Galatians 2.11–14. The dynamics of social attitude had not persuaded them to modify their beliefs in quite the same way, so when challenged about an inconsistency in their behaviour, they changed their behaviour rather than their opinion. At this point, conflict with Paul became inevitable (Galatians 2.14).

The honour-shame code of first-century Graeco-Roman culture then came into play. Loss of face in an argument was costly for Paul, leading to reduced status and personal prestige. Isolated within the group in his attitude and associated beliefs, Paul had little alternative in group-process terms but to 'put up or shut up'. Shutting up in his case would have closed the incident by acknowledging his inferior position: he was in error, and had to submit or withdraw. Putting up, however, amounted to a refusal to accept the outcome. Paul then had two further options, which were social mobility – migration to another group (it would have to be, from his perspective, a 'superior' group), or an internal leadership challenge. Echoes of this latter alternative may be found in the relativizing remarks about 'those supposed to be acknowledged leaders' in Galatians 2.6: Paul protests he is not unduly impressed by their high status. For such a challenge to succeed, however, he needed a persuasive argument with which he could convince enough people in the group that his cognitive attitude was 'correct'. He needed supporters.

It is difficult to tell whether he actually found them in the community in Antioch. The next stage in the story is difficult to unravel because the data is so thin and confusing: Luke suggests that Paul was commissioned by the church and sent out as a missionary delegate (Acts 13.2f), whereas Paul asserts his complete independence. Either way, Paul's major missionary activity came after the incident, suggesting some kind of link.[11] His attitude and beliefs were being modified by experience, and his behaviour subsequently followed suit. Paul's changing attitude is rejected by the leadership of the group, and he responds by moving off to found new dependent communities in which he has the status of founder-benefactor. His honour was thus restored.

Paul's pattern of behaviour is correctly interpreted by his former colleagues as a leadership challenge, and this had the effect of forcing them to defend their position. Unnamed shadows mysteriously appear in an attempt to undermine Paul's position by 'correcting' his teaching (Galatians 1.6ff and 3.1ff). In other words, Paul was haunted by his past as he recruited supporters for his ideal of an open Christian community.

The lists of associates in Romans 16 or 1 Corinthians 16 make it clear that Paul eventually established the network of like-minded supporters he needed. He did not act entirely independently. Nor did he invent the concept of the Gentile mission from scratch – the first tentative steps had already been taken by the Hellenist Jewish Christian radicals back in Jerusalem. It is just that the sheer weight of evidence points in his direction as one of the key figures in the formative process. The amount of material devoted to Paul in the New Testament (thirteen letters associated with his name and 25 per cent of Luke-Acts, or 25 per cent of the entire New Testament) is eloquent testimony to his influence. 2 Peter 3.15ff shows he was remembered as a difficult person. But love him or hate him, you simply could not ignore him.

Much of Paul's subsequent ministry can be seen as the working out of the consequences of this shift in attitudes and beliefs. As well as forcing him to defend the position he adopted in the communities he founded (e.g. Galatians 6.6–17), the Letter to the Romans shows him casting the net far and wide for support of his novel views.[12] Equally, therein lies the significance of his 'collection for the saints', mentioned in all four of his major letters (Romans 15.22–9; 1 Corinthians 16.1ff; 2 Corinthians 8—9; Galatians 2.10)[13] – Paul wanted to use the material resources of his converts to enable him to act as a patron-benefactor of the Jerusalem church. In honour-shame terms, this would create a sense of debt and obligation from the more conservative 'acknowledged pillars' of the community. Acceptance of his charity by these leaders would imply a tacit endorsement of his mission. Their complete absence throughout Acts 21—26, after Paul's arrest in Jerusalem, suggests they did not share his view of the way the game should be played, however.

Case Study One: 1 Corinthians – Social Processes in Action
So, from a practical point of view, what did Paul actually do when he
arrived in a place where he hoped to establish a new mission? How
did he set about building up his contacts? There is no direct account
of his method in any of the letters, but there are enough hints to
piece together an outline, especially when additional information is
cautiously prised from Acts and taken into account.

When Paul first walked into a new location, he was basically
dependent on local goodwill. He might find temporary accommoda-
tion at one of the local inns, but these were notorious places, not
recommended for people with a reputation to establish.[14] His first
port of call, therefore – at least in the early stages of a mission – was
likely to be the most obvious place for any Jewish traveller. He would
call in at the local synagogue and ask for hospitality.

In due course, a few members of the synagogue might be drawn
into his circle, and these would then become the people in a position
to offer Paul a route into the local community – especially if they
were men of substance like Crispus (1 Corinthians 1.14ff and Acts
18.8). The defection of such a prominent figure and the loss of his
patronage had serious financial implications for the local Jewish
community, and doubtless encouraged the Christian congregation.
His conversion would have done little to ease the tension developing
between the two religious movements. But it gave Paul a massive
boost.

Another obvious point of contact was through 'the trade'.[15] In the
pre-industrial city, the network of professional guilds and trade
associations provided routine hospitality for visiting colleagues.
Paul's insistence on working for a living (1 Corinthians 9.15–19) not
only gave him a degree of independence in the honour-shame
culture, but also a simple device for maintaining an alternative
financial support system outside the synagogue.

All this suggests a certain opportunism, with Paul looking for new
openings and then exploiting them. Something like this may lie
behind the only two comments on mission found in 1 Corinthians, a
letter which otherwise deals with internal matters relating to ethics
and doctrine. These references crop up almost in passing. The first
occurs in 1 Corinthians 7.1–16, where in response to a question
raised by the Corinthians, Paul works through his policy on marriage

in the light of his dominant eschatological perspective. In the previous chapter, Paul had argued that sex with a prostitute pollutes the body of Christ (1 Corinthians 6.12–20), but in 1 Corinthians 7.12–16 he argues the opposite case: sex with an unbelieving spouse extends the sphere of God's influence. In the first instance, the uncleanness associated with prostitution pollutes the church, yet in the second, sex with an unbelieving partner within marriage provides an opportunity to extend the Kingdom. For Paul the opportunist, even the most intimate relationship can be turned to missionary advantage.

The second comment on mission in 1 Corinthians arises out of the 'over-realized eschatology' of the spiritual élite who are causing disruption within the church with their exaggerated emphasis on speaking in tongues (1 Corinthians 12.1–31).[16] Paul responds not by criticizing the practice as such, but by drawing out the implications for opportunist contact with non-believers (1 Corinthians 14.13–19): spiritual self-indulgence undermines effective mission. In both these cases, Paul is perhaps framing an argument on the basis of his established custom: he was used to thinking of every encounter as an opportunity for evangelism.

Not surprisingly, Paul's tactics were perceived by others as unfair or even unwelcome. Members of the local synagogue, for example, were in dispute with Paul on at least five occasions – the number of times in 2 Corinthians 11.2 he says he received the thirty-nine lashes. Given that outside Palestine this punishment could only be inflicted on people who accepted the jurisdiction of the synagogue, Paul must have subjected himself to the beating. Was this, perhaps, because he needed the contacts in the synagogue?

In due course, intra-group rivalry within the Jewish community reached breaking point, and the nucleus of Christian believers recruited from the synagogue needed to look for a new base. They found one, sometimes in a local public meeting hall (Acts 19.9), but more often in local houses. These had to be of sufficient size to accommodate (say) twelve to forty people, so necessarily had to be the properties of the better off. Paul now needed to find other influential contacts outside the Jewish community with cash and hospitality to spare: precisely the sort of constituency open to him by virtue of his Roman citizenship.

Paul found such contacts in Gaius and Stephanus, the other two people mentioned in 1 Corinthians 1.14. According to Meeks, these two characters must also have had a relatively high social status, because Gaius was a householder with a property large enough to play host for the local church (Romans 16.23), and Stephanus had a 'household', the normal expression for domestic servants and slaves (1 Corinthians 16.15). Like Crispus, in Graeco-Roman terms these men were benefactors, lending the church status and protection. In return, their cultural values would lead them to expect enhanced esteem from the *ekklēsia*. This appears to be precisely the problem addressed in 1 Corinthians 11.17–34, where one group of élite believers (not necessarily Gaius and Stephanus) are receiving privileged treatment at the expense of the rest of the community, which is excluded from a fair share of the eucharistic meal. In a fascinating demonstration of the interaction between culture and theology, Paul works through his proposed solution: the élite are to hold back from conspicuous consumption in the gathered meeting but they are allowed to indulge themselves privately. By their public display of superiority they are failing to discern the body (of Christ, the church).[17]

In the game of social exchange, things rarely stand still for long. Having attracted a handful of supporters, the mechanics of congruence theory suggest that Paul's reputation as a leader would start to decline in proportion to the growing commitment of his converts. 1 Corinthians shows the process in action. In his absence, his charismatic power was no longer available to hold the community together, and the old social divisions began to undermine group bonding. Paul was forced to attend to these internal divisions in order to protect the fledgling community from disintegration (1 Corinthians 1—4). In the continuing social processes through which early Christian mission was developed, Paul had to pay close attention to internal group dynamics and patrol the boundaries (1 Corinthians 5—11).

The combination of the shadows from Antioch (Galatians 1.7) and internal division at Corinth meant that Paul was constantly facing leadership challenges. These challenges are already apparent in 1 Corinthians 1.10—2.16, but they obviously did not go away and come right to the fore in 2 Corinthians 1.8—3.18 and 10—13.

Since it is the task of the public leader to set the goals and priorities which determine group identity, a leadership challenge necessarily triggers another round in the ongoing cycle of social definition: the threefold processes of social categorization, self-location and social comparison. As Paul's reputation came under question, the pressure grew on the Pauline communities to re-examine their options: were they Jewish associates (as the Anthiochene agents thought they should be), Gentiles (by birth) or de facto a new category of Christian? Then, with the benefit of local feedback, they had to decide whether this was a 'good' thing or not: how did Pauline Christians compare with Jews, pagans and other Christians? Perhaps something of this re-evaluation can be seen to be at work in the debate in 1 Corinthians 15. Some members of the community were apparently having second thoughts about the value of Paul's teaching on the resurrection. Paul is quick to reassure them, however, that they are in the best possible place (1 Corinthians 15.50–8).

Whilst all this was taking place at a group level, personal patterns would continue to adapt at an individual level. Thus, Paul's mission needs to be read against a complex dialogue between belief, attitude and experience in the context of the exchanges between individuals and groups which shape and define social location. Paul's changing attitude towards the community and their changing attitude towards him gave energy to them both. But in the process, Paul was compelled to re-examine the roots of his authority and defend his attitude towards Jewish and Gentile Christianity. Paul needed a rational explanation of his position.

Case Study Two: Galatians and Romans – Rationalizing Experience

Rationalizing belief is related to the final phase of group formation – legitimation, or the subsequent need to present a coherent foundation for the emerging social unit. To support his intuitive belief gained from reflection on experience that God had called Jews and Gentiles 'without distinction' (Romans 3.22, author's translation) Paul eventually needed plausible arguments to enforce the boundary around his new community.

Galatians is perhaps the example par excellence in the New

Testament of the legitimation process in action. The seriousness of the threat faced by Paul is immediately evident from the structure of the letter: unlike his other surviving correspondence, Galatians skips over the usual blessing and thanksgiving section and launches straight into an attack on the readers (Galatians 1.6ff).[18] Paul denounces his opponents in 1.8; 3.1; 5.7–12, and draws a sharp antithesis between faith and works, circumcision and uncircumcision, life in the Spirit versus life under 'the flesh'. He reappropriates the Scriptures for his deviant view (from the perspective of more conservative forms of Jewish Christianity) through extensive quotation, and tries to construct an argument on what he assumes to be common ground. He claims that 'true' continuity with the inherited tradition lies through his teaching, not with that of his forceful opponents.

The shape of the argument demonstrates that Paul's beliefs were rooted in personal experience rather than transmitted tradition (Galatians 1.13—2.14). This is the thrust of the opening chapters of Galatians, which are not meant to be read as an interesting biographical aside, but as critical evidence in the rhetorical argument Paul is hoping to construct.[19] Paul knows his views on mission were a radical departure from the accepted Christian practice, but he argues vigorously that he had been directly authorized by God to initiate the change. Mere human leaders like Peter or James are sharply relativized (Galatians 2.6) in a move to minimize their influence.

Galatians 2.15–21 is the first sketch of the opening rationale: the Jewish Torah divided Jews from Gentiles, yet (Christian) experience shows that the Law was (somehow) ineffective in establishing a positive relationship with God. The role of bringing people into a right relationship with God has therefore been transferred from the Torah to Christ, which has the knock-on effect of rendering redundant the old ethnic distinctions enforced by the Law. God revealed that Christ displaced the Torah, and a mission to all people without distinction was therefore a new possibility.

Paul then sets out to substantiate his case. The evidence is presented in two stages. The first is another brief but telling argument from the experience of the Galatian readers (Galatians 3.1–6). In a series of rhetorical questions (showing perhaps how irritated he felt about the questioning of his authority), Paul demands to know 'did you receive the Spirit by doing works of the law or by believing what you heard?' (Galatians 3.2). He takes it for granted that the readers will acknowledge the evidence of their own charismatic tradition.

The second stage seeks to make a connection between the acknowledged phenomenon of the Spirit and the open mission to the Gentiles. This is more complicated, however, because Paul knows well enough that there was no ready-made link in existing Jewish thought. He therefore has to construct his own.

He achieves this by threading together a composite sequence of ideas. He gets part of the way by drawing on a belief circulating in some Jewish circles that the Spirit had fallen silent and had only been heard as a faint echo since the time of the great prophets (the *bath gōl* or literally 'daughter of a voice'). On this view, the return of the Spirit in power would be a clear sign that the promised new age of redemption had actually arrived (e.g. Isaiah 44.3; Joel 2.28).[20] This gives him a link between the Spirit and eschatology.

But he still has to establish a further link between eschatology and the Gentiles. In scriptural terms, an argument from eschatology should strictly lead to an argument for the renewal of Israel, but this is, of course, the very outcome Paul is most anxious to avoid – he does not want to confirm Jewish exclusivity. Hence, he does not draw a theological conclusion from the presence of the eschatological Spirit, but an ethical one (Galatians 5.16–26).

This is why in Galatians 3—4 Paul sets out in a different direction. Instead of following the Spirit connection, he constructs another argument from Scripture to forge the missing link between eschatology and the Gentiles. He does this via Abraham. It is a tortuous route, and one which might well leave the average Jewish reader reeling from the audacity of his reading of Scripture.

The logic only works if the conclusion is first conceded, that 'for freedom Christ has set you free' (Galatians 5.1) – if Christ is the answer, then clearly the Mosaic Covenant was not. Consequently, there must have been something wrong with the Torah, and Paul concludes that the problem was circumcision, the symbol of the separation between Jew and Gentile. This is the divisive issue which has to be set aside if there is to be one community in Christ (Galatians 5.6). But if the commands of the Torah are annulled, does that not mean that had God abandoned his promise to Israel? Not a bit, says Paul, because before the limited covenant with Moses, God had entered into a more basic relationship with Abraham, and this covenant is loyally maintained by a faithful God.

It is possible Paul had been drawn to the Abraham narrative by the same opponents who were attempting to undermine his authority: Jews (and Jewish Christians?) saw themselves as the elect children of Abraham[21] (see, for example, the reference in Matthew 3.7ff and its parallel in Luke 3.8ff, as well as the oblique claim implied in Matthew 1.1). On the Jewish reading, however, part of the covenant with Abraham had been an instruction to circumcise Isaac. It follows, therefore, that circumcision was a primary sign of elect status: Gentiles who want to become part of the Covenant must be circumcised.

But in his reading of the narrative, Paul is struck by two points overlooked by the pro-circumcision lobby: the promise to Abraham was that he would be the ancestor of many nations (Genesis 17.5 – LXX *patera pollōn ethnōn*), not just the patriarch of Israel; and the promise to be a blessing to all the families of the earth (Genesis 12.2f) preceded the command to circumcise Isaac (Genesis 17.9f). This allows Paul to develop the crucial missing link: the covenant with Abraham was independent of the later Mosaic Torah, and was a covenant with the Gentiles as well as Israel.

However, this exposes Paul to the potentially embarrassing position of having to account for the later Torah. Why did God give the Law through Moses if he had always intended to build a relationship with the descendants of Abraham on the basis of faith (meaning trust or loyalty)? This question alone, perhaps more than anything else, betrays Paul's lasting commitment to his Jewish heritage. Anyone else would simply have agreed and swept the Law aside. But not Paul. He is still sufficiently Jewish to feel the need to account for God's gift of the Mosaic Covenant.

So he sets out to deal with the problem in the most tortuous section of his letter – Galatians 3.19–26. The speed at which Paul fires off the evidence reveals the extent to which he is struggling with different exegetical models in the hope that one might actually work. The result is a stream of half-digested suggestions: the Law was added because of transgression (v.19a), an extraordinary statement which might mean anything (see Romans 5.20); or it was an unnecessary extra given via intermediary angels, not directly by God (vv.19b–20); or the Law was a strict guardian for a privileged minority until they reached the age of majority and could take responsibility for themselves vv.23–5). In fact, Paul is not quite sure what it was, except that it is a problem.

What is crystal clear (at least to Paul), is that God's new revelation in Christ had (in a limited sense) rendered the Law redundant. Indeed, he argues that the Law had always pointed towards its own limitations. According to Galatians 3.10–18 and 4.21–31, the main story line in Scripture ran straight from Abraham to Jesus, who was the (one and only) 'true seed', heir to the promise that all the nations of the world would be blessed. But this 'flow' of promise had been interrupted by human sin, and forced God to protect his chosen people Israel from the worst excesses of disaster by giving them the Law. The Gentiles had been left to fend for themselves. In due course, God acted in Christ to remove the divisive effects of sin, and this also removed the need for the Torah. The 'flow' of blessing had been restored.

The theological sequence could be set out as in Figure 4. The primary function of the Law, therefore, was simply to relay the narrative of God's promise, so the 613 commands of the Torah are

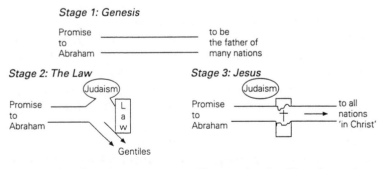

Stage 1: Genesis

Stage 2: The Law

Stage 3: Jesus

Torah has the effect of diverting the 'flow' of God's promised blessing to all nations. Judaism is placed in a privileged position, but the Gentiles are on their own.

The cross has the effect of removing the temporary ethnic barrier of Torah. 'Normal' service resumed: all nations able to receive Abraham's blessing.

Figure 4

essentially a sideline. In effect, Paul invites the reader to skip over most of Genesis 18—Deuteronomy 34, save only for a few personalities and select ethical principles which continue to resonate with his evolving Christian experience. Everything else is relegated to the second division.

In Galatians 3.17 Paul attempts to relativize the Torah even further by driving a temporal wedge between the promise to Abraham and the subsequent arrival of the Law supposedly 430 years later. This argument will not work, however, for the simple reason that although Abraham was obviously not able to keep the Mosaic Covenant, he was still under an obligation to obey the command to circumcise Isaac (Genesis 17.9–14). Abraham was thus bound by the law of circumcision, the key ethnic identity marker Paul is attempting to eliminate. This is another indication Paul was thinking on his feet: he knows the point he wants to make, but cannot quite marshal the evidence to prove it. As on other occasions, Paul is arguing 'from solution to plight'.[22] He supplies the spectacular gaps in the logic of his exegesis by reading Genesis in a christological sense; he already 'knows' that Christ has fulfilled the eschatological promise to Abraham.[23]

Wisely, therefore, he drops the temporal argument in the parallel passage in Romans 4.9–12. Overall, Romans 4 is a thoroughly toned down version of Galatians, as Paul is careful to choose his language as diplomatically as possible – after all, he is writing to solicit the support of the Romans, some of whom he suspects may be uneasy about his rumoured attack on Judaism.[24] In this revised version of the argument, he wants only to establish the general point that the promise to bless the Gentiles through Abraham came before the command to circumcise Isaac. Given that Galatians almost certainly preceded Romans, this suggests that Paul continued to modify his attitude and behaviour in response to an ongoing dialogue with experience.

Romans 9—11 is sufficient testimony to his continuing anxiety to come up with a convincing scriptural argument for his attitude towards the Gentiles. This provides yet another astonishing catena of quotations from the Scriptures quite unlikely to convince anyone who was not already predisposed to accept it. What Paul actually demonstrates through these texts is the 'intransigence' of the Jews. The case for the Gentiles is presented by Paul, not by Scripture.

In the course of this extended dialogue between Scripture and experience, Paul is driven to produce one of the most extraordinary statements in his letters: 'Do we then overthrow the law by this faith? By no means! On the contrary, we uphold the law' (Romans 3.31). Many readers are left breathless by this. In what sense can Paul claim to uphold the Law when he purposely sets out to demonstrate the irrelevance of the Mosaic Covenant? His answer is – as in Galatians – to reach back to Abraham, whom he sees as the supreme paradigm of God's saving activity (Romans 4.1–25).[25] The Torah Paul upholds is again reduced to a prophetic narrative of God's promise to the nations – a promise which is confirmed and completed in Christ. Faith was the basis of the promise to Abraham, not obedience to the law of circumcision. In Christ, therefore, the flow of promise between Abraham and the nations had been resumed. The Mosaic Covenant was never more than a temporary holding operation which protected the Jews from the worst excesses of sin (see also 2 Corinthians 3). This was the 'Jewish privilege' of Romans 3.1. But the effect of the Torah had been to drive a wedge between the children of Abraham, who were not only the Jews, but Gentiles as well.

The curse of that ethnic distinction had finally been torn down by the cross (Galatians 3.10–14); because of Jesus, all are now equal before God. Once this theological connection has been made, the rest falls neatly into place. Legitimation is possible because Paul feels able to reclaim both the tradition of election and the promise of blessing via Abraham, and thus avoid the embarrassment of Moses. Circumcision and the Torah were never meant to be anything more than a temporary diversion.

Armed with this insight, Paul was able to go back to Deutero-Isaiah and re-read those passages about the eschatological flow of Gentiles into Zion. The link in the chain is now complete. Read in the light of the Abraham paradigm, Isaiah takes on a whole new meaning: the Gentiles no longer come in subjection, but as co-heirs to the promise. Paul has recycled the promise of Scripture and turned it into a justification of his mission. The divine basis for the Law is affirmed, and the promise to Israel to be the people of God acknowledged. The true Israelites of Romans 9.6f were still the children of Abraham. But so were the Gentiles.

Putting this together, the logic of Paul's rationale for legitimizing the Gentile mission came together in cumulative steps. Believers know they are part of the eschatological people of God because they have experienced the Spirit. The Spirit comes in fulfilment of God's promise of renewal, not just to Israel, but to the Gentiles as well by virtue of their inclusion in the corporate figure of Abraham. This ancestor of all people provides the theological link: the promise to bless the nations was fulfilled in Christ, the true seed of Abraham (Galatians 3.16) who brought about the age of reconciliation (Romans 3.21ff) and released the Spirit which revealed the power of God (Romans 8.1–27). Paul works out his theology of mission in the light of his experience and in response to the social pressure which forced him to crystallize his beliefs. He rationalizes his pattern of behaviour and attitude in an appeal to Abraham.

According to Acts, Paul was the central figure most intimately linked in the memory of the church with the evolution of the Gentile mission. Maybe this was because he was the first person to provide a working model for a development which had actually been forged through the processes of attitude and behaviour transaction. The theology of Christian mission was a product of controversy as Paul was compelled to think through a plausible conceptual framework which relativized the divisive Torah. By looking over the shoulder of Moses, Paul found in Abraham the paradigm he needed for the Christian reading of Scripture: through the 'true seed', God's promise to bless the Gentiles had finally been fulfilled.

✤ 9 ✤

And So to the Gospels

A round the turn of the century, the great German scholar William Wrede suggested that Paul was 'the second founder of Christianity'.[1] The extent to which he overstated the case has been much debated ever since, but Wrede was obviously correct to point out the towering significance of Paul during the crucial period when early Christian attitudes, beliefs and behaviour were being formed. Paul's experience of preaching to the Gentiles and the impact of his theology and practice were clearly key factors in reshaping the missionary thinking of the first Jewish Christian communities.

On the other hand, it simply is not true (as some scholars after Wrede have tried to argue) that Paul invented Christianity as such. His writings show he was already the heir to an established tradition, and Paul freely acknowledges this dependence on several occasions (e.g. 1 Corinthians 11.23ff; 15.3ff). Although his letters contain surprisingly few direct references to the teachings of Jesus, there are probably a number of indirect quotations, including the ethical teaching in Romans 12—13 which reflects material similar to that now presented in Matthew's Sermon on the Mount.[2] Further, Paul occasionally hints at his dependence on other early Christian sources (e.g. many scholars suspect that a pre-Pauline hymn lies behind Philippians 2.5–11). Paul's anxiety to remain in contact with the Jewish-Christian community in Jerusalem is also worth noting. Although the rhetoric of Galatians 2.9 shows him trying to distance himself from those said to be 'acknowledged pillars' of the church, Paul nevertheless seeks their approval for his mission (Galatians 2.2). He also put a considerable amount of energy into the collection for 'the saints in Jerusalem' (e.g. 1 Corinthians 16.1–4).

It is curious that he still wanted to maintain diplomatic relations with Palestinian communities after the dramatic confrontation with Peter and Barnabas precipitated by the 'people from James'. Whatever his reason for this, Paul's concern to maintain the link and build on the Jesus tradition shows that he had no wish to operate in a theological or a social vacuum. Paul was not a 'second founder of Christianity' in any sense that would make him appear to be an unrestrained or totally independent agent.

Nevertheless, without the Pauline mission, the church would have almost certainly remained a tiny minority sect on the fringes of Judaism, ready to be wiped out along with other such movements in the aftermath of the Jewish rebellion. Paul's insistence on the Law-free gospel open to all without ethnic distinction probably preserved Christianity from oblivion.

The measure of his impact on early Christianity, therefore, is the extent to which the Gentile mission came to be accepted as an integral part of Christian belief. Obviously, it was not all downhill from Antioch onwards: the level of anger in Galatians is evidence enough that Paul thought the battle was far from over. Outside the Pauline corpus, the Letter of James is further evidence of the continuing tension over the Law (James 2.8–26) as the author engages in some sort of debate with a form of distorted Pauline Christianity.[3] The Book of Revelation possibly reflects a similar background – Jezebel in Revelation 2.20 looks remarkably like a Pauline Christian (see 1 Corinthians 8 and 10), and Revelation 13, 17 and 18 are a clarion call to the church to withdraw from compromise with pagan Gentile culture. One wonders what Paul would have made of it all (see, for example, 1 Corinthians 5.9ff and Romans 13.1–7).[4] Finally, the classic remark in 2 Peter 3.15ff places beyond doubt the continuing struggle with the Pauline heritage.

But the primary battle was apparently won by the time the second generation of believers came to be established.[5] The author of Ephesians (almost certainly not Paul) looks back on the ethnic division as a thing of the past (Ephesians 2.11—3.6). The author takes it for granted that Jews and Gentiles belong together, for Christ 'is our peace; in his flesh he has made both groups into one and has broken down the dividing wall, that is, the hostility between us' (Ephesians 2.14).

Because of Paul's rigour (perhaps stubbornness) the later church absorbed most of his theology, albeit in a toned down and modified form under the influence of Luke-Acts and the deutero-Pauline Letters. His claim to be the 'apostle to the Gentiles', previously the subject of so much angst (e.g. 1 Corinthians 9), was finally accepted without further question. If Paul lost the battle at Antioch, he certainly won the war.

The gospels belong to this post-Pauline generation. Despite the best endeavours of a few scholars to argue for an early date,[6] the overwhelming weight of evidence suggests that Mark was written between 65 and 75 CE, and Matthew and Luke perhaps some ten to twenty years after that. The canonical gospels in their present form thus witness to the way the teaching of Jesus was adapted by the post-Pauline Christian church. In the process, Paul's distinctive emphasis on universal mission was woven into the fabric of later Christian thought as appropriated by the wider community of believers. This change in missionary outlook is presented as the work of the risen Christ – perhaps as a word from the Lord spoken through an early Christian prophet (Matthew 28.19ff etc.). But mission had in fact grown out of a controversial dialogue between faith and experience in the particular social context of the first-century Graeco-Roman world. And it continued to be modified in the light of the distinctive social experiences of each of the four communities represented by the gospels.

Mark: The First Evangelist

Mark's Gospel was probably the first of the canonical gospels to be written.[7] There may have been earlier precursors (some would say 'Q'), but in the absence of evidence to the contrary, it would seem that Mark invented the written gospel genre. This raises an interesting question: why? Until Mark, the gospel was an oral proclamation, not a written form (e.g. Romans 1.1). So what prompted Mark to produce his text?

A study of the major themes in the Gospel suggests a possible explanation. Mark seems to reflect a high level of concern over what is seen as a distorted view of Jesus and of Christian discipleship. These twin themes are closely related throughout the Gospel – true disciples realize that Jesus had to suffer, and understand that they too must 'take up their cross' and follow Jesus in the way of the cross (Mark 8.34). In practice, alas, most of them fail to make the connection, and Mark's portrait of the disciples is singularly unsympathetic. A master of ambiguity, Mark deliberately resists closure and leaves open the question whether the disciples might eventually understand. To the end of the narrative, the reader is left to ponder whether they are good, bad, or simply dense. In Mark's opinion, the signs are not encouraging.[8]

At no point is the reader off the hook. Mark never reveals whether Peter and the others went to Galilee as they have been instructed (Mark 16.7). Did they remain as obtuse and disobedient as they had always been, even after the resurrection (notice that Luke assumes they did not return to Galilee but stayed in Jerusalem – Luke 24.52 and Acts 1.4)? Mark leaves only a handful of clues to ponder.

The first is the significance of the curious Marcan geography already noted. This is strangely wayward, difficult to follow on a real map. In an important series of studies published in the mid 1950s, Willi Marxsen suggests that the reason for this was because the evangelist was really working with a theological map – he modified his underlying sources in order to make a point. For Marxsen, the point was that Galilee had been appointed by Jesus as the place where the Gentile mission would eventually be launched (Mark 14.28).[9]

Marxsen's thesis has been much criticized over the years. His work is perhaps remembered more for the contribution he made to the development of redaction criticism than for his lasting contribution to the understanding of Mark. Nevertheless, Marxsen makes a number of telling points. In broad terms, Galilee is the place of success in the first Gospel, whereas Jerusalem is the place of conflict. Even though the shadow of conflict falls across Jesus as early as Mark 3.6, Jesus continues to be enthusiastically received in Galilee (Mark 3.7f etc.).

And it is a border area. Galilee was firmly established in Jewish thought as a slightly eccentric place, on the fringe of things. Matthew was only spelling it out when he added the 'Galilee of the nations' quotation from Isaiah 9.1–2 to the brief introduction to the Galilean ministry found in Mark (Matthew 4.15f). So perhaps this is why the disciples are told to return to Galilee after the resurrection

(Mark 14.28): Jerusalem was where Jesus had to suffer, but thereafter the focus had to shift back to the place where his ministry had been successful, clearly demonstrated in power.

Mark, however, has to work hard to provide material for the Gentile mission he wants to support: the Jesus tradition he inherited had little or nothing to say about it. His solution, as Marxsen observed, was to distort the geography of the Galilean ministry: Jesus is forever crossing the lake in order to move in and out of Gentile territory. On the 'other side', he exorcises a Gerasene demoniac, and drives the demons out of the Gentile lands of Decapolis. Tellingly, these demons end up in a herd of swine, a powerful symbol of impurity in the Jewish symbolic universe. Thus are the purity laws exorcised which divide Jew from Gentile (Mark 5.1–20).

After this, Jesus leaves Jewish territory to go to Tyre, where he meets not only a Gentile, but a woman with a daughter possessed by an unclean spirit (Mark 7.24ff). Her faith saves the child, unlike the Jewish disciples who cannot cast out the demon possessing the epileptic boy (Mark 9.9–29). This healing of a Gentile is followed by an extraordinary detour as Jesus travels back to Galilee via Sidon – a glance at a map shows the unlikeliness of the proposed route (Mark 7.31). Even then, Jesus does not return to Jewish territory – he goes to the 'regions of Decapolis' where he heals a deaf man (presumably a Gentile) and prompts the admiration of the crowd (Mark 7.37). He repeats the earlier feeding miracle in practically every detail except the arithmetic (Mark 8.1–9).[10] Jesus miraculously meets the needs of both Jews and Gentiles.

Only then does Mark allow Jesus to return to Jewish soil (Mark 8.10), though only briefly, because he sets out again without stopping for Bethsaida – the original destination in Mark 6.45, but not reached until now. Bethsaida is in the territory of Philip the Tetrarch, on the edge of Palestine proper. From here, Jesus moves to the other end of Philip's jurisdiction to Caesarea Philippi, which places him on the frontier in the region of a major Hellenistic city. This provides the setting for the important confession of faith by Peter, on the borders between the Jewish and Gentile worlds. Here, on the margins, the disciples first stumble towards the truth about Jesus. Peter's attempt to rescue Jesus for a nationalistic Jewish Messiah draws only a stinging rebuke: he is starting to act like Satan (Mark 8.27–33).

Mark thus shows every sign of bending his source material to bring Jesus into extended and sympathetic contact with the Gentiles. The evangelist wanted to present Jesus as a model for the later universal mission (Mark 13.10). But why?

The second clue concerns the role of the Roman centurion, who is the only person at the crucifixion to perceive the true significance of Jesus' death (Mark 15.39). Or does he? Even at the moment of supreme revelation, Mark cannot bring himself to drop the ambiguity: what does the centurion say? Is it 'This man was [past tense] *a* Son of God' or 'This man was [and still is] *the* Son of God'? The Greek of the text allows for both possibilities in various combinations. This continuing ambiguity draws attention to the fact that although it was a Gentile who first saw Jesus tear down the barrier which kept God safely locked up in an exclusively Jewish holy of holies, Gentiles also kill Jesus (Mark 10.33) and threaten the disciples: 'As for yourselves, beware; for they will hand you over to councils; and you will be beaten in synagogues; and you will stand before governors and kings because of me, as a testimony to them. And the good news must first be proclaimed to all nations' (Mark 13.9f). The Little Apocalypse shows the Gentile mission under threat from Gentile rulers. The evangelist is quietly pointing out that looking beyond Judaism is not necessarily going to make things any less costly in terms of Christian discipleship.

For Mark, therefore, mission to the Gentiles is about commitment. From the point of view of the Gentiles 'whoever gives you a cup of water to drink' (that is, shows hospitality towards those engaged in mission) 'because you bear the name of Christ will by no means lose the reward' (Mark 9.41). From the point of view of the disciples, 'Truly I tell you, there is no one who has left house or brothers or sisters or mother or father or children or fields, for my sake and for the sake of the good news' – which presumably means give up family commitments to 'go out' on mission – 'who will not receive a hundredfold now in this age [...] and in the age to come eternal life' (Mark 10.29f). Reception of the Christian mission is the basis of final judgement: 'Those who are ashamed of me and of my words [...] of them the Son of Man will also be ashamed when he comes in the glory of his Father' (Mark 8.38).

Noting the strong emphasis on suffering in the Gospel, many

scholars posit that Mark was written against a background of tension. For some, that tension was the terror instigated by Nero following the fire of Rome in 64 CE.[11] But the link between Mark and Rome depends largely on the supposed association with Peter claimed by Papias (*c.* 130 CE), a tradition which there are good grounds to question. A growing number of scholars therefore prefer to argue for a Syrian provenance – they believe the clues in the Gospel itself point to a location somewhere north of the border with Palestine.[12] This, of course, is exactly the area around Damascus, Antioch and Cilicia in which Paul began his early ministry. Is it coincidence that the Gospel which speaks most powerfully about suffering may perhaps come from the area where Paul first preached the centrality of the cross (1 Corinthians 2.1f)? Was Mark deliberately building on that preaching in order to explore the meaning of the death of Jesus for those who would be his followers? True disciples must 'take up their cross' (8.34) and follow Jesus into Galilee and beyond.

If the Syrian provenance is accepted, the theme of suffering witness in Mark could not have been a response to the Neronian persecution in Rome, but was more likely to reflect concern about the Jewish rebellion in nearby Palestine from 66 to 74 CE. As a fringe sect with strong Jewish associations, Mark's community would have been under intense scrutiny from their Gentile neighbours as potential rebels. On the other hand, their refusal to support the rebellion would have brought down the hostility of their more radical Jewish neighbours. Squeezed between the two political forces, Mark urges his readers to ponder the cost of discipleship. His Gospel is a call to follow Jesus in the way of the cross.

Mark's shaping of the Jesus tradition reflects his commitment to costly witness. It is this the historical disciples constantly fail to understand. For Mark, the mission to the Gentiles inherited from Paul is an inescapable part of the gospel, but it leads inevitably to suffering and rejection. Disowned by the parent Jewish community, Mark calls on his readers to imitate Jesus and seize the opportunity to preach to the Gentiles (Mark 13.9ff). He turns to mission into an alternative strategy to the violence of the Jewish–Roman conflict. He believes it is better to suffer in the way of the cross than to take sides or fight. The Good News is that in the ambiguity of conflict, the Kingdom of God is proclaimed.[13]

Reclaiming the Tradition for Judaism: Matthew's Gospel

Assuming Marcan priority, Matthew revised his version of Mark in order to supplement and modify the earlier account. Perhaps like later generations of Christians, Matthew felt Mark was somehow inadequate to meet the needs of the developing church. Matthew updates the narrative and weaves into it additional material from other sources[14] in order to produce a new account which reflects his own particular concerns and interests.

One of the many obvious signs of his activity is the repeated formula 'Now when Jesus had finished saying these things' found in Matthew 7.28; 11.1; 13.53; 19.1 and (in slightly modified form) 26.1. Since the formative work of B. W. Bacon,[15] it has been widely accepted that this is an editorial device to signal the end of the five major blocks of teaching created by Matthew. The first and perhaps most famous of these is the Sermon on the Mount (Matthew 5.1—7.27),[16] but the others are the Mission discourse (10.1–42), the Parables discourse (13.1–52), the much briefer Teaching on the Church section (18.1–35), and the Eschatological discourse of Matthew 24.1—25.46 (or does this include Matthew 23 as well?).

Matthew clearly did not create all the material in these blocks of teaching. A good example would be the Sermon on the Mount: a comparison between this and the parallel Sermon on the Plain in Luke (6.17–49) suggests that both evangelists drew on a briefer version of the sermon found in the underlying double tradition. Much the same could be said about the Mission discourse which appears to be an expanded narrative based on an earlier version (see Luke 9.1–6 and 10.1–22). The Parables and Eschatological discourses are developments of Marcan material, and perhaps only the Teaching on the Church section is a thoroughly Matthean construction, based on sayings brought together by the evangelist for the first time.

This approach to teaching highlights one of Matthew's obvious interests – he is concerned to augment the rather sparse material provided by Mark. Although Mark draws attention to the general content of Jesus' teaching and the admiration of the audience (Mark 1.22f; 2.13; 6.6) he provides surprisingly few examples. Matthew more than makes up for this deficiency: he seems to find Marcan ambiguity intensely frustrating, and prefers to make sure the reader is left in no doubt. He is anxious to be perfectly clear about everything.[17] Including mission.

But Matthew also knows his original sources contained little material directly on the subject. The double tradition had already worked on the teaching to a degree, but the discourse Matthew found in his sources remained sharply focused on Jesus' exclusive mission to Israel.[18] It spoke only about the closeness of God's Kingdom, the role of Jesus as the agent of the kingdom, and the appointment of apostles ('missionaries' in Greek) to share in Jesus' charismatic ministry.

Matthew seems to be rather conservative by nature, so he preserved the format of the original discourse but made one important change: he moved the collection of sayings predicting persecution in the Gentile mission from the Marcan Little Apocalypse (Mark 13.9–13) to his expanded discourse on mission (Matthew 10.1–42). By this simple rearrangement, he prepares the ground for his post-Easter missionary perspective.

But there are signs Matthew felt uneasy about this shift in missionary horizons. At least since the time of Ernst von Dobschültz, the background to this Gospel has been well explored,[19] and although not everyone is convinced, there is wide agreement that Matthew comes from a Jewish-Christian background.[20] His Jewish credentials are writ large in the concern he shows over the continuing relationship between Christianity and the Torah (see especially Matthew 5.17–48 and 22.15–46),[21] as well as the way he continues to use 'Gentile' as a form of abuse (e.g. Matthew 5.47; 6.7).

But perhaps one of the most interesting tell-tale signs in Matthew is his use of the Pharisees, identified as the primary opponents of Jesus. Due mainly to the pioneering research of E. P. Sanders, it is now crystal clear that Judaism at the time of Jesus was fragmented into a number of competing parties. The attention Matthew gives to the Pharisees is thus way out of proportion to the extent to which they had power and influence during the first half of the century.[22] During Jesus' lifetime, the Pharisees were merely one group among many competing for power and influence. Although they were certainly in the ascendant, they had no legal authority as such (though individual Pharisees might have been on the Sanhedrin(s)). To say that Jesus argued with Pharisees, therefore, is to say little more than he was a first-century Jewish religious teacher who disagreed with other rival first-century Jewish teachers. But disagreement was (and still is) a prime theological method. It does not (normally) lead to crucifixion. Many Jews (including the Sadducees and Essenes) argued with Pharisees, and came to no harm. Come to that, most Pharisees argued with Pharisees (Hillel versus Shammai is the obvious example).

Therefore, the prominence Matthew chooses to give to the dispute between Jesus and the Pharisees is anachronistic and does not reflect the reality of Jewish groupings during Jesus' ministry. However, by the time Matthew wrote, after the debacle of 70 CE, most Jewish groups had been destroyed or scattered in the aftermath of the war. Only the Pharisees survived in working order, though even they needed time to recover. But they were able to regroup, with the result that they were in the process of becoming the dominant religious and social power in Judaism towards the end of the first century. In other words, Judaism was undergoing a major upheaval at precisely the same time Matthew was writing his Gospel. The times, they were a-changing.

Matthew was almost certainly a Jew. He comes from a strongly Jewish-Christian movement trying to define itself in relation to continuing Judaism, itself in disarray after defeat by the Romans. Pharisaic Judaism was in the ascendant, a vibrant form of Judaism well able to adapt to the new circumstances facing Judaism following the destruction of the temple. This is the context within which the Gospel was written: a Jewish-Christian community in the process of extracting itself painfully from a parent religion which was also trying to regroup. It is hardly surprising that the Pharisees emerge in Matthew as the major debating partners. The two groups are both competing with each other for potential (Jewish) recruits (Matthew 23.15) to support their claim to be heirs to the Jewish tradition. This is why Matthew feels so passionately about the Pharisees in the fearsome polemic throughout Matthew 23.[23] The social processes of inter-group dynamics had forced a competition for recognition within Judaism which led to a polarization of attitudes as Matthew sought to affirm the integrity of his Jewish identity. He wants the best of the old and the new (Matthew 13.52).

It is against this background that Matthew's teaching on mission must be read. The evangelist, like Mark, knows that post-Pauline Christianity has moved into a new world, and he wants to show the growing relationship between the Jesus movement and the Gentiles in the best possible light. However, there is a sense in which they remain peripheral to his thinking. Matthew is deeply concerned that the reader still understands the priority of Israel (e.g. Matthew 15.21–8).[24] Thus, Gentiles are included simply by default because the Jewish leaders have rejected Jesus.

This is spelt out in a further significant modification Matthew made to his Marcan source. In the parable of the vineyard (Mark 12.1–12 paralleled in Matthew 21.33–46), Matthew adds a saying which is unique to his Gospel: because Israel rejected Jesus 'Therefore, I tell, the kingdom of God will be taken away from you and given to a people' – *ethnos*, the same word in Greek which is used in the plural for 'Gentiles' – 'that produces the fruits of the kingdom' (Matthew 21.43).

The language points towards the situation in the future post-resurrection era. Even so, Matthew is nervous lest the Gentile members of the Kingdom forget their Jewish roots: thus, disciples are to practise traditional forms of Jewish piety (Matthew 6.1–18), and to see their faith as the righteousness required by a Jewish God. But above all, they are to remember Jesus came to fulfil Torah, not to destroy it.[25] In a wonderfully involved passage in 5.17–20, Matthew brings together all these competing cross-currents in his thinking. Despite the complications in the text, his general point is clear enough: Jesus both preserves the Torah and creates a radically new perspective through (from Matthew's point of view) his final and definitive interpretation of how the Law is to be observed. This christological interpretation of the Law is spelt out in the so-called antitheses of Matthew 5.21–48 which define the 'righteousness which exceeds that of the scribes and Pharisees' required in Matthew 5.20. Matthew expects the members of his community, Jews and Gentiles alike, to keep this modified form of Torah (Matthew 5.48). He drives the point home no less than three times in the parables of the wheat and tares (13.24–30 and 36–43), the dragnet (13.47ff) and the sheep and the goats (25.31–46). The church, like ancient Israel, stands under the judgement of God's command and must remain faithful to the Law as interpreted by Jesus.

Matthew is struggling with shifting boundaries. He is concerned to be true to the post-Pauline Gentile mission, but he is also deeply aware of his rich Jewish heritage. He knows that universal mission is essentially a post-Easter innovation (Matthew 28.19ff), yet, for him, it was the rejection of Jesus by Israel that forced the change (Matthew 21.43). So be it: but this does not change by one iota the heart of the matter presented in the Torah as interpreted by Jesus (Matthew 5.18). The new ethnically mixed church is also under judgement, and had better be more faithful than their erstwhile sparring partners, the Pharisees, with whom they were competing for attention. Unlike them, they must be obedient to all the commands taught by Jesus, who is God-with-us even to the end of time (Matthew 28.19f).

Lingering Doubts: Luke-Acts

That Luke, like Matthew, reshaped his underlying sources is beyond doubt. The renewed debate about a 'Q'-less double tradition[26] only concerns the number of the sources he had available, not whether he had any at all.

Hans Conzelmann was perhaps the first scholar in the modern era to identify the redactional features of Luke and thus draw attention to his probable theological agenda. For Conzelmann, Luke was concerned about the way in which Christianity lived with the reality of unfulfilled eschatological hope as the church adjusted to the continuing world order. As might be expected, the details of Conzelmann's thesis have also been challenged and modified over the years,[27] but at the very least his main point stands: Luke, like the other evangelists, was a creative theologian. He shaped the Jesus tradition to reflect his particular needs and interests.

By carefully comparing the way Luke tells the Jesus story with the accounts in the other gospels, it is not difficult to highlight some of those Lucan concerns. For example, repentance was clearly high on his agenda, though this may come as surprise to Christians who will take it for granted that repentance is a key part of the Christian message. Curiously, though, repentance is not a particularly prominent theme in other parts of the New Testament.[28] The statistics are telling: all told, the 'repent' group of words (*metanoeō*) is found approximately 54 times in the New Testament as a whole, but about 23 of these are in Luke-Acts alone – getting on for half the total. Further, repentance is not a peculiarly Christian idea – many other religions stress the need for it, especially first-century Judaism (including John the Baptist, and, long before him, the Hebrew prophets). Arguably, therefore, if Jesus' teaching on repentance caused offence, it was because he took a decidedly different view from other popular piety at that time – perhaps because he believed in a gracious God who would invite even Jews like the 'tax collectors and prostitutes' (e.g. Matthew 21.31) to enter the Kingdom of God *before* they had repented.[29]

If this was the received Jesus tradition, then Luke was clearly anxious to modify it. His Jesus is certainly the 'friend of sinners' (e.g. Luke 14.15–24), but one who first calls them to repentance and to make proper restitution (e.g. Luke 15.7, 10). Such teaching was unlikely to cause offence to any pious Jew, least of all the Pharisees.

Another distinctive Lucan theme is poverty and wealth. Mary proclaims that 'he has filled the hungry with good things and sent the rich away empty' (Luke 1.53); Lazarus the pauper rests in paradise whilst the rich man is in torment (Luke 16.19–31). Much used by liberation theologians to show the Gospel has a 'bias to the poor', these Lucan stories appear to present a powerful case, though on closer inspection it seems likely that Luke was less concerned with the destitute than about Christian commitment.[30] His major remedy, therefore, is generosity rather than the restructuring of socio-political power which institutionalizes poverty (e.g. Luke 12.33). To take but one example, Luke modifies a double tradition pericope about cleaning the inside and outside of dishes and turns it into a saying about true disciples who 'give for alms those things that are within' so that 'everything will be clean for you' (Luke 11.41). Only one person in the Gospel is required to give up all his wealth (Luke 18.22), and he is the exception who proves the rule – he was so rich that he allowed his wealth to stand in the way of his commitment to Jesus. Zacchaeus, on the other hand, was also immensely rich, but he responded to the demand of Jesus by making the fourfold restitution demanded by Torah, plus an additional half of his remaining possessions. This is traditional Jewish teaching and hardly anything new. In any case, a rich man can presumably still live comfortably on what is left! So perhaps Luke is not so radical after all. When the gospel is preached to

161

potential converts in Acts, the question 'What should we do?' is predictably answered 'Repent and be baptized' (Acts 2.37f), rather than 'Repent and give up all your possessions'.

Yet another characteristic theme of the Gospel which resonates with contemporary Christian experience is the role of women.[31] Luke has two unique stories about 'fallen' women who find forgiveness (of course) for their 'sin' (Luke 7.36–50 and 13.10–17). In addition, Luke alone tells the story about the widow at Nain (7.11–17) and Martha and Mary (11.38–42). But again, it is unlikely that Luke was a radical theologian before his time. His women are not leaders, and generally stereotyped as peripheral, fussy and probably 'fallen' (Luke 7.11–17). They are probably only one more example of Luke's overriding interest in the marginalized and powerless within his society.

This connection between traditional piety and the marginalized is spelt out in the otherwise rather odd treatment of the divorce pericope in Luke 16.18. This is a vastly streamlined version of the discussion found in Matthew and Mark. Further, it is moved into a new framework and surrounded by two long stories about the use of wealth (Luke 16.1–15 and 16.19–31). It is immediately preceded by an equally brief comment on keeping the Torah (the Lucan parallel to Matthew 5.17–20). Putting these changes together, the evidence suggests Luke saw a real connection between divorce, undermining God's will, and these other units on the use of wealth. It is difficult to think of any other common thread than his belief that divorced women simply represent one more vulnerable group among the poor and neglected. Care for those on the margins of society is, from Luke's point of view, the essence of the Law.

This is the power of the gospel for Luke – that even women and other marginalized members of society can come into the Kingdom – provided they repent, of course. Thus Luke reshapes his Gospel to show how Christian disciples must live in a world where the parousia has been delayed – by practising traditional and uncontroversial forms of piety such as repentance and almsgiving. Christianity is no more revolutionary than any other humane society in the ancient world, and certainly no threat to the status quo: Jesus, Stephen and Paul, Luke insists, are innocent of any charge of fomenting social unrest (e.g. Luke 23.47).

Right at the beginning, Luke flags up his concern for decency and good order (Luke 1.1–4). There is an orderly progression from Judaism (Zechariah in the temple, visions of angels, prophets, psalms and concern to be obedient to the Law in Luke 1—2) through to a powerful yet unthreatening presence in the heart of the Empire (Acts 28). The Lucan manifesto in 4.18–21 says it all in a nutshell: although Jesus is initially received with enthusiasm, his teaching (in a slightly bizarre about-turn in Luke 4.22ff) provokes a sharp response and he has to move on quickly (Luke 4.22–30). Jesus is to be rejected by his own and only in this way can the prophecy of Simeon be fulfilled (Luke 2.30ff) – the glory of Israel (Jesus) is to lighten the Gentiles. It is all part of God's foreordained plan (*dei*, 'it is necessary').

But why? Perhaps Robert Maddox points in the right direction when he draws attention to the recurring theme of reassurance which runs through most of Luke.[32] Philip Esler, in his hugely important study of Luke-Acts,[33] builds on this by seeking to unravel the social code underlying the Gospel. This is symbolized in the number of meals Jesus has both with friends and opponents – in the honour-shame culture of the Graeco-Roman world, as well as in the purity world of first-century Judaism, the issue of table fellowship was crucial: social and religious boundaries are determined by the question of who may eat with whom. Reading this code alongside the other narrative signals, Esler finds a key to unlock the Gospel. Luke wants to reassure his readers on two fronts simultaneously: on the one hand, the innocence of Jesus and Paul show that Christianity was not politically subversive whilst, on the other hand, the pattern of changing table fellowship spells out the adjustments taking place in the relationship between the Jewish parent and the Christian sibling. Through his telling of the story, Luke seeks to reassure his Jewish-Christian readers that the God who offered salvation to Gentiles is the same as the God of the Hebrew Scriptures, whilst reassuring his Gentile readers that they too now have a place in the Kingdom of God. In short, Luke is about continuity and discontinuity: how to change things fundamentally without threatening anyone.

Luke's teaching on mission, therefore, must be read against this matrix of underlying concerns. The Jesus tradition has been reshaped in Luke-Acts to show how an essentially Jewish movement progressed in an orderly fashion towards the predominantly Gentile church known to Luke's readers. This is the real purpose of the two volumes together: neither history, nor biography, nor even gospel as such, but legitimation – the concern to justify social change. Yet again, Luke's teaching on mission would appear to be a function of his response to internal group dynamics.

The Introverted Community: The Gospel of John

John's Gospel is manifestly not the 'seamless robe' it is often said to be.[34] Although the present form of the Gospel reads perfectly well as a satisfactory narrative, a closer inspection establishes there are a number of displacements which suggest that the text has evolved over an extended period of time.[35]

In his brief but important study, J. Louis Martyn concluded that the present form of the Gospel reflected the changing perspective of the Johannine community.[36] The strongest part of his argument are his comments on the use of the word *aposynagōgos* in John 9.22, 12.42 and 16.2 (literally 'put out of the synagogue', in the sense of 'excommunicate'). The point is that Judaism had no means of expelling anyone from a synagogue until after the Pharisaic reforms of the post-Jewish War era. At the time of Jesus' ministry, synagogues were meeting places within the control of the local community: there was no centralized authority which had the right to come in from outside and impose discipline. It follows, therefore, that the word *aposynagōgos* in John is anachronistic, and the conditions assumed by the Gospel did not exist at the time the narrative is set.

This leads Martyn to suggest that John's Gospel operates at two different levels: on the surface, at the narrative level, it presents the story of Jesus; but beneath the surface, the subtext is about the experience of the later Johannine community. Thus, although John speaks at length about the conflict surrounding Jesus, his account is actually coloured by the experience of conflict in the life of the later Johannine community – especially the trauma of ejection from the synagogue on the grounds of strongly held Christian belief. The Gospel is therefore a 'two-level drama' in the sense that it is a 'window' on to the life of Jesus and also a 'mirror' reflecting the painful experience of the Johannine church.

This is the point which was then taken up and expanded by another magisterial figure in the world of Johannine scholarship, Raymond Brown. In his book *The Community of the Beloved Disciple*,[37] Brown freely concedes that much of his reconstruction is speculative, and that he would be happy to settle for simply 60 per cent accuracy.[38] Perhaps even that degree of certainty is questionable, but there is more than enough evidence in his book to support the broad outline of his thesis.

Brown argues that it is possible to detect four stages in the life of the Johannine church behind the Gospel. Phase one was the period of the oral tradition, when the material in the later text was shaped and conditioned. This is the time of the Beloved Disciple, a prominent leader whose influence on the community was formative. Phase two was the period when these traditions were written down and revised into the shape of the present Gospel. Phase three was a post-Gospel period of conflict and reform, represented in the New Testament through the Johannine Epistles. Phase four is even later, after the Epistles, when the community had been dissolved and finally absorbed into the mainstream Petrine church. This last phase is perhaps represented symbolically by the acted-out parable in John 21, a later appendix to the main text.

Brown focuses largely on phase one, when the oral tradition was being shaped. Noting the burning interest over the question of Jesus' identity, Brown argues that the Johannine community was formed in the heat of an ongoing christological dispute. The debating partners were the Johannine movement, which was originally a Hellenist Jewish Christian community still attached to the synagogue, and continuing Judaism, lumped together en masse as 'the Jews' – as if Jesus and his disciples were not. As with Paul and Matthew, these inter-group exchanges forced a polarizing of attitude as both sides were compelled to articulate their beliefs more precisely. For the Johannine Christians, this meant a move from the relatively low Christology of John 1.19–42 through to the soaring heights of the Prologue (John 1.1–14). This moving passage is more like an epilogue, probably tacked on to the original introduction (John 1.6–8 and 19ff), and designed to sum up years of reflection on the significance of Jesus.

In the earliest layer of this tradition, Jesus is seen in traditional Jewish terms as an agent of God – he is rabbi, Messiah, prophet like Moses, King of Israel (John 1.35–9). In the process of an interaction with the disciples of John the Baptist, all these titles are tried and tested. By John 1.51 a breakthrough has been achieved: Jesus is now the 'Son of Man', a title inherited from the pre-Synoptic tradition but developed by John in a significantly new way. He is the one sent by God to form a link between heaven and earth by his 'lifting up' on the cross. Through this mission, the plain water of Judaism is transformed into the new wine of Christianity (John 2.1–11) and the new temple of his body (John 2.13–22).

John's Gospel is all about christology – from the profound *logos* doctrine in the Prologue, and the *ego eimi* or 'I am' sayings, to the all important 'agency' motif identified by Peder Borgen.[39] But at the heart of the Gospel lie four chapters of increasingly bitter christological dispute with 'the Jews'. The outcome of this confrontation is the chilling comment in John 8.44 that all Jews are 'children of the devil'. By John 9.1–34 the Jewish element attached to the Johannine community are forced to make up their minds: it is no longer possible to be a closet believer. In terms of the narrative, echoing the light and darkness antithesis in the later Prologue, the choice facing the community is between sight and blindness.[40] Jesus gradually withdraws to be alone with his disciples (from John 10 onwards), and eventually reveals himself as the sole 'way' to life with God (John 14.1–6). The Farewell Discourses (John 13—17) are full of foreboding, but written from the perspective of the post-Easter church. In the world, the disciples will be vulnerable and exposed. But they are not left like orphans: they have the protection of the Paraclete, Jesus' alter ego. Amidst the anxiety surrounding Jesus' departure, the tiny Johannine community is to have confidence: 'In the world you face persecution. But take courage; I have conquered the world!' (John. 16.33). Once again, these texts are designed to offer reassurance to a community facing an uncertain changing world.

In short, the Community of the Beloved Disciple (to use Brown's phrase) was formed around a core group of Jewish-Christian believers. At an early stage, these founder members came into contact with the disciples of John the Baptist, some of whom were subsequently attracted into membership. This Jewish community then embarked on a long series of debates within itself and with continuing Judaism about the role of Jesus. Some of Jews, like Nicodemus, were broadly sympathetic, but too timid to do anything except come to Jesus 'by night'. Others were more hostile and forced the church through their aggressive behaviour to think through their central christological beliefs. Continuing hostility served as the catalyst for development until the final parting of the ways was marked in the expulsions of John 9.22, 12.42 and 16.2. By John's time, it was no longer possible to be both a Christian and a Jew.

So far, like the intra-Hellenist dispute of Acts 6—8, this has been an almost entirely Jewish affair. But, like the experience of the Hellenists in Acts 8.1, the split with Judaism forced the community to look beyond the boundaries, and they began to attract new converts from precisely the same areas – the Samaritan woman who then acts as a missionary to her own people (John 4.39), and the Hellenists who ask to see Jesus (John 12.20-6). They never get to meet him during his lifetime, of course. John knows that only when the grain of wheat has fallen into the earth and died is it possible for the post-Easter community to bear fruit among the Gentiles.

The Farewell Discourses in John 13—17 reflect the uncertainty facing the later community (e.g. John 15.18–25; 17.11–19). The Johannine community turns in on itself to retreat from this external threat: the disciples are to be in the world, but not of the world (John 17.11–15). The Johannine community is left alone at the end of the first draft of the Gospel to contemplate its own distinctive faith behind closed doors (John 20.19–29).

This reading of John confirms the emerging pattern of development in early Christian missionary horizons. Universal mission to the Gentiles was not immediately on the agenda, and the Johannine community was rather fearful of it. They had been driven out from Judaism through sustained conflict, and responded by struggling to come to terms with their new social environment. Mission comes in only at the tail-end of this process (John 20.21). It is a post-Easter response to the otherwise unwelcome experience of regrouping after the death of Jesus.

Conclusion

The study of the gospels comes full circle. Far from providing a starting point for mission, they turn out to be post-Pauline texts which reflect the perspectives and concerns of late first-century Christianity. In all four gospels, the twin themes of mission and the Gentiles have been linked to the redactional interests of the evangelists, which in turn reflect the immediate social context of the communities that helped to nurture and shape the evolving Jesus tradition. What began as a collection of isolated sayings showing Jesus in contact with lone individuals on an occasional basis has been worked by experience into a systematic theme of mission to the Gentiles.

In each case it is possible to trace the impact of continuing social conflict on these texts. The conflict surrounding Jewish Christian Hellenist communities in Palestine and Syria was driven with renewed energy through the controversial ministry of Paul and his colleagues. But by the time the gospels were written, the debate over the admission of Gentiles was becoming past history, and the evangelists were more concerned about the adjustments this new perspective demanded in terms of social definition and group identity. In all four gospels, it is possible to watch this process in action, and to demonstrate the connection between mission to the Gentiles and the social dynamics which shaped the Christian communities behind the evangelists.

The gospels are a product of a changing world order where the Gentile mission is simply taken for granted and read back into the ministry of Jesus. Christianity is struggling to establish a new identity in the Hellenistic environments outside Palestine, but Judaism is a continuing debating partner as it recovers from the shock of defeat after the Jewish War. The origin of universal mission, therefore, lies in this experience of the early church and the fierce arguments fought out in the life of competing first-century communities.

❀ 10 ❀
Preaching to the Nations: Conclusion

Mission is a contested concept.[1] It was contested during the earliest phase of the formation of the Christian community, and remains contested in the life of the contemporary church. There are many different models of mission, some of which are incompatible with the other competing alternatives on offer. All of these operate within a complex framework of theological presupposition which is usually taken for granted by those engaged in mission – as if repeating well-rehearsed theological clichés loudly is enough to mask the elusive content.

To put it crudely, what is the 'Good News' Christians are asked to proclaim? Even at a superficial level, people from different theological traditions give quite different answers: evangelicals tend to speak about the 'Good News' of 'salvation', whereas those of a more liberal persuasion are probably more inclined to speak about the 'Good News' of 'God's reign on earth'. Behind the rhetoric of both traditions there is a host of unexamined assumptions. Some evangelicals place an emphasis on the personal dimension of 'salvation', whereas others speak with genuine passion about the God who acts to save his people from social injustice and oppressive powers. Likewise, many liberals see their incarnational missiology embedded in a pattern of practical care focused on the individual, whereas more radical Christians speak with equal passion about the 'reign of God' reflected in the 'social gospel'.

A further layer of complexity is added when the orientation of attitude towards the world is taken into account. On this spectrum of opinion, the two pole positions are *world-affirming* and *world-denying* attitudes. World-affirmers are the theological optimists: they tend to see the world as essentially a 'good place', perhaps flawed by human imperfection, but nevertheless essentially positive. When all is said and done 'God saw everything that he had made, and indeed, it was very good' (Genesis 1.31).

Whatever the impact of sin, God 'likes matter – he invented it'.[2] By contrast, world-deniers are the theological pessimists: they tend to see the world as utterly corrupt, so much so that the best thing that could happen is that it should be replaced as quickly as possible. Thus, world-deniers characteristically think in terms of two spheres of being ('this world and the world to come') and adopt a predominantly eschatological outlook.

Thus, there are twin axes of underlying theological attitude which have a direct impact on the content of the 'Good News': one relates to the role of the individual within society, the other relates to the value placed on the existing world of everyday experience. Putting these two scales together, it is possible to form a grid of possible attitudes towards Christian mission, as in Figure 5.

World-affirming attitudes

(positive view of creation; incarnational theology)

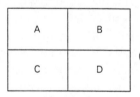

Focus on individuals
(pastoral care ministry)

Focus on community
(prophetic/social ministry)

World-denying attitudes

(two worlds; eschatological theology)

Figure 5

Individual attitudes towards evangelism can be plotted within these quadrants (A to D) at any position reflecting the strength of the view taken.

The definition of key terms relating to mission will be dependent on the orientation adopted. For example, someone who combines a world-denying attitude with a focus on the individual (quadrant C) is most likely to use the language of salvation, which will be seen as the rescue of a person from the threatening situation of sin and evil. On the other hand, someone who combines a world-affirming attitude with a strong social conscience (quadrant B) is more likely to be comfortable with 'reign of God' language, and will see this primarily in terms of social liberation. And so on.

Of course there are many other important factors to consider. Arguably, there has been a subtle shift in the underlying focus of attention assumed in modern western culture: attitudes may be based on an increasingly privatized view of life which is centred on the free-standing individual rather than the individual-in-community. This would be represented on the grid as a drift towards quadrant A, and would imply a significant move away from the dyadic relationships assumed in the New Testament. 'Self-fulfilment' in the first century (to use a hopelessly anachronistic term) would be defined as satisfactory feedback from the salient peer group about the role of the individual within the group. In the late twentieth century, self-fulfilment is driven primarily by interior values and aspirations, and social feedback is increasingly marginalized ('Blow that for a game of soldiers: I'll do what *I* want to do, thank you').

A classic example would be the reading of the 'Love Command' (Mark 12.31 and parallels): in the dyadic world of the New Testament, this has a primary focus on the satisfaction of self-giving service in relation to the external community, whereas the tendency in the twentieth century would be to psychologize and internalize the text. The emphasis is now placed on the second half of the command, and it is argued that you cannot begin to love your neighbour unless you are first prepared to love yourself.

This drift towards quadrant A has had a marked influence on the understanding of mission in all other sectors of the grid. Thus, every shade of contemporary opinion tends to assume the language of personal 'wholeness' or 'integrity' rather than the idea of eschatological rescue from the fires of hell.[3] In New Testament times, there had been a major shift from rural Palestinian perceptions with its hope for the renewal of Israel to the values of the Graeco-Roman pre-industrial city with its hope for rescue from blind fate. Now, the focus of the 'Good News' is once again changing in the Christian community. Salvation has taken on new shades of meaning.

Paradoxically, alongside the generally privatized local world of the individual, the late twentieth century has also witnessed a shattering of global boundaries. Actually, the two tendencies are almost certainly related: as individuals become aware of the greater international context, so the immediate world is narrowed down in an attempt to reduce experience to more manageable proportions. Social feedback on a global scale is simply too much to cope with.

However, the 'world' into which the disciples are sent in Matthew 28.19f is almost certainly the more limited world of the Roman Empire. Obviously, some people in the first century were aware of the wider scene, but this has had remarkably little impact on the New Testament. Colossians mentions the Scythians (Colossians 3.11), but otherwise there are really only broad comments about 'tribes' and 'nations' (mostly in the book of Revelation). There is an ancient tradition that the apostle Thomas went to India, though this is almost certainly apocryphal – Eusebius says only that he was dispatched to Parthia. Apart from that, contacts in the early stages of Christian expansion were limited to the tribes around the fringes of the Empire, such as Ethiopia and Georgia.[4] And yet, by the end of the second century both Irenaeus and Origen could claim that the 'whole world' had been evangelized.[5] Such was their perspective: the world, by and large, was coterminous with the Roman Empire.

In one sense, our worlds are worlds apart. Modern perceptions have changed almost beyond recognition. Part and parcel of the change is not only the global communications explosion, but the dramatic increase in awareness of other cultures and belief systems this has brought with it. The authors of the New Testament had only two major debating partners: continuing Judaism and the polytheistic world of Graeco-Roman paganism. Islam had yet to appear on the horizon, and the ancient religions of India and China made no obvious impact on their religious environment. The issue which concerns the authors of the Gospels and Epistles is the relationship between Jews and Gentiles, competing cultural groups within the Empire. The debate with Hinduism, Buddhism and Confucianism lay far in the distant future.

However, some things have not changed. Between the New Testament communities and the present day, the history of Christian mission has been a mixed tale. Alongside the examples of unbelievable courage and heroic commitment shown in the lives of particular believers, there are disturbing stories of triumphalist church expansion which, with the benefit of 'enlightened hindsight', seem rather sordid and distasteful.[6] In practice, the most common method of organized evangelism throughout Christian history turns out to be 'church planting' – that is, the formation and reinforcement of local church structures at a diocesan and parochial level. Alternative models have been tried occasionally, for example by the informal Celtic *perigrinati* (wanderers), small clusters of monks who left the monastery to move around the wider community, living alongside the local people and setting up small satellite communities before moving on. But these brave experiments were usually smothered by the institutional interests of a church more concerned with power, control and influence. Too often, the 'Good News' has been that you can join the church on its terms or be consigned to eternal damnation.

For centuries Christian mission has been characterized by such power struggles: from Gregory the Great anxious to extend Roman authority over the Celtic Church in Britain, through Charlemagne, with his chilling diktat to conquered Saxons in 785 ('be baptized or die'), on to the crusades and the machiavellian manoeuvres of the sixteenth-century papacy, designed to support the imperial aspirations of Spain and Portugal. The history of Christian missions is sometimes quite sobering.

Not that mission has always been high on the church's agenda. From earliest times, the most effective form of evangelism (other than enforced mass baptism) has been osmosis – witness by presence alone. Christianity is generally caught, not taught. Indeed, at the time of the Reformation, the Protestant emphasis on the prevenient grace of God and the doctrine of predestination even worked against more active forms of evangelism: what was the point of preaching to non-believers if they could only come to faith by the grace of God, and might well be predestined to eternal damnation anyway?

The first signs of a more systematic approach to evangelism emerge during the Counter-Reformation, when the Roman Catholic Church saw foreign mission as a heaven-sent opportunity to compensate for the loss of the Protestants. By contrast, when the Protestant missions eventually started, they tended to operate outside the formal structures of the denominational churches, and were organized by groups of like-minded individuals. Thus, the first known mission agency in England was founded in 1695 by the Revd Thomas Bray as the 'Society for the Propagation of Christian Knowledge' (this book's publisher!). Such independent organizations represent a markedly different ecclesiology from the Catholic approach, where mission could never be a freelance activity. Action and reaction strike again, as they did in the time of Paul.

During the period of colonial expansion, knowingly or unknowingly, many of these missionary organizations worked in support of colonial powers, and tended to take a low view of the capabilities of indigenous 'natives'. Christianity, for a while, was virtually synonymous with western colonial culture. It was only at the turn of this century that mission began to extract itself from the imperial mindset. In 1910 the Edinburgh World Missionary Conference heard the first call to ecumenism in recent centuries (at least within the Protestant orbit) in the form of a speech from Dr Chang, one of the Chinese delegates. He pleaded with the denominational groups to stop confusing potential converts by competing with each other: instead, they should work together for the greater good of Christianity. The conscientious struggle for a balance between Christian idealism and social reality lives on.

From this first tentative move, the World Council of Churches was eventually born in 1948, though its progress has not been unchallenged either by the Catholic Church or by more conservative fundamentalist groups.[7] Conflict between conservative theologians and radical pioneers is nothing new, however. It was already there in the community in Antioch.

Throughout the history of mission, New Testament texts have been used and abused in support of these competing interests. If it is true that the first generation of Jewish Christian believers had to struggle to work through their Hebrew Scriptures living with the tensions generated by the Gentile mission, it is also true that their response helped to shape and support the developing patterns of later church engagement. In a real sense, the New Testament Scriptures have become normative for Christian evangelism,[8] but only as interpreted by the competing power groups laying claim to their own particular model of mission. More often than not, these

Scriptures have been treated with a superficial naivety and moulded into the shape which suits the interests of a particular viewpoint. New Testament texts are basically used as ammunition, a pretext for the real agenda.

Somewhere in all this there is a nagging feeling that God ought to be allowed to get a word in edgeways. Authority does not rest in any interpretation of a text, however influential or normative it may become. It exists in the elusive glimpse of the transcendent which is present in the possibility that the text and the reader may challenge each other.

But this presupposes that both the text and the reader are able to respect the integrity of each other. This is the task of historical criticism, not as an academic exercise but as a contribution to faith. The intention (however inadequately achieved) is to create the distance needed to allow a New Testament text to speak for itself before moving the dialogue to a premature closure. Paul and his churches may need to speak to each other before later Christian theologians muscle in and try to take over.

So the question for faith becomes 'Where in the mess of Christian formation and in the later history of mission is it possible to discern the presence of God?' If mission has been consistently rooted in conflict and mixed motives, in what sense is it possible to speak with integrity of a theology of mission? With these questions in mind, it is time to revisit the argument of this book.

The Origins of Universal Mission

The first-century Christian communities did not inherit a concept of universal mission either from Judaism or from the historical Jesus. As David Wenham writes: 'There is little doubt that the church, which was to become self-consciously international, was well aware that Jesus' own ministry focused almost exclusively on the Jews.'[9] The first Christians had to be persuaded to develop the Gentile mission, therefore, and it has been argued that this process was driven not by a theological rationale so much as by practical experience interpreted in the light of an evolving framework of early Christian belief. Pragmatism and reflection fired the commitment to mission; theology followed later.

Christianity began as a Jewish renewal movement, and only subsequently became a distinct social grouping. Initially, most Palestinian Jewish Christians were reluctant to allow the socio-religious boundaries to be redrawn, and resisted all attempts to push the movement outside the established orbit of first-century Judaism. This was already capable of supporting a rich diversity of groups along with their competing theologies – but on its own terms. There was no 'official' definition of Jewish belief, but most people inside and outside the community recognized the distinctive ethos which characterized Judaism. These core values were symbolized by the Sabbath, kosher food laws, circumcision and the temple in Jerusalem, but these things as such did not establish the Jewish identity.[10] Rather, they combined with other implicit core attitudes at a social level to produce a sense of identity which was widely recognized on both sides of the ethnic divide. It was this basic sense of belonging that actually set the Jews apart, not an established doctrinal code.

It was only when the first Christians started to undermine some of these received values that controversy began. The catalyst was almost certainly christology: competing views about the nature of the relationship between Jesus and the Jewish God began to push against the limits of toleration.[11] This blurring of the theological boundaries prompted a new round in the ongoing debate about 'Jewishness', and in turn helped to sharpen the definition.[12] It also led to an increasing polarization of views. At some point, the more extreme members of the new movement were expelled from their synagogues, and the parting of the ways had begun.[13] After that, it was not long before Gentile sympathizers began to knock at the door of this interesting variant of first-century Judaism.

The growing Christian community, however, was ill-equipped to deal with the trickle of interest from Gentile God-fearers. Like most of his Jewish contemporaries, Jesus had probably responded to individual Gentiles on a one-off basis, and he might occasionally be persuaded to act on their behalf. But he believed passionately that his primary mission was to the people of Israel. He is remembered as feeling strongly about the outcast and marginalized, but only within Judaism. His concern for fringe members, therefore, did not provide a link for the first Christians to make the connection between a Jewish God and the Gentiles. Neither were the passages in the post-

exilic prophets much help, even when they spoke about an eschatological influx of the Gentiles into Zion (how ever much twentieth-
century apologists for mission insist on appealing to them). There
was no ready-made concept of universal mission waiting to be taken
off the peg.

Rather, the evidence suggests that the origins of mission lie buried
in the incident behind the expulsion of Jewish Christian radicals
from the Hellenist synagogue in Jerusalem. Disowned by their host
community, these Jewish believers looked for new support around
the existing fringes of first-century Judaism. They attracted Samaritans, Gentile sympathizers like the Ethiopian eunuch, and benefactors like Cornelius. A trickle of these God-fearers were drawn into
membership of the embryo movement, and enabled the Hellenist
Jewish Christian community to survive. But they brought with them
Greek ideas and values, and these began to exercise a subtle influence
over the development of early Christian belief. The very presence of
these (few) Gentiles in the community was enough to alter the
ethnic balance within the movement as a whole.

Their arrival triggered a new round of the dynamic interaction
between competing social and religious groups within Judaism. As a
result, the Jesus movement was able to achieve a distinctive social
identity for the first time (Acts 11.26). Recognition of such an
identity is a complex operation, and involves different levels of
exchange between in-group and out-group members. But the friction
generated by conflicting cognitive and emotional values within first-
century Judaism forced the pace of change.

There were at least four parties to the dialogue. One was the
Christian community itself; the others were continuing Judaism, the
host culture of the Graeco-Roman world, and the individual
potential converts. Each party was involved in discrete processes of
exchange and adjustment at different levels of understanding and
experience, and only when circumstances conspired to bring these
multidimensional influences together was it possible for Christian
mission to succeed.

The process of inter- and intra-group exchange was already well
under way by the time Paul was drawn into membership of the
Christian movement. He appeared first as a Hellenist Jew violently
opposed to the Jesus movement (1 Corinthians 15.9; Galatians 1.14;

Philippians 3.6). But as someone sympathetic to the language and values of the Hellenist Jewish Christian radicals associated with Stephen, he was persuaded through a visionary experience to change sides (1 Corinthians 15.8; Galatians 1.15 etc.). He was initiated into Christianity via the Hellenist Jewish Christian community in and around Syria.

At first, Paul continued the established Hellenist Jewish Christian practice, and preached only to Jews in the Diaspora synagogues. But like Philip and the other radicals before him, he found that by preaching in synagogues he was also addressing a small number of Gentile sympathizers. In due course, he found that some of these were attracted by his teaching, and eventually drawn into the Jesus movement.

By the same token, not many Hellenist Jews were attracted to Christianity (a fact which continued to puzzle Paul in Romans 9—11). Paul learnt from experience that pro-Jewish Gentile sympathizers provided more fertile ground. It is important not to exaggerate the size of his 'mission', of course: only a tiny handful of Jews and Gentiles responded at all. Nevertheless, the growing number of Gentiles started to upset the ethnic balance in the community at Antioch where Paul was based. This was to have far-reaching consequences for the church.

The first report of tension appears in Galatians 1—2. Unease over the steady erosion of the Jewish identity of Christianity precipitated a debate within the leadership about kosher food laws and circumcision, two of the key markers which set Judaism apart in the ancient world. Participants in the argument were compelled to justify their respective positions, and this articulation of opinion accelerated the process of polarization. Peter and Barnabas were persuaded to change course and withdrew from the open Gentile mission, whereas Paul was provoked into an angry and defensive response. He challenged the leadership, and although it is impossible to be sure, it seems likely he lost and was effectively expelled. Under the social code of the honour-shame culture, this left Paul with three options: apology and consequent loss of face, resigned acceptance of his rejection, or counterattack. Characteristically he chose the last, and the first full-scale independent Pauline mission can be dated from precisely this period.

Religion and culture were intimately connected in the ancient world (and still are). The Hellenistic cities Paul chose to target were places where loyalty to pagan religion was often nominal and superstitious, and reflected more the concept of obligation to the local gods who protected the community than personal religious devotion. To defect from a local cult, therefore, was tantamount to cultural treason. For this very reason, Jewish dismissal of local gods was considered offensive, though Judaism was generally tolerated (sometimes under protest) on the grounds of ancient ancestral custom. Christianity was similarly protected so long as it was seen as a Jewish subculture. But when it was rejected by mainstream Hellenistic Judaism, it was out on its own. As a monotheistic religion in a polytheistic environment, it looked decidedly vulnerable in an increasingly hostile society.

In order to succeed, therefore, Paul had to persuade potential converts that Christianity was sufficiently attractive to overcome social disapproval as well as personal inertia. He had to identify a target audience which was prepared to consider the possibility of abandoning cultural and family links in favour of a radical movement disowned by its parent religion and preaching an eccentric doctrine of a crucified (and therefore failed) leader. By his own reckoning, this was sheer foolishness (1 Corinthians 2.1–13). It is probably not surprising that he attracted only a handful of followers – perhaps as many as twenty to thirty people in a large cosmopolitan city like Corinth. It is remarkable that he attracted any at all.

Left on his own without visible means of support, Paul operated an opportunist ministry in which he exploited the natural contacts he had in the cities he visited. He relied on Jewish hospitality and preached in the synagogues until he could find his feet. He also sought out contacts 'within the trade' in order to support himself and widen his network of contacts. It seems that, from time to time, the Jewish community which initially received him was either split by his teaching, or driven to take hostile action against him. When his presence in the synagogue became intolerable, Paul turned to the core group he had established, and like everyone else in the Graeco-Roman world, looked to them for the support and protection he needed.

As a charismatic leader with an energetic drive, Paul continued to attract a handful of recruits. Realistically, however, his target audience was severely restricted: on the whole, he was going to appeal to individuals who were attracted to a derivative of Judaism, looking for some sort of personal religious affiliation, and prepared to take on the consequences of sharp social disapproval. He found such people not only on the fringes of the synagogue, but also among those who in some sense were experiencing social ambivalence. Many of these were from relatively low-status social backgrounds, but not all: people like Gaius, Stephanus and Crispus had some wealth and position, but were dissatisfied in some other way with their current social context.

Several factors contributed to the success of the Pauline mission. Much of the theological spadework had been provided by the Jewish Diaspora which led to a widespread awareness of Judaism throughout the Graeco-Roman world. The advent of mystery cults created the novel possibility of a religious market place in which individuals could express a personal preference and choose from competing religious groups. And the ubiquitous network of clubs and guilds operating throughout the Empire provided a mundane but essential cultural infrastructure.

However, it is difficult to say what finally persuaded individuals among the target audience to convert to Christianity. The emphasis in the New Testament on liberation from tyrannical cosmic forces suggests a widespread fear of *daimonia* and *tychē*, or fate. In an age of uncertainty, Christianity offered salvation in which initiation (baptism) was experienced as personal liberation. Thereafter, the distinctive cultic meal (the Eucharist) served to reinforce group bonding. Together, these two rituals redrew the social boundaries around the new recruit and enabled in-group and out-group members alike to recognize the change in personal status. Sharing the meal consolidated the values and beliefs of the group and gave the members a sense of unique identity and privilege.

Once Paul secured what he felt was a reasonable base for the group, he moved on and began all over again. He assumed that the local grapevine operating within the network of communities clustered around the urban centres where he ministered would do the rest. But the dynamics of social interaction did not stop when he left. Part of the cost of charismatic styles of leadership is a trade-off between affective bonds and growing self-confidence in newly acquired beliefs. The initial emotional attraction to a powerful personality such as Paul is likely to diminish as new recruits 'begin to think for themselves' and establish their own identity.

Further, the local host culture continues to exercise a considerable influence over new converts through the symbolic universe or framework of cultural attitudes they take for granted. In the first-century Graeco-Roman context, this meant the honour-shame code, dyadic relationships, everyday exchanges between benefactors, patrons and clients, and social structures within the pre-industrial city. Believers therefore lived in the tension generated between Christian idealism and social reality. Paul was himself subject to precisely the same cultural pressure, as witnessed for example in his continued anxiety over status (e.g. 2 Corinthians 1—3, 10—13). He responds by asserting his independence and authority as forcefully as he can whilst moderating the demands of Christian idealism through the mechanism of love-patriarchalism.

Yet another factor in the equation is the evidence of continuing intra-group rivalry. Hellenist Jewish Christian opponents apparently shadowed Paul as they tried to undermine his teaching. This contributed significantly to the shifting balance between attitudes, beliefs and behaviour and demanded that Paul paid careful attention to the needs of group maintenance in order to preserve his effective leadership. He achieves this through a personal visit whenever possible, but where necessary through his correspondence as well (e.g. Galatians and 1 Corinthians).

In this complex exchange between culturally conditioned attitudes and belief, Paul was forced to defend his concept of universal mission. He attempted to authenticate his position by recalling the crucial role of experience – his own, and that of his converts. He regards the persuasive force of these charismatic and visionary experiences as self-evident. But as he attempts to rationalize the argument, he returns to the Hebrew Scriptures which nurtured his outlook. Forced to ask new questions about the Gentiles, he now reads the text afresh and finds a new focus in the figure of Abraham. This novel reading of Scripture gives him the permission he requires to relativize the divisive Mosaic Covenant (Galatians 4 and Romans 4).

As Paul rereads the story, it occurs to him that his opponents have overlooked two important details – the promise that Abraham would be the father of many nations, and the fact that Abraham received the promise before he was commanded to circumcise Isaac. For Paul, the pieces finally fell into place. The Mosaic Covenant beloved of the Judaizers forced an artificial division between Jew and Gentile. But it was a secondary issue, never meant to be more than a temporary expedient to deal with the sin of disobedience. The Jews had been privileged to be protected from the worst effects of sin through the Torah. By contrast, the providence of God had left the Gentiles to wander alone, though still under the offer of God's protection to Ishmael (Genesis 21.19ff). But now this interim period had finally passed: 'Christ is the end (*telos*) of the law' (Romans 10.4). God's intention had always been to bless the nations regardless of the divisive issue of circumcision, because Abraham had been the ancestor of Jew and Gentile alike. The 'flow' of the promised blessing had been interrupted by the Torah, but had been decisively re-established by Christ who removed 'the curse of the law' (Galatians 3.10–14).

Abraham thus became the root metaphor for faith and mission for Paul through his christological rereading of Scripture.[14] Armed with the insight, Paul turns back to the prophets and rereads the passages about the eschatological influx of the nations. Read in the light of the Abraham paradigm, the point becomes obvious: God always intended to include the Gentiles in his plan of salvation (Romans 11.1–32).

In short, Paul's theology of mission was driven thoroughly by experience. His rationale developed out of the heady cocktail of social interaction and theological reflection fuelled by controversy.

It is not possible to trace developments with any certainty during the period between the Pauline Letters and the later canonical Gospels. It is only possible to speculate on the basis of Acts 21—28, which suggests that the grand eschatological gesture planned by Paul (the 'collection') almost certainly failed.[15] One of the most striking features of Acts is the number of absent friends – where were James and the rest of the Jerusalem church when Paul was arrested? Little had changed to modify the outlook of the Palestinian movement. Paul was on his own on the road to Rome.

Acts provides a curiously unsatisfactory ending: the reader is never allowed to know the outcome of the proceedings against Paul. Perhaps it is assumed they already know. All Luke suggests is that Paul continued to stir up controversy right to the end (Acts 28.23–8/9[16]).

Whether in Rome or Syria, Mark presented his distinctly Pauline account of the story of Jesus – the gospel of the suffering Messiah. Mark skilfully wove together the thread of his narrative to show how Jesus foreshadowed the development of the later Christian mission through his sympathetic contact with Gentiles and numerous unlikely excursions into Gentile territory. Matthew, Mark's first known editor, is more cautious and seems to want to roll back some of the growing Gentile influence. Nevertheless, he is aware where the future lies as he engages with his major sparring partner, Pharisaic Judaism. In the heat of the controversy which developed between these competing forms of Judaism in the aftermath of the Jewish War, Matthew accepts that times had changed. The post-Easter Lord is pointing towards the Gentiles (Matthew 28.19f), provided they remember they too are under judgement.

By the time Luke wrote his two-volume work, the ethnic mix in the Christian movement had shifted dramatically, and the boot was on the other foot: it was the Jewish element in Luke's community who felt marginalized and threatened. On the other hand, Luke did not want to take sides, and was anxious to reassure both groups. There is continuity and discontinuity, he says, but Jews and Gentiles alike are honoured under the providence of God's plan to bring salvation to all.

Meanwhile, the Johannine community was developing independently as a small introverted Hellenist Jewish Christian group. It had experienced a slightly different history, but mirrored the experience of the Hellenist group around Stephen. Driven by conflict within the synagogue to define its belief, this group developed one of the strongest Christologies in the New Testament. They recruited a few former disciples of John the Baptist, as well as Samaritans and other marginalized groups. They acknowledged that the death of Jesus had changed the religious horizon, and that it was now possible for even Greeks to see Jesus (John 12.20ff). Meanwhile, the intensity of the christological controversy with Judaism drove the community in on itself, symbolized in the strongly introverted nature of the Farewell

Discourses in John 13—17. About to be swallowed up by an immensely threatening *kosmos*, the community eventually had to turn to the 'great church' associated with Peter (John 21).[17] But it bows out in style with a passionate reminder that although the future lay with Peter, their community had been founded by the disciple Jesus really loved.

Controversy over the balance between Jews and Gentiles, therefore, continued well after Paul as social dynamics continued to shape group experience and theological reflection. The teaching of Jesus was adapted in the light of the experience as the post-Easter church found a new focus in the work of charismatic leaders such as Paul. The gospels are all post-Pauline. The concept of a universal mission to all people was a product of this multidimensional conversation between experience, values and beliefs, as the first Christians came to believe that the risen Jesus had commanded his followers to stretch the horizons of faith and preach to the nations.

Mission and Evangelism: Appropriating the Text

So what? In what way does this reading of Christian mission contribute to a dialogue between Scripture and faith in the context of late twentieth-century belief?

At the very least, it seeks to establish a degree of honesty. A 'mission imperative' cannot be asserted simply on the basis of the New Testament texts, still less on the majority evidence of later church history. The Gentile mission was a highly controversial enterprise in the life of the early Christian communities, and these texts reflect the heat of the debate. It did not occur to most Jewish Christians before Paul that they should preach to the nations. Nor, in fact, did it occur to many other Christians thereafter.

Further, Christianity makes a number of substantial truth claims about history – that at a particular place at a particular time, a particular person uniquely presented the human face of God. As soon as Christianity moves into this kind of territory, it is open to precisely the same scrutiny as any other historical discipline. It is a simple matter of respect to pause before superficially imposing later belief structures on the text. As soon as Christians make the claim that God acted in history through Jesus they invite questions like 'how?', 'when?' and 'why?'. What kind of evidence is there to support the claim? It may be important (I speak as a believer) to get it right. As Lesslie Newbigin suggests: 'Any attempt to deal with the present without awareness of what has gone before can only lead to distorted vision and false judgement.'[18]

Beyond that, however, it may be possible to abstract a number of other theological principles on the basis of this study. The first concerns the ever-present role of conflict in theology. Controversy in the church can be a cause of real anxiety in the church, especially if it is whipped up by hungry media keen to generate a story where there is none. Far from running away from conflict, however, a study of the origins of mission would suggest that controversy is the life blood of creative theology. It is an essential theological method, as competing views push the whole church towards a greater under- standing of the mystery of faith. God is always greater than human beings can conceive or imagine, so the debate is bound to go on. The only absolute truth of faith is the absolute assurance that when we are absolutely certain about anything to do with God, we are absolutely wrong. There is always more.

The point about controversy is well made by Ken Leech:

> Linked with the view of prayer and the spiritual life as essentially analgesic and peace-inducing, is the assumption that [. . .] our primary concern is with the reduction of conflict and tension. This is based on two false assumptions: that it is possible, and that it is desirable. In fact, the nature of the pastoral relationship is one which does not allow us to escape from inner struggle, but rather intensifies it.[19]

Paul was not renowned for his analgesic or peace-inducing qualities. On the contrary, he was perceived as a rather unyielding person determined to be difficult. And yet it was apparently because of the energy he released through his refusal to compromise that a new model of mission eventually emerged. Theology thrives on controversy. It shows there is life in the old church yet.

This points to the crucial importance of allowing for the possibility of divine providence: the ability to detect the hand of God within the mess and not despite it. The moral of the story is simple: the God made known in Christ is the elusive God of ordinary human experience. The trick is to see through the heat of conflict and the mixed motives to discern the presence of a God who is constantly meddling in the mundane affairs of life. That is surely part of the meaning of incarnation.

This leads on to a point concerning the significance of social context for understanding theology. The concept of mission in the New Testament developed out of a dynamic exchange between Jewish, Hellenistic and Christian subcultures. Contemporary Christian mission also operates against a background of dynamic exchange in the context of cultural upheaval. The church in western society is increasingly marginal to the perceptions and aspirations of the overwhelming majority of people. This may be due to any number of factors which may be loosely attributed to increasing secularization and materialism coupled with the rapid decline in the power of Christianity to grip the imagination. For many people, the church appears to be earnestly offering all the answers to the questions nobody is asking. Where, perhaps, is the real point of contact between the church and the everyday experience of most people in contemporary society?

The extent of secularization in modern Britain is open to challenge, since elementary forms of religious outlook are still widely reported. Exaggerated claims are often made on the basis of this evidence about the level of residual faith in Britain, but on closer examination much of this appears to be little more than a form of superstition – not hugely different, perhaps, from the fear of *tychē* found in the ancient world, which drove people to seek the comforting voice of the oracle in order to keep one step ahead of fortune. Rather like the growing interest in astrology, tarot readings and the National Lottery, perhaps.

What is changing, though, is the growing reluctance of many people to take on any form of commitment, including religious affiliation.[20] As in the first century (and perhaps most other periods of history?) religion is reduced to the level of a social function – useful at times of personal or national crisis, but to be treated with nominal indifference most of the rest of time. Christian leaders are keen to clutch at anything that hints at residual power or influence, but there is little evidence that most people most of the time regard the church with anything other than polite amusement bordering on boredom. It is not at all clear that the much-vaunted surge of emotion following the death of Princess Diana will prove very much in the long run – except, perhaps, to confirm the trend towards the church as an occasional service provider (in every sense of the term) when collective emotion demands it.

The most popular form of religious broadcasting – to the relief of those religious commentators desperate to find anything positive to report – turns out to be programmes such as *Songs of Praise*, which requires no response at all on the part of the TV audience. The concept of worship as something other than personal entertainment is not hugely popular at the present time.

Another product of contemporary social change is the shifting relationship between different traditions within the church, particularly associated with the revival of evangelical Christianity, but also found in the dogmatic authoritarianism of conservative Roman Catholicism. It is certainly not very fashionable to be a theological liberal. Yet this growing polarization of theological opinion is almost certainly a reflection of recent social trends.[21] It is part of a response to anxiety over the future role of the church in society, and involves wider issues of social power and influence within an increasingly secular setting.

Similarly, as in New Testament times, many forms of contemporary Christianity are deeply compromised by an ambivalence towards the prevailing culture. Ecclesiastical judgements are almost invariably based on unexamined assumptions of the white, male, middle-class, Anglo-Saxon variety. Deeply critical of either personal moral values (usually related solely to issues of human sexuality), or of social injustice, nevertheless the church draws heavily on the same unspoken cultural assumptions that produced that morality in the first place. This cultural ambivalence is perhaps symbolized perfectly in the ironic symbolism of an élitist (usually male) choir singing the Magnificat (the song of a marginalized woman) in a cathedral context: 'He has filled the hungry with good things, and the rich he has sent empty away.' Or the self-indulgence of certain types of charismatic worship. Or the slightly disturbing versions of the 'health and wealth' gospel.

Also striking in the development of mission in New Testament times is the extent to which personality factors are significant. The image of Paul which emerges from the texts is not one of a plaster-cast saint. Here is a person as much concerned with personal ambition within the honour-shame culture of the Graeco-Roman world as most other people in his time. He was a child of his environment, heavily influenced by the same expectations as his Jewish and Gentile neighbours. The theological premise which may be deduced from this behaviour is the one he reached himself: God's wisdom is made known in our weakness (2 Corinthians 12.9f; see 1 Corinthians 2.2f). Yet without the energy and commitment of his towering personality, the church would almost certainly have disappeared without trace. As with all the genuine saints, the vulnerability of his personality provided the seed for change. Commitment, enthusiasm and sheer determination remain central to the mission task.

It is not too difficult, therefore, to see a number of interesting parallels between the contemporary British church and the fledgling New Testament communities. There are similar patterns of social competition and cultural interchange focused on a flawed humanity engaged in an ambitious power struggle. Mission rose out of the context of conflict as the first Christians strove to establish a new identity in a changing world. Is it entirely surprising, therefore, that the contemporary British church should seek to respond with a Decade of Evangelism?

The question of universal mission only became pressing when Gentiles had already started to join the community; until then, it was largely a non-issue. Experience forced the early Christian communities to think through the theological implications of the changes they faced in key social relationships. Similarly the experience of life in a multifaith environment sets a new agenda for the church to think through again the purpose of mission: what is it trying to achieve? There will be different answers to these difficult questions.[22] But in seeking to focus on this issue, the church may need to listen again to the voice of experience and learn from the insight of others – including the non-Christian religions which should not always be dismissed as inadequate or demonic. On the other hand, the church should not be in too much of a hurry to forget the voice of its own experience – that Christianity offers a unique insight through Christ into the nature of God. An adequate theology of mission will only emerge from within the dialectic holding of both these truths together. We, too, may not know what we believe until we have had time to think about it in the light of our experience.

The contemporary church should acknowledge the extent to which the current surge of interest in mission is itself a product of internal politics between competing wings of tradition, social pressure reflecting continuing decline in membership and influence, and a genuine commitment to renewal. It may be that only when this hidden subtext of mixed motives is honestly acknowledged that it will become possible to formulate a renewed theology. The dialogue between experience, inter-group processes, attitudes and belief is pushing the church to articulate a new 'mission statement':[23] put most simply, it is that God cares about his world and his people and calls on the church to act in his name in a ministry of care and involvement.

But fortunately it is not the mission of the church which is ultimately important, however much it is dressed up in scriptural quotation to make it look respectable. The church remains a deeply flawed institution, a sacramental reminder of the need for a gracious God. It is God's little joke. Far more important is the *missio dei*: the reaching out of God in loving service to humanity. It is this primary insight which leads the Johannine Christ to say 'as the Father has sent me, so I send you' (John 20.21). All mission is rooted in what God has already done for us, not in the absurd pretensions of the church. It is always a serious mistake to confuse the institutional church with the Kingdom of God.

This is the good news. If the development of a universal mission in New Testament times has anything to teach contemporary Christianity it is that God is able to use even the mess of the church. The church has probably always been divided and probably always will be. But it turns out that dissent is crucial in the crystallization of belief. In the paradox of inter-group dynamics there is always the possibility of creative energy – enough, perhaps, to help reshape the church for the next millennium of witness to an increasingly sceptical audience.

Notes

Introduction

1   See D. Bosch, *Transforming Mission* (Orbis 1991); W. Abraham, *The Logic of Evangelism* (Hodder 1989); V. Donovan, *The Church in the Midst of Creation* (SCM 1989).

2   See C. Moody, *Eccentric Ministry* (Darton, Longman & Todd 1992).

3   M. Nazir-Ali, *Mission and Dialogue* (SPCK 1995), p. 28f.

4   See S. Neill, *A History of Christian Missions* (Penguin 1964).

5   Evangelicalism is defined by A. McGrath as 'a major movement, especially in English-language theology, which places special emphasis upon the supreme authority of Scripture and the atoning death of Christ', *Christian Theology: An Introduction* (Blackwell 1994), p. 497.

6   *Book of Common Prayer*, Collect for Good Friday.

7   J. Comby, *How to Understand Christian Mission* (SCM 1996), p. 58f.

8   Bosch, *Transforming Mission*, pp. 302–13.

9   G. Davie, *Religion in Britain since 1945* (Blackwell 1994), pp. 8 and 70.

10 See, for example, the *Church Times*, 7 February 1997.

11 All quotations from Scripture, unless otherwise stated, are from the *New Revised Standard Version*, Anglicized Edition (OUP 1989, 1995).

12 See especially E. P. Sanders, *Jesus and Judaism* (SCM 1985); and G. Vermes, *Jesus the Jew* (SCM 1973; rev. edn, SCM 1983).

13 Vermes, *Jesus the Jew*, pp. 192–213.

14 See Sanders, *Jesus and Judaism*, pp. 61–119.

15 P. Borgen, 'God's Agent in the Fourth Gospel' in J. Ashton (ed.), *The Interpretation of John* (SPCK 1986), pp. 67–78.

16 R. Brown, *The Gospel according to John: XIII–XXI* (Doubleday 1970), p. 613.

17 A. Yarbro Collins, *Crisis and Catharsis: The Power of the Apocalypse* (Westminster 1984), pp. 124ff.

18 See A. Le Grys, 'Conflict and Vengeance in the Book of Revelation', *Expository Times*, Vol. 104 No. 3 (December 1992), pp. 76–80.

19 See Sanders, *Jesus and Judaism*, pp. 174–211. Sanders notes the relative paucity of references to repentance in the authentic gospel sayings, and suggests that part of the scandal of Jesus' teaching was precisely that he offered the truly 'wicked' entry into the Kingdom *without* prior repentance.

20 *Pace* E. Schnabel, 'Jesus and the Beginnings of the Mission to the Gentiles'

in J. Green and M. Turner (eds), *Jesus of Nazareth: Lord and Christ* (Eerdmans 1994), p. 53.

21 See J. L. Houlden, *The Public Face of the Gospel: New Testament Ideas of the Church* (SCM 1997), pp. 15–25.

22 See R. Maddox, *The Purpose of Luke-Acts* (T. & T. Clark 1982).

23 The title of a book on 1 Peter by J. Elliott: *A Home for the Homeless: A Social-Scientific Criticism of 1 Peter, Its Situation and Strategy* (Fortress 1981).

1 Mission and the Hebrew Scriptures

1 The more common term for the Hebrew Scriptures is perhaps 'The Old Testament'. However, 'old' is a relative adjective which implies the 'new' – in other words, the description already implies a Christian understanding of the text. Further, it is not clear that there was a complete collection of books which were commonly accepted by all Jews as 'Scripture' at this time: that involved a long process of canonization which was almost certainly not complete by the time of Jesus, and a number of different documents had the status of 'inspired writing' in different Jewish communities. See J. Barton, 'Canon' in *The Dictionary of Biblical Interpretation* (SCM 1990). The collection of Greek texts known as the Septuagint also contained a number of different texts from those known in the Hebrew Bible. The situation was therefore altogether more fluid than the 'traditional' term 'Old Testament' might suggest, and the expression 'Hebrew Scriptures' is therefore used to try to avoid this confusion of perspectives.

2 See E. P. Sanders, *Judaism: Practice and Belief 63 BCE–66 CE* (SCM 1992).

3 Sanders, *Judaism*, pp. 315–490.

4 Josephus, *Jewish Antiquities* XVIII.11–22 (Loeb Classical Library, Harvard 1965).

5 The Mishnah is, of course, a full documentation of late Pharisaic and early rabbinic Jewish disputes over Jewish life and practice.

6 G. Vermes, *The Dead Sea Scrolls in English* (Penguin 1962), p. 13.

7 Josephus, *Antiquities* XVIII.23–25.

8 Josephus, *The Life* 11 (Loeb Classical Library, Harvard 1926).

9 J. P. Meier, *A Marginal Jew*, Vol. 2 (Doubleday 1994), pp. 19–176.

10 This assumes a date of *c.* 1200 BCE for some of the earliest fragments of written sources now incorporated into scriptural texts down to a date of *c.* 167 for the Book of Daniel. See J. Soggin, *Introduction to the Old Testament* (SCM 1976), pp. 57–75.

11 See, for example, D. Senior and C. Stuhlmueller, *The Biblical Foundations for Mission* (SCM 1983).

12 See M. Goodman, *Mission and Conversion* (Clarendon 1994).

13 The final form of the Pentateuch is commonly dated to the post-exilic period. See R. N. Whybray, *The Making of the Pentateuch* (Sheffield 1987).

14 The established view(s) of Deutero-Isaiah is under attack in much current Old Testament scholarship, according to R. Coggins, 'Recent Continental Old Testament Literature' in the *Expository Times*, Vol. 104 No. 10, p. 298.

15 G. von Rad, *Old Testament Theology*, Vol. 1 (SCM 1975), p. 136.

16 W. Brueggemann, *A Social Reading of the Old Testament* (Fortress 1994), pp. 254–8.

17 See W. Schmidt, *Introduction to the Old Testament* (SCM 1984), p. 79.

18 It forms the basis of the 'second Adam' Christology in Paul, for example (e.g. Romans 5.15–21).

19 E.g. Ezekiel 40—48.

20 G. Bertram, article on 'Ethnos' in TDNT, p. 201.

21 See H. Ringgren, *Israelite Religion* (SPCK 1966), pp. 66ff.

22 J. Eaton, *The Psalms Come Alive* (Mowbray 1984), pp. 1–9.

23 J. Day, *Psalms* (Sheffield 1992), pp. 123f.

24 L. Legrand, *Unity and Plurality: Mission in the Bible* (Orbis 1990), pp. 22ff.

25 See C. North, *The Second Isaiah* (OUP 1964), pp. 20ff.

26 See Legrand, *Unity and Plurality*, p. 20.

27 The 'centripetal'/'centrifugal' image comes from Senior and Stuhlmueller, *Biblical Foundations*, pp. 315ff.

28 Daniel 7.14; 1 Enoch 90.30.

29 Legrand, *Unity and Plurality*, p. 36f.

30 Senior and Stuhlmueller, *Biblical Foundations*, pp. 36–80 and pp. 110–36.

31 See P. Ackroyd, *Exile and Restoration* (SCM 1968) and *Israel under Babylon and Persia* (OUP 1970).

32 Senior and Stuhlmueller, *Biblical Foundations*, pp. 105–8.

33 See also J. Dunn's discussion of the important work carried out by E. P. Sanders in 'The New Perspective on Paul: Paul and the Law', reprinted in K. Donfried (ed.), *The Romans Debate* (T. & T. Clark 1991), pp. 299–308.

34 For further discussion see E. P. Sanders, *Paul and Palestinian Judaism* (SCM 1977), pp. 329–418.

35 See, for example, J. A. Soggin, *Introduction to the Old Testament* (rev. edn, SCM 1980), p. 395.

36 An echo of this 'protest' may lie behind the genealogy attributed by Matthew to Jesus in Matthew 1.1–17. This also associates Jesus 'the Son of David' with Gentile ancestors.

37 Soggin, *Introduction*, pp. 355–9.

38 Soggin, *Introduction*, p. 403.

39 Senior and Stuhlmueller, *Biblical Foundations*, pp. 105–8.

40 Legrand, *Unity and Plurality*, p. 14.

2 Judaism and Mission: Jewish and Gentile Perceptions of One Another

1 M. Goodman, *Mission and Conversion: Proselytizing in the Religious History of the Roman Empire* (Clarendon 1994).
2 J. Jeremias, *Jesus' Promise to the Nations* (SCM 1956), p. 17.
3 R. Brown, *Group Processes* (Blackwell 1988), pp. 19–28.
4 A. Cohen, *The Symbolic Construction of Reality* (Routledge 1985).
5 W. Meeks, *The First Urban Christians* (Yale 1983), p. 34.
6 B. Holmberg, *Sociology and the New Testament* (Fortress 1990), p. 22.
7 A detailed account of the geographical distribution of Jewish communities at this period can be found in E. Schürer, *The History of the Jewish People in the age of Jesus Christ*, rev. G. Vermes, F. Millar and M. Black (T. & T. Clark 1979), Vol. III, pp. 3–86.
8 F. Dexinger, 'Limits of Tolerance: The Samaritan Example' in E. P. Sanders (ed.), *Jewish and Christian Self-Definition* (SCM 1981), Vol. 2, pp. 88–114, argues that it is important not to exaggerate the extent of the Assyrian deportations. It is likely that significant portions of the indigenous population remained in Israel.
9 Cited by S. McKnight, *A Light among the Nations* (Fortress 1991), p. 32.
10 J. Gager, *The Origins of Anti-Semitism* (OUP 1983).
11 M. Hengel, *Judaism and Hellenism* (2 vols., SCM 1974).
12 See J. Goldstein, 'Jewish Acceptance and Rejection of Hellenism' in *Jewish and Christian Self-Definition*, Vol. 2 (SCM 1981), p. 75.
13 B. Malina, *The New Testament World* (SCM 1983), pp. 71–5, notes the tendency in pre-industrial cities for social élite groups – represented by the aristocratic priestly castes in Jerusalem – to be the cultural 'trend-setters' in contrast to the 'old-fashioned' urban non-élites and even more 'quaint' villagers. This fits in well with the evidence from 1 and 2 Maccabees that Jason – a priest who manoeuvred himself into a position where he was appointed high priest by the Seleucid Emperor Antiochus IV – was one of the leading figures in the pro-Hellenistic movement. He was resisted by the Maccabeans, who came originally from Modein, a small town midway between Jerusalem and the coast. Several of their initial successes were in essentially rural areas, such as Galilee (see 1 Maccabees 1.11—2.28 and 2 Maccabees 4.7—5.27).
14 See G. Nickelsburg, *Jewish Literature between the Bible and the Mishnah* (SCM 1981), pp. 71–99, for a brief account of the background to the Maccabean revolt, and some of the Jewish literature produced at that time.
15 Citations from Gager, *Origins*, p. 55f.
16 Gager, *Origins*, pp. 55–66.
17 A Jewish colony had been established on the island of Elephantine in mid

Egypt since at least this time. What is particularly interesting from the point of view of Jewish studies is that the community apparently operated a fully operational sacrificial cult around their own temple – despite the insistence in Deuteronomy (e.g. 12.13) that sacrifice could only be legitimately offered at the one place chosen by God – i.e. Jerusalem. This is yet further evidence of varieties of Judaism in the period prior to the downfall of Jerusalem in 70 CE.

18 Gager, *Origins*, p. 41. See pp. 35–54 generally for further background material for Gentile–Jewish relationships at this time.
19 D. Crossan, *The Historical Jesus: The Life of a Mediterranean Jewish Peasant* (T. & T. Clark 1991), pp. 43–71.
20 Suetonius, *Tiberius* 36, tr. C. K. Barrett in *The New Testament Background: Selected Documents* (SPCK 1956), p. 10.
21 Josephus, *Jewish Antiquities* XVIII.82–3 (Loeb Classical Library, Heinemann 1930).
22 See G. Lüdemann, *Paul Apostle to the Gentiles* (SCM 1984), p. 6.
23 Suetonius, *Life of Claudius* XXV.4, cited by J. Stevenson, *A New Eusebius* (SPCK 1957).
24 Cited by J. Jeremias, *Jesus' Promise to the Nations* (SCM 1955), p. 41.
25 See G. Vermes, *The Dead Sea Scrolls in English* (rev. edn, Penguin 1987), and for the more recently published material (though not the more eccentric scholarship), R. Eisenman and M. Wise, *The Dead Sea Scrolls Uncovered* (Element 1992). Eisenman and others posit a connection between the Dead Sea Community and primitive Christianity. For a more reliable account of the Scrolls, see J. C. Vanderkam, *The Dead Sea Scrolls Today* (SPCK 1994). For a discussion of some of the fragments which, it is sometimes claimed, show a link with Mark's Gospel see Chapter 2 in G. Stanton, *Gospel Truth?* (HarperCollins 1995).
26 Eisenman and Wise, *Dead Sea Scrolls*, pp. 185ff, 236ff and *passim*.
27 Nickelsburg, *Jewish Literature*, pp. 202–9.
28 Nickelsburg, *Jewish Literature*, pp. 280–305.
29 McKnight, *Light among the Nations*, pp. 43ff.
30 Nickelsburg, *Jewish Literature*, pp. 62–169.
31 Nickelsburg, *Jewish Literature*, p. 165, my italics.
32 Nickelsburg, *Jewish Literature*, pp. 165–9.
33 McKnight, *Light among the Nations*, pp. 12–19.
34 E. P. Sanders, *Paul and Palestinian Judaism* (SCM 1977), p. 210.
35 E. P. Sanders, *Jesus and Judaism* (SCM 1985), pp. 212–21.
36 Josephus, *Antiquities* XX.39.
37 Josephus, *Antiquities* XIII.257.
38 Malina, *New Testament World*, p. 25f.
39 This point should not be pressed too far, however. Crossan, *Historical*

Jesus, notes that Nazareth was part of a web of villages in Lower Galilee, one of the most densely populated areas in the entire Roman Empire. A fair degree of assimilation between Hellenistic and Jewish cultures was therefore unavoidable.

40 Josephus, *Against Apion* (Loeb Classical Library, Heinemann 1926), II.282–6.

41 See F. Millar, 'Gentiles and Judaism: Godfearers and Proselytes' in Schürer, *History*, Vol. 3.1, pp. 150–76.

42 McKnight, *Light among the Nations*, p. 89.

43 The full text of the story may be found in J. Charlesworth (ed.), *The Pseudepigrapha of the Old Testament*, Vol. 2 (Darton, Longman & Todd 1985). A description and summary of the text is in Nickelsburg, *Jewish Literature*, pp. 258–63.

44 Millar, 'Gentiles and Judaism', p. 150, comments on the lack of information about first-century proselytes.

45 See also A. Segal, *Paul the Convert* (Yale 1990), pp. 72–114 for a description of the social consequences of conversion.

46 McKnight, *Light among the Nations*, p. 98f.

47 McKnight, *Light among the Nations*, p. 44f.

48 McKnight, *Light among the Nations*, p. 45.

49 See especially Millar, 'Gentiles and Judaism', pp. 65–175.

50 McKnight, *Light among the Nations*, pp. 98ff.

51 McKnight, *Light among the Nations*, pp. 49–77 and Goodman, *Mission and Conversion*.

3 The Historical Jesus 1: Jesus and the Concept of Universal Mission

1 M. Goodman, *Mission and Conversion* (Clarendon 1994), p. 105.

2 So M. Hengel, *Judaism and Hellenism* (SCM 1974).

3 G. Vermes, *Jesus the Jew* (rev. edn, SCM 1983), pp. 42–57.

4 Josephus, *Jewish Antiquities* XVIII.4–10 (Loeb Classical Library, Heinemann 1930).

5 See Vermes, *Jesus the Jew*, pp. 69–82.

6 See Vermes, *Jesus the Jew*, p. 70.

7 Vermes, *Jesus the Jew*, pp. 210ff.

8 A brief study of the texts, together with some reflections for the modern church, can be found in M. Arias and A. Johnson, *The Great Commission* (Abingdon 1992). This study should be used with care, however, as it does not really engage with modern critical scholarship at any real depth.

9 See P. Avis (ed.), *The Resurrection of Jesus Christ* (Darton, Longman & Todd 1993), especially pp. 39–134.

10 For example, see L. Newbigin, *The Open Secret* (SPCK 1995), p. 122.

11 R. T. France, *Matthew* (IVP 1985), p. 413.

12 C. H. Scobie, 'Jesus or Paul – the Origins of Universal Mission in the Christian Church' in P. Richardson and J. Hurd (eds), *From Jesus to Paul* (Wilfrid Laurier 1984).

13 See the major commentaries on Matthew, in particular D. Hill (New Century Bible, Marshall, Morgan & Scott 1972), E. Schweizer (SPCK 1976) etc.

14 See G. Bornkamm, G. Barth and H. Held, *Tradition and Interpretation in Matthew* (SCM 1963), pp. 15–164 for a crucially important discussion of Matthew's understanding of the Torah.

15 Goodman, *Mission and Conversion*, p. 94.

16 C. E. B. Cranfield, *The Gospel according to St Mark* (CUP 1959).

17 M. Hooker, *The Gospel according to Mark* (Black 1991), p. 387.

18 See C. F. Evans, *Luke* (SCM 1990), p. 923f.

19 See I. Howard Marshall, *Luke: Historian and Theologian* (Paternoster 1992).

20 J. Fitzmeyer, *Luke X—XXIV* (Vol. 2 of the Anchor Bible Commentary, Doubleday 1985), p. 1581.

21 See B. Lindars, *The Gospel of John* (New Century Bible, Marshall, Morgan & Scott 1972), p. 611.

22 R. Brown, *John XIII—XXI* (Vol. 2 of the Anchor Bible Commentary, Doubleday 1970), p. 1036.

23 Brown, *John XIII—XXI*, p. 1039.

24 See, for example, the evidence set out in R. Maddox, *The Purpose of Luke-Acts* (T. & T. Clark 1982).

25 B. Throckmorton, *Gospel Parallels* (4th edn, Nelson 1979).

26 For a discussion of the 'tests' used by many scholars to assess the historicity of the gospel traditions see J. Meier, *A Marginal Jew*, Vol. 1 (Doubleday 1991), pp. 167–84.

27 See E. P. Sanders, *Jesus and Judaism* (SCM 1985), pp. 98–106.

28 E. P. Sanders and M. Davies, *Studying the Synoptic Gospels* (SCM 1989), pp. 74–82.

29 D. Catchpole, *The Quest for Q* (T. & T. Clark 1993), pp. 151–88.

30 Hooker, *Mark*, p. 111.

31 Cranfield, *Mark*, p. 200.

32 See S. van Tilbourg, *The Jewish Leaders in Matthew* (E. J. Brill 1972), pp. 163ff.

33 D. Garland, *Reading Matthew* (SPCK 1993), p. 143f.

34 See Evans, *Luke*, p. 444f.

35 Evans, *Luke*, p. 396.

36 D. Pennington, *Essential Social Psychology* (Arnold 1996 – *sic*), pp. 220–39.

4 The Historical Jesus 2: Jesus and the Gentiles

1 C. Myers, *Binding the Strong Man* (Orbis 1988), pp. 190ff and 426ff.
2 W. Kelber, *Mark's Story of Jesus* (Fortress 1979), p. 30. See the whole chapter (pp. 30–42) for a further discussion of this section of Mark.
3 Myers, *Binding the Strong Man*, pp. 188ff and 241f.
4 See H. Räisänen, *The Messianic Secret in Mark's Gospel* (T. & T. Clark 1990).
5 For comment on the sources Mark may have used see M. Hooker, *The Gospel according to Mark* (Black 1991), p. 141f. On the narrative skill of Mark generally, see D. Rhoades and D. Michie, *Mark as Story* (Fortress 1982).
6 As J. Meier is inclined to believe: *A Marginal Jew*, Vol. 2 (Doubleday 1994), p. 653.
7 See B. Throckmorton, *Gospel Parallels* (4th edn, Nelson 1979), Section 115, pp. 82–83.
8 See, for example, C. E. B. Cranfield, *The Gospel according to St Mark* (CUP 1959), p. 248.
9 So Meier, *A Marginal Jew*, Vol. 2, p. 660.
10 Hooker, *Mark*, p. 185f.
11 See Hooker, *Mark*, p. 187f.
12 E. Best, *Following Jesus* (Sheffield 1981), pp. 134–43.
13 See further W. D. Davies and D. Allison, *The Gospel according to Matthew*, Vol. 1 (International Critical Commentary, T. & T. Clark 1988), pp. 161–90; and R. Brown, *The Birth of the Messiah* (Doubleday 1977), pp. 57–95.
14 See K. Stendahl, *The School of Matthew and Its Use of the Old Testament* (rev. edn Philadelphia 1968); or R. France, *Matthew: Evangelist and Teacher* (Paternoster 1989), for a summary and discussion.
15 Unlike the story of the Syrophoenician woman, however, Meier (*A Marginal Jew*, p. 726) thinks there are grounds for accepting that the healing of the centurion's servant may be based on an historical incident.
16 As France seems to indicate in his commentary, *Matthew*, pp. 205ff.
17 B. J. Malina, *New Testament World* (SCM 1983), p. 79.
18 See C. F. Evans, *Luke* (SCM 1990), p. 623.
19 B. Lindars, *The Gospel of John* (New Century Commentary, Marshall, Morgan & Scott 1972), p. 175f.
20 R. Brown, *The Community of the Beloved Disciple* (G. Chapman 1979), p. 36.
21 See Lindars, *Gospel of John*, pp. 195ff.
22 R. Fortna, *The Fourth Gospel and Its Predecessor* (Fortress 1988).
23 See the discussion of the incident, and the literary unit of which it is part, in Hooker, *Mark*, pp. 260–70.
24 E. P. Sanders, *Jesus and Judaism* (SCM 1985), *passim*; but see especially pp. 270–93.
25 Hooker, *Mark*, pp. 297–303.

26 Cranfield, *Mark*, p. 390.

27 The woman is named as Mary Magdalene by later (fourth century CE) tradition – possibly by association with the equivalent story in John 12.1–8, which names the woman as Mary, the sister of Lazarus, and with the (possibly) equivalent story in Luke 7.36–50, where the incident recording the repentance of an unnamed woman is followed a couple of verses later (8.2) with a reference to several women, including Mary Magdalene.

28 See E. S. Fiorenza, *In Memory of Her* (SCM 1983), pp. xiii and 128ff.

29 See, for example, I. H. Marshall, *Luke: Historian and Theologian* (Paternoster 1992).

30 So, for example, C. K. Barrett, *The Gospel according to John* (SPCK 1955), pp. 34–45. I also believe, from conversations overheard, that a number of other scholars are working on other theories of dependence between John and the Synoptic tradition.

31 See, for example, Lindars, *Gospel of John*, pp. 25ff.

32 Hooker, *Mark*, p. 330.

33 For further important discussion about this way of reading John's narrative see J. L. Martyn, *History and Theology in the Fourth Gospel* (2nd edn, Abingdon 1979); and Brown, *Community of the Beloved Disciple*, *passim*.

34 The relationship between the Johannine discourses and the teaching of the historical Jesus is enormously complex, and should be followed up by reading the relevant sections in the standard commentaries – e.g. Lindars, *Gospel of John*, pp. 46–56; R. Brown, *The Gospel according to John*, 2 vols. (Anchor Bible, Doubleday 1970), *passim*. An excellent overview of recent discussions of Johannine scholarship may be found in B. Lindars, *John* (NT Study Guides, Sheffield Academic Press 1990); but perhaps the most impressive book on practically every aspect of modern Johannine research is J. Ashton's *Understanding the Fourth Gospel* (OUP 1991).

35 Lindars, *John*, p. 159.

5 The First Christian Communities: Controversy over the Law

1 Assuming Jesus was executed *c.* 30 CE and the gospels were written between 65 and 90 CE, the maximum period of time available for a change of attitude would be around 60 years. It was almost certainly rather less.

2 The image comes from G. Stanton's lectures.

3 See R. Jewett, *Dating Paul's Life* (SCM 1979); and G. Lüdemann, *Paul Apostle to the Gentiles: Studies in Chronology* (SCM 1984).

4 H. Conzelmann, *The Theology of St Luke* (Faber 1960).

5 J. D. G. Dunn, *1 Corinthians* (Sheffield 1995), p. 13f.

6 E. Haenchen, *The Acts of the Apostles* (ET, Blackwell 1971), pp. 81–90.

7 Some scholars continue to argue that Luke's main source of information was his own experience as a travelling companion of Paul, of course. The queries already raised about the reliability of Luke's account of Paul, however, throw this into serious doubt.

8 For example, F. Watson, *Paul, Judaism and the Gentiles* (CUP 1986), p. 28.

9 As perhaps M. Hengel does in *Between Jesus and Paul* (SCM 1983).

10 See, for example, I. H. Marshall, *The Acts of the Apostles* (Sheffield 1992).

11 L. Alexander, *The Preface to Luke's Gospel* (CUP 1993).

12 See especially R. Maddox, *The Purpose of Luke-Acts* (T. & T. Clark 1982).

13 P. Esler, *Community and Gospel in Luke-Acts* (CUP 1987).

14 C. H. Talbert, *Reading Luke* (Crossroad 1992), p. 3f.

15 Haenchen, *Acts*, p. 102.

16 D. J. Bosch, *Transforming Mission: Paradigm Shifts in Theology of Mission* (Orbis 1992), pp. 15–52.

17 E. P. Sanders, *Jesus and Judaism* (SCM 1985), pp. 174–241.

18 For example, J. D. G. Dunn, *Romans 9—16* (Word Biblical Commentary, Word Books 1991), p. 572.

19 See C. H. Scobie, 'Jesus or Paul? The Origins of the Universal Mission of the Christian Church' in P. Richardson and J. C. Hurd (eds), *From Jesus to Paul* (Wilfrid Laurier Press 1984), pp. 47–60.

20 The *Didache* in *Early Christian Writings* (Penguin 1968), tr. M. Stanisforth, p. 232f.

21 See M. Simon, *St Stephen and the Hellenists in the Primitive Church* (London 1958); and Hengel, *Between Jesus and Paul*, pp. 1–29.

22 M. Goulder, *A Tale of Two Missions* (SCM 1994). Goulder, however, still seems to think in terms of only two independent Christian traditions, the Petrine and the Pauline. It seems to me that the evidence points rather more strongly in the direction of Christianity as a continuing reform movement in the earliest stages of development, existing only as localized interest or 'ginger' groups within Judaism. Although Acts only mentions two – the Hebraists and the Hellenists – I see no reason to limit it to these. Indeed, I am not so sure as Goulder that Peter and James can be put into exactly the same category.

23 The letters of Paul, the Johannine Epistles and the Book of Revelation, to name but a few texts, also, of course, point to division in the early church. Later church history is beyond the scope of this book, but this author has yet to be convinced that the church has ever been united. Division appears to be the normal state of the church.

24 H. Cadbury, *The Making of Luke-Acts* (Macmillan 1927), pp. 184–93; and E. Schweizer, 'Concerning the Speeches in Acts' in L. E. Keck and J. L. Martyn (eds), *Studies in Luke-Acts* (Yale 1976), pp. 208–16.

25 C. C. Hill, *Hellenists and Hebrews: Reappraising Division within the Earliest Church* (Fortress 1992).

26 On this point about different Christian communities within the primitive Jerusalem church see also Goulder, *Tale of Two Missions*.

27 L. Hurst, *The Epistle to the Hebrews* (CUP 1990), pp. 89–106.

28 Hurst, *Hebrews*, p. 41f and *passim*; and B. Lindars, *The Theology of the Letter to the Hebrews* (CUP 1991), pp. 1–25.

29 Philo, *Concerning Noah's Work as a Planter* (*De Plantatione*) XXV.107–9 and XXX.126–9 (Loeb Classical Library, Heinemann 1929–1962).

30 Josephus, *Jewish Antiquities* XX.219 (Loeb Classical Library, Heinemann 1930).

31 See F. Dexinger, 'Limits of Tolerance in Judaism: The Samaritan Example' in E. P. Sanders with A. I. Baumgarten and A. Mendelson (eds), *Jewish and Christian Self-Definition*, Vol. 2 (SCM 1981).

32 See R. Witherup SS, 'Cornelius Over and Over Again: "Functional Redundancy" in the Acts of the Apostles', JNTS 49 (March 1993).

33 This, however, looks suspiciously like Lucan embarrassment again – there is not a shred of evidence anywhere else that there was such a thing as an 'apostolic decree', and had there been, Paul would have been the first to use it. The issues linked to it by Luke were real enough, however (see 1 Corinthians 8—10 and Revelation 2—3).

34 If conversion it was: see K. Stendahl, *Paul among the Jews and Gentiles* (Fortress 1976), pp. 7–23. For an alternative view, however, see A. Segal, *Paul the Convert* (Yale 1990).

35 Watson, *Paul, Judaism and the Gentiles*, p. 29.

36 I am indebted to Professor Philip Esler for this point.

6 Christianity in a Pagan World

1 *Hellenistas* or 'Hellenist' is supported by B (fourth-century MS), D (fifth-century), E and P (sixth-century) as well as a large number of minuscules and a few fragments of evidence in the form of early church quotations. *Hellenas* or 'Greek' is supported by a later papyrus fragment (seventh-century), one of the revised readings of the important Codex Sinaiticus (fourth-century) and two fifth-century uncials, together with a few more quotations from early church authors. This range   evidence is given the C rating in the United Bible Society's fourth edition of the Greek New Testament, which means the editorial 'Committee had difficulty in deciding which variant to place in the text'!

2 There is, however, remarkably little evidence of actual persecution: see W. H. C. Frend, *Martyrdom and Persecution in the Early Church* (Blackwell 1965). It is entirely possible, however, that local hostility between near neighbours occasionally erupted into a physical threat of some kind, and

that this accounts for the fear of persecution witnessed in many New Testament passages (e.g. 1 Peter etc.). See A. Yarbro Collins, *Crisis and Catharsis* (Westminster Press 1984), pp. 84–110, for a discussion of the importance of perceived social threat; and J. Elliott, *A Home for the Homeless* (Fortress 1981), pp. 101–64 on 1 Peter.

3 F. Watson, *Paul, Judaism and the Gentiles* (CUP 1986), pp. 88–105.

4 S. Price, 'The History of the Hellenistic Period' in J. Boardman, J. Griffin and O. Murray (eds), *The Oxford History of Greece and the Hellenistic World* (OUP 1986), pp. 364–89.

5 For a description of the pre-industrial cities of the Graeco-Roman world see R. Rohrbaugh, 'The Pre-Industrial City in Luke-Acts' in J. Neyrey (ed.), *The Social World of Luke-Acts* (Hendrickson 1991).

6 Rupert Brown, *Group Processes* (Blackwell 1988), p. 88.

7 B. Malina, *The New Testament World: Insights from Cultural Anthropology* (SCM 1983), pp. 51–70.

8 R. Lane Fox, *Pagans and Christians* (Penguin 1986), pp. 27–261.

9 W. Meeks, *The First Urban Christians* (Yale 1983), pp. 77–80.

10 Malina, *New Testament World*, p. 48f.

11 See S. Bartchy, *'Mallon Chrēsai*: First Century Slavery and the Interpretation of 1 Corinthians 7.21' (Society of Biblical Literature Dissertation Series 11).

12 Statistics from B. Holmberg, *Sociology and the New Testament* (Fortress 1990), p. 22f.

13 Most of the details used in this section are culled from Malina, *New Testament World*; G. Theissen, *Social Setting of Pauline Christianity* (T. & T. Clark 1982); and Holmberg, *Sociology and the New Testament*.

14 Theissen, *Social Setting of Pauline Christianity*, p. 139.

15 E. Judge, *The Social Pattern of the Christian Groups in the First Century* (London 1960).

16 See M. Hengel, *The Pre-Christian Paul* (SCM 1991), pp. 1–38.

17 J. Lieu, T. Rajak and J. North, *The Jews among Pagans and Christians* (Routledge 1992), pp. 1–8.

18 Lieu, Rajak and North, *Jews among Pagans*, p. 3.

19 Lane Fox, *Pagans and Christians*, p. 30f, argues that 'civilian' is the most likely meaning.

20 J. Ferguson, *The Religions of the Roman Empire* (Thames and Hudson 1970), pp. 65ff.

21 Ferguson, *Religions of the Roman Empire*, p. 34f.

22 R. Parker, 'Gods and Men' in J. Boardman, J. Griffin and O. Murray (eds), *The Oxford History of the Classical World* (Oxford 1986, TSP edn, 1995), p. 261.

23 Ferguson, *Religions of the Roman Empire*, pp. 88–98.

24 Ferguson, *Religions of the Roman Empire*, pp. 99–123.
25 T. tam Tinh, 'Sarapis and Isis' in B. Meyers and E. P. Sanders (eds), *Jewish and Christian Self-Definition*, Vol. 3 (SCM 1982).
26 Brown, *Group Processes* (Blackwell 1988), pp. 20–27.
27 Ferguson, *Religions of the Roman Empire*, pp. 104–6.
28 Meeks, *Urban Christians*, p. 162f.
29 J. Stambaugh and D. Balch, *The Social World of the First Christians* (SPCK 1986), pp. 45ff.
30 Ferguson, *Religions of the Roman Empire*, p. 184.
31 See especially F. G. Downing, *Christ and the Cynics* (Sheffield 1988).
32 Ferguson, *Religions of the Roman Empire*, pp. 190ff.
33 See, for example, C. H. Dodd, *The Interpretation of the Fourth Gospel* (CUP 1968), pp. 263–85.
34 Ferguson, *Religions of the Roman Empire*, p. 193f.

7 The Social Mechanics of Early Christian Mission: Christianity in the Religious Market Place

1 Rupert Brown, *Group Processes* (Blackwell 1988), pp. 103–6.
2 C. H. Talbot, *Reading Luke* (Crossroad 1992), pp. 4ff.
3 G. Fee, *The First Epistle to the Corinthians* (Eerdmans 1987), p. 6 and *passim*.
4 In order to receive the 39 lashes five times, he would have had to submit to the authority of the Diaspora synagogue voluntarily: outside Palestine the Jews had no legal right to flog those who did not accept their jurisdiction. Paul thus wants to retain a foothold in the synagogue.
5 Brown, *Group Processes*.
6 H. Tajfel, 'Social Categorization, Social Identity and Social Comparison' in H. Tajfel (ed.), *Differentiation between Social Groups* (Academic Press 1978).
7 J. D. G. Dunn, *The Partings of the Way* (SCM 1991).
8 M. Hengel, 'Christology and New Testament Chronology' in *Between Jesus and Paul* (SCM 1983), p. 45.
9 Brown, *Group Processes*, pp. 59–67.
10 See, for example, W. Meeks, *The Origins of Christian Morality* (Yale 1993), pp. 86–8.
11 Tajfel, 'Individual Behaviour and Inter Group Behaviour' in Tajfel (ed.), *Differentiation between Social Groups*.
12 See Tajfel, 'Individual Behaviour and Inter Group Behaviour'.
13 E. Barker, *New Religious Movements* (HMSO 1989), p. 19.
14 E. Erikson, *Childhood and Society* (Paladin 1950).
15 The phrase comes from W. Conn, *Christian Conversion* (Paulist Press 1986), p. 68.
16 See, for example, 'Christology and Social Experience: Aspects of Pauline

Christology in the Light of the Sociology of Knowledge' in G. Theissen, *Social Reality and Early Christianity* (T. & T. Clark 1992), pp. 187–201.

17 P. Berger and T. Luckmann, *The Sociology of Knowledge* (Penguin 1967).

18 R. Macmullen, 'Two Types of Conversion in Early Christianity' in *Vigiliae*, Vol. 37 No. 2 (Brill 1983).

19 M. Weber, *Sociology of Religion* (ET, Beacon Press 1963), p. 46f and *passim*.

20 W. A. Meeks, *The First Urban Christians* (Yale 1983), pp. 22–3.

21 B. Holmberg, *Sociology and the New Testament* (Fortress 1990), pp. 56–9, 67–9.

22 Based on the work of L. R. Rambo, *Understanding Religious Conversion* (Yale 1993).

23 Though whether in fact Paul *was* converted in this sense is a moot point. See K. Stendahl, *Paul among Jews and Gentiles* (Fortress 1976), pp. 7–23.

24 D. Snow and R. Machalek, 'The Convert as Social Type' in R. Collins (ed.), *Sociological Theory 1983* (Jossey Bass 1983).

25 B. Wilson, *Religion in Sociological Perspective* (OUP 1982), p. 118f.

26 Rambo, *Conversion*, p. 9f.

27 J. Lofland and N. Skonovd, 'Becoming a World-Saver: A Theory of Conversion to a Deviant Perspective' in *The American Sociological Review*, Vol. 30, pp. 862–75.

28 Rambo, *Conversion*, p. 16f.

29 On the importance of religious rituals in the early church to mark transition into membership and consolidate the group see Meeks, *First Urban Christians*, pp. 140–63.

30 Barker, *New Religious Movements*, p. 35.

31 P. Esler, *Community and Gospel in Luke-Acts* (CUP 1987), pp. 220–3.

32 B. Lindars, *The Theology of the Letter to the Hebrews* (CUP 1991), pp. 4–15.

33 R. Martin in A. Chester and R. P. Martin, *The Theology of the Letters of James, Peter and Jude* (CUP 1994), pp. 120–30 (on 1 Peter).

34 Brown, *Group Processes*, pp. 67–84.

35 Berger and Luckmann, *Sociology of Knowledge*, p. 111.

36 This is another illustration borrowed from G. Stanton's lectures.

37 F. Watson, *Paul, Judaism and the Gentiles* (CUP 1986), pp. 61–72.

38 R. Mohrlang, *Matthew and Paul* (CUP 1984).

39 A. Le Grys, 'The Epistle of James: An Epistle of Straw on a Question of Social Identity' (unpublished paper read at the British New Testament Conference, September 1995).

40 See especially J. Gager, *Kingdom and Community: The Social World of Early Christianity* (Englewood Cliffs 1975).

41 K. Burridge, *New Heaven, New Earth: A Study of Millenarian Activities* (OUP 1969).

42 B. Wilson, *Magic and the Millennium* (Paladin 1973).

43 For further details on these and other models of sectarian behaviour see Holmberg, *Sociology*, in which all these theories are discussed in much greater detail.

44 See J. Beker, *Paul the Apostle* (T. & T. Clark 1980), pp. 135–212, on the crucial importance of eschatology for understanding Paul's thought.

45 See Holmberg, *Sociology*, p. 80.

46 C. Rodd, 'Max Weber and Ancient Judaism', *Scottish Journal of Theology*, 32 (1979); and 'On Applying a Social Theory to Biblical Studies', *JSOT*, 19 (1981).

8 The Birth of a Concept

1 J. R. Eiser and J. van Pligt, *Attitudes and Decisions* (Routledge 1988), p. 179.

2 Eiser and van Pligt, *Attitudes*, p. 22f.

3 D. C. Pennington, *Essential Social Psychology* (Yarnold 1996).

4 Pennington, *Essential Social Psychology*, p. 67f.

5 M. Argyle, *The Psychology of Interpersonal Behaviour* (Penguin 1967), p. 167.

6 Pennington, *Essential Social Psychology*, pp. 69f.

7 H. Maccoby, *Paul and Hellenism* (SCM 1991), especially pp. 129–54.

8 M. Hengel, *The Pre-Christian Paul* (SCM 1991).

9 F. Bruce, *I & II Corinthians* (Marshall, Morgan and Scott 1971), p. 240.

10 K. Stendahl, *Paul among Jews and Gentiles*, pp. 7–23.

11 J. D. G. Dunn, 'The Incident at Antioch' in *Jesus, Paul and the Law* (SPCK 1990), pp. 129–82.

12 A. Wedderburn, *The Reasons for Romans* (T. & T. Clark 1988), p. 141f.

13 K. F. Nickle, *The Collection: A Study in Paul's Strategy* (SCM 1966), p. 72f. Nickle argues that the collection was 'a direct outgrowth of the emerging delicate situation created by the simultaneous diffusion of the gospel in two different yet intermingled directions under the auspices of two conflictingly orientated missionary enterprises' and that Paul was 'revolted' by the unresolved conflict. Although I agree with the drift of the first part of the argument – that there were (at least) two different Christian missions, and that the collection was part of Paul's strategy towards the Jerusalem community – I am not sure that Paul was motivated by a 'revulsion' at the prospect of a permanent division. As suggested in the text, I suspect that in the honour-shame culture, he simply wanted to save face and win.

14 See A. Malherbe, *Social Aspects of Early Christianity* (Fortress 1983), pp. 94–103.

15 See W. Meeks, *The First Urban Christians* (Yale 1983), p. 109, for further discussion of the important issue of hospitality for early Christian missionaries. See also Meeks, pp. 51–73 on the social status of these hosts/

patrons and G. Theissen, *The Social Setting of Pauline Christianity* (T. & T. Clark 1982).

16 Like most commentators, I assume there is a common thread running through 1 Corinthians: a relatively affluent group of believers had understood Paul to preach a form of proto-Gnosticism, and this fitted well with their sense of social élitism: Christians were privileged people initiated into the divine mysteries. This 'freedom' from the common limitations of humanity had given them a false ethic and false doctrine: they believed they had already been raised to a new life, and had therefore died to all the normal constraints on behaviour: hence the array of misbehaviour – incest, prostitution, litigation, problems over marriage, contact with pagan temples and so on. Speaking in tongues was the badge of their élitist status (they spoke like angels); and because they were already risen with Christ, they had no sense of a future resurrection. In other words, they had an 'over-realized eschatology'. See further G. Fee, *The First Epistle to the Corinthians* (Eerdmans 1991), pp. 16–20 and *passim*.

17 Theissen, *Social Setting of Pauline Christianity*, pp. 121–43.

18 See R. N. Longenecker, *Galatians* (Word Biblical Commentary 1990), pp. 11–15.

19 D. J. Verseput, 'Paul's Gentile Mission and the Jewish Christian Community: A Study of Narrative in Galatians 1 and 2' in *New Testament Studies*, Vol. 39 No. 1 (January 1993), pp. 36–58.

20 See also, for example, W. D. Davies, *Paul and Rabbinic Judaism* (rev. edn, SPCK 1970), pp. 215ff.

21 J. Sanders, *Schismatics, Sectarians, Dissidents, Deviants* (SCM 1993), p. 14.

22 The phrase is from E. P. Sanders, *Paul and Palestinian Judaism* (SCM 1977). See especially pp. 474–511.

23 B. Witherington III, *Paul's Narrative Thought World* (Westminster 1994), pp. 41ff.

24 For a discussion of all of the possible 'reasons' for Romans see K. Donfried, *The Romans Debate* (rev. edn, T. & T. Clark 1991); and Wedderburn, *The Reasons for Romans*.

25 This is assuming with many recent commentators that Romans 3.31 points forward to the ensuing argument about Abraham, and is not meant to be a concluding argument to the earlier passage. See, for example, J. Ziesler, *Paul's Letter to the Romans* (SCM 1989), p. 119f.

9 And So to the Gospels

1 W. Wrede, *Paul* (Philip Green 1907), p. 166.

2 D. Wenham, *Paul: Follower of Jesus or Founder of Christianity?* (Eerdmans 1995).

3 J. D. G. Dunn, *Romans 1—8* (Word Biblical Commentaries 1991), p. 197.

4 See A. Le Grys, 'Conflict and Vengeance in the Book of Revelation' in the
  Expository Times, Vol. 104 No. 3 (December 1992); and C. Rowland,
  Revelation (Epworth 1993).
5 See J. C. Beker, *Heirs of Paul* (T. & T. Clark 1992).
6 J. A. T. Robinson, *Redating the New Testament* (SCM 1976); and J. Wenham,
  Redating Matthew, Mark and Luke: A Fresh Assault on the Synoptic Problem
  (Hodder and Stoughton 1991).
7 This is, of course, still the subject of intense academic debate: see
  G. Stanton, *The Gospels and Jesus* (OUP 1989), pp. 34–58.
8 On the central theme of discipleship in Mark see E. Best, *Following Jesus*
  (Sheffield 1981); D. Rhoades and D. Michie, *Mark as Story* (Fortress 1982),
  pp. 122–9; and W. Kelber, *Mark's Story of Jesus* (Fortress 1979).
9 W. Marxsen, *Mark the Evangelist* (ET, Nashville 1969).
10 See M. Hooker, *The Gospel according to Mark* (Black 1991), pp. 187–9.
11 Such as M. Hengel, *Studies in the Gospel of Mark* (SCM 1985), pp. 1–30.
12 C. Myers, *Binding the Strong Man* (Orbis 1990), p. 41.
13 Myers, *Binding the Strong Man*, pp. 413–31. Myers has perhaps allowed his
  own pacifist convictions to colour his interpretation, but there is no
  doubt that he has made a powerful case for reading Mark as a protest
  against a simplistic *either/* (pro-Jewish rebels) *or* (pro-Roman imperialism)
  approach.
14 This includes material from the 'double tradition' (pericopae common to
  Matthew and Luke but not found in Mark) as well as material unique to
  Matthew. The pericopae from the double tradition are often described as
  'Q', though the debate about the existence of 'Q' rumbles on. The present
  author considers it likely that 'Q'-ish sources (plural) existed, some of
  which may have been written down, and some of which remained within
  the oral tradition. He is extremely sceptical about some of the more
  refined reconstructions of 'Q' now on offer. See J. Kloppenborg (ed.), *The
  Shape of Q* (Fortress 1994); and D. Catchpole, *The Quest for Q* (T. & T. Clark
  1993), for arguments in favour of 'Q'; and E. P. Sanders and M. Davies,
  Studying the Synoptic Gospels (SCM 1989), pp. 51–119 *passim*, for a
  discussion and evaluation of the whole 'Q' debate.
15 B. W. Bacon, *Studies in Matthew* (Constable 1930).
16 It often surprises lay members of the church to discover that the Sermon
  on the Mount in its present form is almost certainly a Matthean
  construction rather than a direct report of Jesus' teaching.
17 See P. Minear, *The Teacher's Gospel* (Darton Longman & Todd 1983).
18 See Catchpole, *Quest for Q*, pp. 151–88, for a discussion of the underlying
  'Q' missionary charge – though not everyone would share the author's
  confidence about the precise form of that original discourse.
19 See E. von Dobschütz, 'Matthew as Rabbi and Catechist', originally

published in *Zeitschrift für die neutestamentliche Wissenschaft* in 1928, but now translated by R. Morgan and reprinted in G. Stanton (ed.), *The Interpretation of Matthew* (SPCK 1983).

20 R. France, *Matthew: Evangelist and Teacher* (Paternoster 1989), pp. 81–122.

21 On the hugely important topic of Matthew's christological interpretation of the Law see G. Bornkamm, G. Barth and H. J. Held, *Tradition and Interpretation in Matthew* (SCM 1963).

22 E. P. Sanders, *Judaism: Practice and Belief 63 BCE–66 CE* (SCM 1992), pp. 315–490.

23 See G. Stanton, *A Gospel for a New People* (T. & T. Clark 1992), pp. 113–68.

24 A. J. Saldarini, *Matthew's Christian-Jewish Community* (University of Chicago 1994), p. 196.

25 On the important theme of fulfilment in Matthew, see France, *Matthew*, pp. 166–205. Note also the importance of the 'formula quotes' first studied by K. Stendahl in his *The School of Matthew and Its Use of the Old Testament* (rev. edn, Fortress 1968).

26 A broad overview of the case for 'Luke without Q' is set out in M. Goulder, 'A House Built on Sand' in A. Harvey (ed.), *Alternative Approaches in New Testament Study* (SPCK 1985). The argument is set out in detail in M. Goulder, *Luke – A New Paradigm* (Sheffield 1989).

27 R. Maddox, *The Purpose of Luke-Acts* (T. & T. Clark 1982).

28 E.g. Mark 1.15. A computer search of the *metanoeō* root in the Greek NT showed up only three uses of the group in the undisputed Pauline corpus – which is surely a surprisingly low score for a concept which has come to such prominence in Christian thought.

29 E. P. Sanders, *Jesus and Judaism* (SCM 1985), pp. 106–13.

30 T. Schmidt, *Hostility to Wealth in the Synoptic Gospels* (Sheffield 1987), pp. 135–62; and L. Johnson, *The Literary Function of Possessions in Luke-Acts* (Scholars Press 1977).

31 On some of the important recent feminist readings of the Bible see E. Schüssler Fiorenza, *In Memory of Her* (SCM 1983). See also P. Trible, *Texts of Terror* (Fortress 1984), on the role of women in the Hebrew Scriptures.

32 Maddox, *Purpose of Luke-Acts*.

33 P. Esler, *Community and Gospel in Luke-Acts* (CUP 1987).

34 The quote is attributed to D. Strauss but actually quite difficult to track down. As always, John Ashton comes to the rescue: according to *Understanding the Fourth Gospel* (OUP 1991), p. 28 n. 57, the paragraph from which the phrase comes is cited *in extenso* but not translated in W. Howard, *The Fourth Gospel in Recent Criticism and Interpretation* (London 1931), p. 258.

35 The obvious example is the comment in 14.31 which is then followed by a

further three chapters of discourse before Jesus finally leaves the Upper Room in 18.1. The content of 15—16 revisits and develops the same themes as John 14; so these later chapters look suspiciously like a revised edition of the same discourse. Slightly more debatable is the likely displacement between 5.47 and 7.16. The text reads perfectly well without the intervening chapters, and the movements between Jerusalem and Galilee required by the present arrangement seem somewhat artificial. John 6 was perhaps originally a separate sermon introduced at this point to illustrate the point about Jesus and Scripture set out in 5.46f: Jesus, like the manna in the wilderness, is the 'bread of life' who feeds God's people. Chapter 21 seems like an appendix added after the original ending in 20.30f, and so on.

36 J. L. Martyn, *History and Theology in the Fourth Gospel* (New York 1968). Martyn develops his theory in *The Gospel of John in Christian History* (Paulist Press 1979).

37 R. Brown, *The Community of the Beloved Disciple* (Paulist Press 1979).

38 Brown, *Community of the Beloved Disciple*, p. 7.

39 P. Borgen, 'God's Agent in the Fourth Gospel' in J. Ashton (ed.), *The Interpretation of John* (SPCK 1986), pp. 67–78.

40 The Prologue was almost certainly added at one of the later stages of the Gospel's development. See R. Fortna, *The Fourth Gospel and Its Predecessor* (Fortress 1988), pp. 22–3.

10 Preaching to the Nations: Conclusion

1 W. Saayman, 'Christian Mission in the Current World Situation' in W. Saayman (ed.), *Missiology* (University of South Africa 1992), p. 3.

2 C. S. Lewis, *Mere Christianity* (Fontana 1955), p. 62.

3 D. Bosch, *Transforming Mission* (Orbis 1992), pp. 393–400.

4 J. Comby, *How to Understand the History of Christian Mission* (SCM 1996), pp. 6, 16–17.

5 Comby, *How to Understand the History of Mission*, p. 11.

6 Careful qualification is – as always – needed, of course: it has been suggested, I believe, that there have been more Christian martyrs in the twentieth century than all the other centuries put together. We are not that 'enlightened', it would seem.

7 Much of the material in these paragraphs is drawn from material in Comby, *How to Understand the History of Mission*; and John Finney, *Recovering the Past* (Darton, Longman & Todd 1996).

8 M. Green, *Evangelism in the Early Church* (2nd edn, Eagle 1995), p. 9.

9 D. Wenham, *Paul: Follower of Jesus or Founder of Christianity?* (Eerdmans 1995), p. 169.

10 For a full and detailed account of the range of attitudes found in first-

century Diaspora Judaism see John Barclay, *Jews in the Mediterranean Diaspora* (T. & T. Clark 1996).

11 See J. D. G. Dunn, *Christology in the Making* (SCM 1980).

12 On the social processes which help to define a sense of belonging, see A. Cohen, *The Symbolic Construction of Community* (Routledge 1985).

13 Though the circumstances of the final split are still far from clear, it is probably a mistake to think in terms of a clear 'official' break, and more likely that the breach occurred in different places at different times. See J. D. G. Dunn, *The Partings of the Way* (SCM 1991).

14 Ben Witherington III, *Paul's Narrative Thought World* (Westminster/John Knox Press 1994), p. 45.

15 A. J. M. Wedderburn, *The Reasons for Romans* (T. & T. Clark 1988), pp. 39ff.

16 Acts 28.29 is found only in some MSS.

17 R. Brown, *Community of the Beloved Disciple* (Paulist Press 1979), pp. 81–91.

18 L. Newbigin, *The Open Secret* (SPCK 1995), p. 3.

19 K. Leech, *Spirituality and Pastoral Care* (Sheldon Press 1986), p. 35.

20 G. Davie, *Religion in Britain since 1945: Believing without Belonging* (Blackwell 1994).

21 S. Bruce, *Religion in Modern Britain* (OUP 1995), pp. 29–71.

22 See A. Race, *Christians and Religious Pluralism* (2nd edn, SCM 1993); and L. Newbigin, *The Gospel in a Pluralist Society* (SPCK 1989), for two rather different responses.

23 Is it not interesting the way the commercial world has adopted this theological language to provide a focus for activity by formulating statements of intent and purpose?

Select Bibliography

Ackroyd, P., *Exile and Restoration*. SCM 1968.

Ackroyd, P. and Evans, C. F. (eds), *Cambridge History of the Bible*, Vol. 1. CUP 1970.

Alexander, L., *The Preface to Luke's Gospel*. CUP 1993.

Argyle, M., *The Psychology of Interpersonal Behaviour*. Penguin 1967.

Arias, M. and Johnson, A., *The Great Commission*. Abingdon 1992.

Ashton, J. (ed.), *The Interpretation of John*. SPCK 1986.

Ashton, J., *Understanding the Fourth Gospel*. Oxford 1991.

Avis, P. (ed.), *The Resurrection of Jesus Christ*. Darton, Longman & Todd 1993.

Bacon, B. W., *Studies in Matthew*. Constable 1930.

Barclay, J. M., *Jews in the Mediterannean Diaspora: from Alexander to Trajan (323 BCE–117 CE)*. T. & T. Clark 1996.

Barker, E., *New Religious Movements*. HMSO 1989.

Barrett, C. K., *The Gospel According to John*. SPCK 1955.

Barrett, C. K. (ed.), *The New Testament Background: Selected Documents*. SPCK 1956.

Bartchy, S., 'Mallon Chrēsai: First-Century Slavery and the Interpretation of 1 Corinthians 7.21'. Society of Biblical Literature Dissertation 1973.

Beker, J. C., *Paul the Apostle*. T. & T. Clark 1980.

Beker, J. C., *Heirs of Paul*. T. & T. Clark 1992.

Berger, P. and Luckmann, T., *The Sociology of Knowledge*. Penguin 1967.

Best, E., *Following Jesus: Discipleship in the Gospel of Mark*. Sheffield 1981.

Boardman, J., Griffin, J. and Murray, O. (eds.), *The Oxford History of the Classical World*. Oxford 1986, TSP 1995.

Bornkamm, G., Bath, G. and Held, H., *Tradition and Interpretation in Matthew*. SCM 1963.

Bosch, D. J., *Transforming Mission: Paradigm Shifts in Theology of Mission*. Orbis 1992.

Bromiley, G., *Theological Dictionary of the New Testament Abridged in One Volume*. Eerdmans 1985.

Brown, R., *The Gospel According to John* (2 volumes). Doubleday 1970.

Brown, R., *The Birth of the Messiah*. Image, Doubleday 1977.

Brown, R., *The Community of the Beloved Disciple*. G. Chapman 1979.

Brown, R., *Group Processes: Dynamics within and between Groups*. Blackwell 1988.

Bruce, F., *I and II Corinthians*. Marshall, Morgan and Scott 1971.

Bruce, S., *Religion in Modern Britain.* OUP 1995.

Brueggemann, W., *A Social Reading of the Old Testament.* Fortress 1994.

Burridge, K., *New Heaven, New Earth: A Study of Millenarian Activities.* OUP 1969.

Cadbury, H., *The Making of Luke-Acts.* Macmillan 1927.

Catchpole, D., *The Quest for Q.* T. & T. Clark 1993.

Charlesworth, J. (ed.), *The Old Testament Pseudepigrapha* (2 volumes). Doubleday/DLT 1983 and 1985.

Chester, A. and Martin, R. P., *The Theology of the Letters of James, Peter and Jude.* CUP 1991.

Coggin, R. J. and Houlden, J. L. (eds), *A Dictionary of Biblical Interpretation.* SCM 1990.

Cohen, A., *The Symbolic Construction of Community.* Routledge 1985.

Collins, R. (ed.), *Sociological Theory 1983.* Jossey Bass 1983.

Conn, W., *Christian Conversion.* Paulist Press 1986.

Conzelmann, H., *The Theology of St Luke.* Faber 1960.

Cranfield, C. E. B., *The Gospel According to St Mark.* CUP 1959.

Crossan, D., *The Historical Jesus: The Life of a Mediterranean Jewish Peasant.* T. & T. Clark 1991.

Davie, G., *Religion in Britain since 1945: Believing without Belonging.* Blackwell 1994.

Davies, W. D., *Paul and Rabbinic Judaism* (revised edition). SPCK 1970.

Davies, W. D. and Martin, D., *The Gospel According to Matthew* (2 volumes). T. & T. Clark 1988.

Day, J., *Psalms.* Sheffield 1992.

Dodd, C. H., *The Interpretation of the Fourth Gospel.* CUP 1968.

Donfried, K. (ed.), *The Romans Debate.* T. & T. Clark 1991.

Downing, F. G., *Christ and the Cynics.* Sheffield Academic Press 1988.

Dunn, J. D. G., *Christology in the Making.* SCM 1980.

Dunn, J. D. G., *Jesus, Paul and the Law.* SPCK 1990.

Dunn, J. D. G., *The Partings of the Way.* SCM 1991.

Dunn, J. D. G., *Romans 9—16.* Word Biblical Commentary 1991.

Dunn, J. D. G., *1 Corinthians.* Sheffield Academic Press 1995.

Eaton, J., *The Psalms Come Alive.* Mowbray 1984.

Eisenman, R. and Wise, M., *The Dead Sea Scrolls Uncovered.* Element 1992.

Eiser, J. R. and van Pligt, J. (eds), *Attitudes and Decisions.* Routledge 1988.

Elliott, J. H., *A Home for the Homeless: A Social-Scientific Criticism of 1 Peter, Its Situation and Strategy.* Fortress 1981.

Erikson, E., *Childhood and Society.* Paladin 1950.

Elser, P. E., *Community and Gospel in Luke-Acts.* CUP 1987.

Elser, P. E., *The First Christians in their Social Worlds: Social-Scientific Approaches to New Testament Interpretation.* Routledge 1994.

Evans, C. F., *Luke*. SCM 1990.

Fee, G., *The First Epistle to the Corinthians*. Eerdmans 1991.

Ferguson, J., *The Religions of the Roman Empire*. Thames and Hudson 1970.

Fitzmeyer, J., *Luke* (2 volumes). Doubleday 1985.

Fortna, R., *The Fourth Gospel and Its Predecessor*. Fortress 1988.

France, R. T., *Matthew*. Inter Varsity Press 1985.

France, R. T., *Matthew: Evangelist and Teacher*. Paternoster 1989.

Frend, W. H. C., *Martyrdom and Persecution in the Early Church*. Blackwell 1965.

Gager, J., *Kingdom and Community: The Social World of Early Christianity*. Englewood Cliffs 1975.

Gager, J., *The Origins of Anti-Semitism*. Oxford 1983.

Garland, D., *Reading Matthew*. SPCK 1993.

Goodman, M., *Mission and Conversion: Proselytizing in the Religious History of the Roman Empire*. Clarendon 1994.

Goulder, M., *Luke: A New Paradigm*. Sheffield Academic Press 1989.

Goulder, M., *A Tale of Two Missions*. SCM 1994.

Green, J. and Turner, M. (eds), *Jesus of Nazareth: Lord and Christ*. Eerdmans 1994.

Green, M., *Evangelism in the Early Church*. Eagle 1995.

Haenchen, E., *The Acts of the Apostles*. Blackwell 1971.

Hahn, F., *Mission in the New Testament*. SCM 1965.

Harvey, A. (ed.), *Alternative Approaches in New Testament Studies*. SPCK 1985.

Hengel, M., *Judaism and Hellenism* (2 volumes). SCM 1974.

Hengel, M., *Between Jesus and Paul*. SCM 1983.

Hengel, M., *Studies in the Gospel of Mark*. SCM 1985.

Hengel, M., *The Pre-Christian Paul*. SCM 1991.

Hill, C. C., *Hellenists and Hebrews: Reappraising Division within the Earliest Church*. Fortress 1992.

Holmberg, B., *Sociology and the New Testament*. Fortress 1990.

Hooker, M., *The Gospel According to Mark*. Black 1991.

Houlden, J. L., *The Public Face of the Gospel: New Testament Ideas of the Church*. SCM 1997.

Hurst, L., *The Epistle to the Hebrews*. CUP 1990.

Jeremias, J., *Jesus' Promise to the Nations*. SCM 1956.

Jewett, R., *Dating Paul's Life*. SCM 1979.

Johnson, L., *The Literary Function of Possessions in Luke-Acts*. Scholars Press 1977.

Josephus, *Against Apion*. Loeb Classical Library, Heinemann 1926.

Josephus, *The Life*. Loeb Classical Library, Heinemann 1926.

Josephus, *The Jewish Antiquities*. Loeb Classical Library, Heinemann 1930; Harvard 1965.

Judge, E., *The Social Pattern of the Christian Groups in the First Century: Some*

Prolegomena to the Study of New Testament Ideas of Social Obligation. Tyndale 1960.

Keck, E. and Martyn, J. L. (eds), *Studies in Luke-Acts.* (Yale 1976).

Kelber, W., *Mark's Story of Jesus.* Fortress 1979.

Kloppenborg, J., *The Shape of Q.* Fortress 1994.

Lane Fox, R., *Pagans and Christians.* Penguin 1986.

Le Grys, A., 'Conflict and Vengeance in the Book of Revelation'. *Expository Times*, Vol. 104 No. 3, December 1992.

Legrand, L., *Unity and Plurality: Mission in the Bible.* Orbis 1988.

Lieu, J., Rajak, T. and North, J. (eds), *The Jews among Pagans and Christians.* Routledge 1992.

Lindars, B., *The Gospel of John.* Marshall, Morgan and Scott 1972.

Lindars, B., *John.* Sheffield Academic Press 1990.

Lindars, B., *The Theology of the Epistle to the Hebrews.* CUP 1991.

Lofland, J. and Skonovd, N., 'Becoming a World-Saver: A Theory of Conversion in a Deviant Perspective'. *American Sociological Review*, Vol. 30.

Longenecker, R. N., *Galatians.* World Biblical Commentary 1990.

Lüdemann, G., *Paul Apostle to the Gentiles: Studies in Chronology.* SCM 1984.

Maccoby, H., *Paul and Hellenism.* SCM 1991.

MacMullen, R., 'Two Types of Conversion in Early Christianity', *Vigiliae Christianae*, Vol. 37 No. 2. Brill 1983.

Maddox, R., *The Purpose of Luke-Acts.* T. & T. Clark 1982.

Malherbe, A., *Social Aspects of Early Christianity.* Fortress 1983.

Malina, B. J., *The New Testament World: Insights from Cultural Anthropology.* SCM 1983.

Marshall, I. H., *Luke: Historian and Theologian.* Paternoster 1992.

Marshall, I. H., *The Acts of the Apostles.* Sheffield Academic Press 1992.

Martin, R., *Mark: Evangelist and Theologian.* Paternoster 1972.

Martyn, J. L., *History and Theology in the Fourth Gospel* (2nd edn). Abingdon 1968.

Martyn, J. L., *The Gospel of John in Christian History.* Paulist Press 1979.

McGrath, A., *Christian Theology: An Introduction.* Blackwell 1994.

McKnight, S., *A Light among the Nations.* Fortress 1991.

Meeks, W. A., *The First Urban Christians: The Social World of the Apostle Paul.* Yale 1983.

Meeks, W. A., *The Origins of Christian Morality.* Yale 1993.

Meier, J. P., *A Marginal Jew: Rethinking the Historical Jesus.* Doubleday 1994.

Meyers, B. and Sanders, E. P. (eds), *Jewish and Christian Self-Definition*, Vol. 3. SCM 1982.

Minear, P., *The Teacher's Gospel.* Darton, Longman & Todd 1983.

Moody, C., *Eccentric Ministry.* Darton, Longman & Todd 1992.

Morhlang, R., *Matthew and Paul.* CUP 1984.

Myers, C., *Binding the Strong Man: A Political Reading of Mark's Story of Jesus.* Orbis 1988.

Nazir-Ali, M., *Mission and Dialogue: Proclaiming the Gospel Afresh in Every Age.* SPCK 1995.

Neill, S., *A History of Christian Missions.* Penguin 1964.

Newbigin, L., *The Open Secret: An Introduction to the Theology of Mission.* SPCK 1995.

Neyrey, J. (ed.), *The Social World of Luke-Acts.* Hendrickson 1991.

Nickelsburg, G., *Jewish Literature between the Bible and the Mishnah.* SCM 1981.

Nickle, K. F., *The Collection: A Study in Paul's Strategy.* SCM 1966.

North, C., *The Second Isaiah.* Oxford 1964.

Pennington, D., *Essential Social Psychology.* Arnold 1996.

Philo, *De Plantatione.* Loeb Classical Library, Heinemann 1929–1962.

Race, R., *Christians and Religious Pluralism* (2nd edn). SCM 1993.

Räisänen, H., *The Messianic Secret in Mark.* T. & T. Clark 1990.

Rambo, L. R., *Understanding Religious Conversion.* Yale 1993.

Rhoades, D. and Michie, D., *Mark as Story.* Fortress 1982.

Richardson, P. and Hurd, J. (eds), *From Jesus to Paul.* Wilfrid Laurier 1984.

Riches, J., *Jesus and the Transformation of Judaism.* Darton, Longman & Todd 1980.

Ringgren, H., *Israelite Religion.* SPCK 1966.

Robinson, J. A. T., *Redating the New Testament.* SCM 1976.

Rodd, C., 'Max Weber and Ancient Judaism'. *Scottish Journal of Theology,* 32, 1979.

Rodd, C., 'On Applying a Sociological Theory to Biblical Studies'. *Journal for the Study of the Old Testament,* 19, 1981.

Rohrbaugh, R. (ed.), *The Social Sciences and New Testament Interpretation.* Hendrickson 1996.

Rowland, C., *Radical Christianity.* Polity Press 1988.

Saayman, W. (ed.), *Missiology.* University of South Africa 1992.

Saldarini, A., *Matthew's Jewish-Christian Community.* University of Chicago 1994.

Sanders, E. P., *Paul and Palestinian Judaism.* SCM 1977.

Sanders, E. P., Baumgarten, A. I. and Mendelson, A. (eds), *Jewish and Christian Self-Definition,* Vol. 2. SCM 1981.

Sanders, E. P., *Jesus and Judaism.* SCM 1985.

Sanders, E. P. and Davies, M., *Studying the Synoptic Gospels.* SCM 1989.

Sanders, E. P., *Judaism: Practice and Belief 63 BCE–66 CE.* SCM 1992.

Sanders, J., *Schismatics, Sectarians, Dissidents, Deviants.* SCM 1993.

Schmidt, W., *Introduction to the Old Testament.* SCM 1982.

Schmidt, T., *Hostility to Wealth in the Synoptic Gospels.* Sheffield Academic Press 1987.

Schüssler Fiorenza, E., *In Memory of Her*. SCM 1983.

Segal, A., *Paul the Convert*. Yale 1990.

Senior, D. and Stuhlmueller, C., *The Biblical Foundations for Mission*. SCM 1983.

Simon, M., *St Stephen and the Hellenists in the Primitive Church*. Longmans 1958.

Soggin, J. A., *Introduction to the Old Testament*. SCM 1976.

Stambaugh, J. and Balch, D., *The Social World of the First Christians*. SPCK 1986.

Stanisforth, M. (tr.), *Early Christian Writings*. Penguin 1968.

Stanton, G. (ed.), *The Interpretation of Matthew*. SPCK 1983.

Stanton, G., *The Gospels and Jesus*. OUP 1989.

Stanton, G., *A Gospel for a New People*. T. & T. Clark 1992.

Stendahl, K., *The School of Matthew and Its Use of the Old Testament* (rev. edn). Philadelphia 1968.

Stevenson, J. (ed.), *A New Eusebius*. SPCK 1957.

Tajfel, H., *Differentiation between Social Groups: Studies in Social Psychology of Intergroup Relations*. Academic Press 1978.

Talbert, C. H., *Reading Luke*. Crossroad 1992.

Theissen, G., *The Social Setting of Pauline Christianity*. T. & T. Clark 1982.

Theissen, G., *Social Reality and the Early Christians: Theology, Ethics and the World of the New Testament*. T. & T. Clark 1992.

Throckmorton, B., *Gospel Parallels* (4th edn). Nelson 1979.

Trible, P., *Texts of Terror*. SCM 1984.

van Tilbourg, S., *The Jewish Leaders in Matthew*. E. J. Brill 1972.

Vermes, G., *The Dead Sea Scrolls in English*. Penguin 1962.

Vermes, G., Millar, F. and Black, M. (eds), *The History of the Jewish People in the Age of Jesus* (rev. Schürer). T. & T. Clark 1979.

Vermes, G., *Jesus the Jew* (rev. edn). SCM 1983.

von Rad, G., *Old Testament Theology*. SCM 1975.

Watson, F., *Paul, Judaism and the Gentiles*. CUP 1986.

Weber, M., *Sociology of Religion*. Beacon Press 1963.

Wedderburn, A., *The Reasons for Romans*. Sheffield Academic Press 1989.

Wenham, J., *Redating Matthew, Mark and Luke: A Fresh Assault on the Synoptic Problem*. Hodder and Stoughton 1991.

Wenham, D., *Paul: Follower of Jesus or Founder of Christianity?* Eerdmans 1995.

Whybray, R. N., *The Making of the Pentateuch*. Sheffield Academic Press 1987.

Wilson, B., *Magic and Millennium: A Sociological Study of Religious Movements of Protest among Tribal and Third World Peoples*. Paladin 1973.

Wilson, B., *Religion in Sociological Perspective*. OUP 1982.

Witherington III, B., *Paul's Narrative Thought World*. Westminster 1994.

Wrede, W., *Paul*. Philip Green 1907.

Wright, N. T., *The New Testament People of God*. SPCK 1992.
Yarbro Collins, A., *Crisis and Catharsis: The Power of the Apocalypse*. Westminster 1984.
Ziesler, J., *Paul's Letter to the Romans*. SCM 1989.

Index

Esther, book of 17
exclusivism xv, 6, 14–19
exile, Babylonian 6–7, 14–15, 22
Ezra 14–16
Ezra: 4 Ezra, book of 16, 29

families xix, 31, 34, 35, 92, 96, 100, 113, 114, 116–17, 120, 144, 154
fate or *tyché* xix, 92, 107, 171, 180

Galatians, Paul's letter to xvii, 42, 72–3, 85–7, 89–90, 95, 97, 108, 111–12, 118, 124, 125, 135–7, 141–8, 149, 150, 178, 181–2
Genesis, book of 6–7, 144, 146, 170, 182
Gentiles xiii, xv–xix, 5–19, 20, 22, 23, 24, 27–36, 37, 38, 40–3, 45, 46, 48, 49, 50, 51, 52–67, 88–90, 97, 99, 105, 107, 112, 116–17, 124, 125, 126, 128, 135–6, 137, 141–8, 149–51, 152, 153, 154, 155, 157, 159–60, 163–4, 167, 168, 172, 174, 175, 176, 177, 178, 181, 182, 183, 184, 188
God-fearers xvi, 35, 84, 85, 176, 177
Graeco-Roman culture xvii, xviii, 21, 22, 90–106, 107, 114, 118, 128, 136, 140, 151, 163, 171, 172, 177, 179, 180, 181, 188
Greek gods xviii, xix, 89, 92–3, 99–105, 179
Greek language 90

Hebrew Scriptures xviii, 3, 5–6, 11, 16, 23, 30, 75, 143–4, 163, 174, 181
Hebrews, letter to 81–2, 106, 122, 125
Hellenistic culture xvii, 22–3, 29, 32, 38, 48, 53, 90–8, 99, 105, 108, 168, 186
Hellenistic Judaism 21–2, 62, 80–4,

85–6, 90, 111, 117, 124, 125, 168, 177–8
Hellenists 79–84, 88, 167, 177
hermeneutics 174–5
Herod and Herodians 32, 48, 55–6, 59, 63
honour–shame culture 85, 94–8, 99, 100, 101, 107, 112–13, 119, 136, 138, 163, 178, 181, 188

Isaiah, book of 6, 10–12, 14, 16, 21, 59, 84, 143, 147, 152
Isis xviii, 101–3, 111
Israel xiii, 6–19, 21, 29, 42, 43, 47, 48, 49, 50, 51, 52, 55, 59, 64, 71, 76, 77, 78, 82, 106, 126, 128, 143–5, 147–8, 157, 159–60, 163, 166, 171, 176
Izates 31–2

Jerusalem/Zion xvii, 4, 12, 14, 16, 22, 23, 24, 27, 28, 32, 50, 56, 61, 63, 73, 74, 77–8, 79, 80–4, 86, 88, 89, 95, 97, 112, 137, 147, 149, 152, 153, 176, 177, 182
Jesus ix, x, xii, xiii, xiv, xv, xvi, xvii, xx, 3–6, 37–51, 52–68, 71, 72, 74, 76, 77, 81, 82, 88, 95, 99, 101, 102, 104, 106, 128, 145, 147, 149, 150, 151–5, 156–68, 175, 176, 177, 178, 183, 184
Jews xi, xiii, xv, xvi, xvii, xviii, 3, 7, 15–18, 20–31, 32, 34–5, 40, 41, 42, 43, 45, 50, 54, 55, 56, 57, 58, 59, 60, 61, 62, 71, 73, 77, 78, 79, 80, 81, 82, 84, 85, 86, 88, 89, 90, 101, 126, 150, 153, 158, 159, 161, 165, 166, 167, 172, 175, 176, 177, 178, 183
John, Gospel of xiv, xv, xx, 40, 41, 43, 45–6, 60–3, 67–8, 95, 105, 164–7
John the Baptist 5, 161, 166, 167